IMAGES
of America

LOST RAYNE

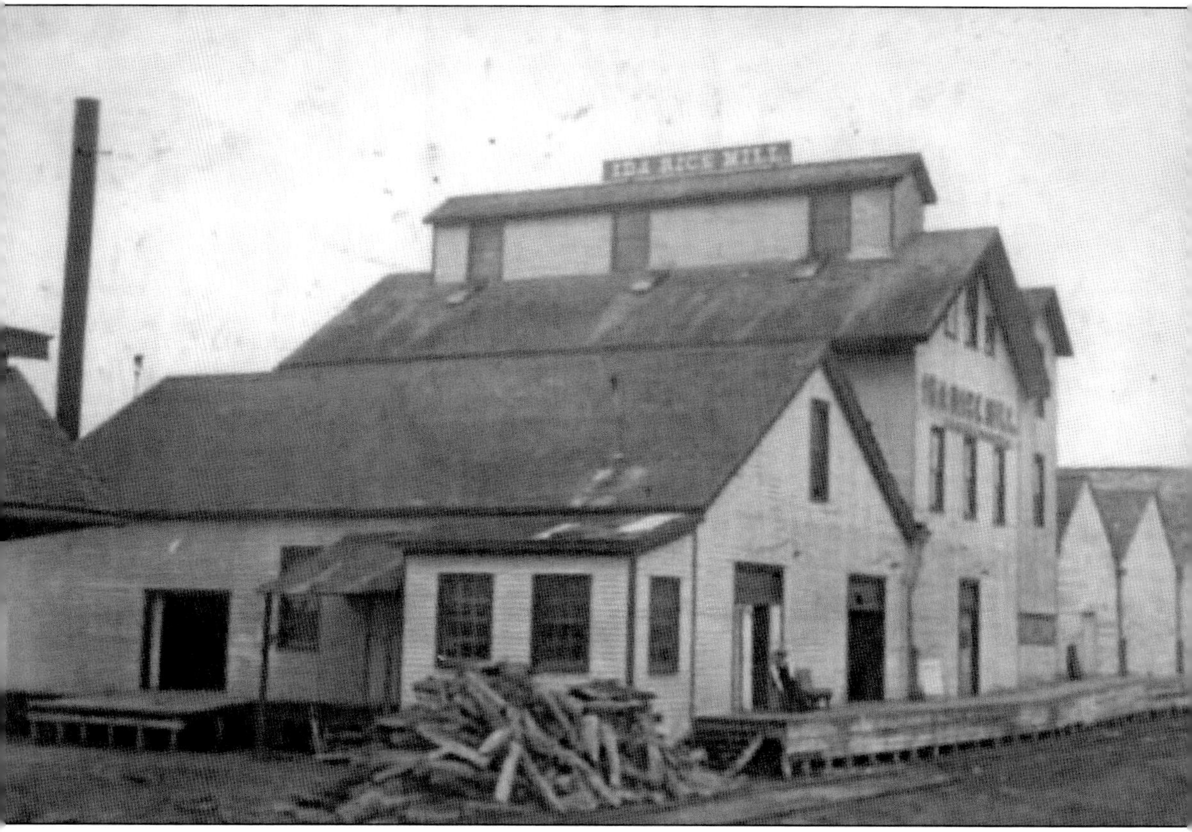

The Ida Rice Mill is seen here in 1904 along the Texas & New Orleans Railroad tracks. Jefferson Davis Marks built the mill and named it after his daughter Ida. It was the first rice mill built in Louisiana outside of New Orleans. Before the mill was erected in 1889, rice had to be shipped to New Orleans to be milled. The Ida was bought out later, and the name was changed to the Acadia Rice Mill. It was located along the railroad tracks on East Texas Avenue, across from where the Rayne Post Office is now.

ON THE COVER: The Mervine Kahn Company general merchandise store is pictured after one of its numerous expansions. The store was expanded in 1924, 1936, 1945, and 1953. In 1884, Mervine Kahn and his brother-in-law Michel Schmulen were heading to Beaumont, Texas, when a Rayne booster convinced them to check out the new growing town of Rayne. They bought a general merchandise store from Anselm S. Chappuis and named it Schmulen & Kahn. In 1886, it was renamed Mervine Kahn's after Schmulen's death. It was incorporated in 1924 and operated continually until it closed its doors for the final time in 1989.

IMAGES
of America

LOST RAYNE

Tony Olinger
with an introduction by Charles Sidney Stutes

ARCADIA
PUBLISHING

ISBN 978-1-4671-1459-2

Published by Arcadia Publishing
Charleston, South Carolina

Printed in the United States of America

Library of Congress Control Number: 2015944268

For all general information, please contact Arcadia Publishing:
Telephone 843-853-2070
Fax 843-853-0044
E-mail sales@arcadiapublishing.com
For customer service and orders:
Toll-Free 1-888-313-2665

Visit us on the Internet at www.arcadiapublishing.com

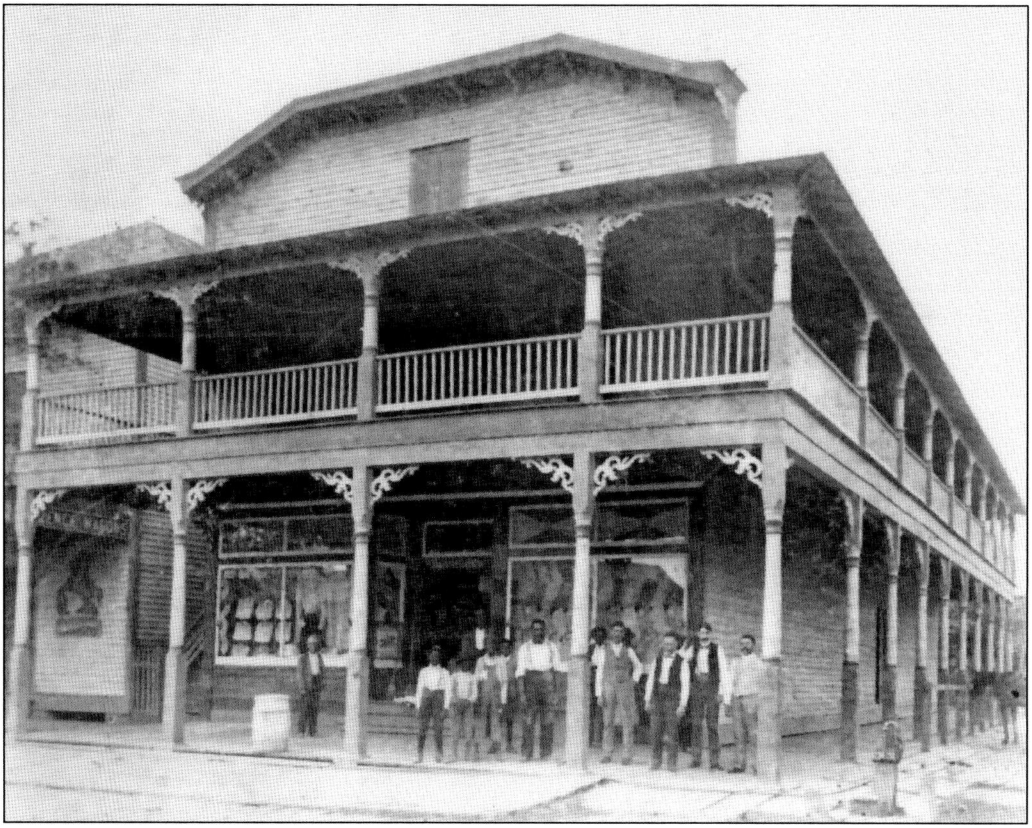

No book about Rayne would be complete without a photograph of the historic Mervine Kahn Company Store, located on the corner of North Adams and East Louisiana Avenues. The store was on the bottom floor, and the family lived on the second floor. The great businessman Mervine Kahn grew his establishment until it took up almost the entire city block. It was credited as being the first store to sell German diatonic accordions to Cajun musicians. (Courtesy of *Rayne Independent.*)

Contents

Acknowledgments

We all have people in our lives who influence our actions and help us accomplish our goals. In my journey discovering the history of Rayne, I have had many inspirational people guide me along the way.

The first person helping me to discover Rayne's history is Charles Sidney Stutes, whom I consider the ultimate Rayne historian. Being a history teacher, he has a fire inside when discussing our marvelous past. Many hours have been spent in his kitchen, discussing locations of buildings, businesses, and trying to identify photographs. I would also like to thank his wife, Monica, for allowing me into their home to "talk Rayne."

My next influence is Fair Craig Hash, who has afforded me the opportunity to go through all of her mother, Myrta Fair Craig's, files and copy information and photographs as needed. Her unique perspective on Rayne and her knowledge of our city is unbelievable. The Craig name will always be mentioned when the history of Rayne is discussed.

In 2015, with social media playing such an important part in all of our lives, my next influence is a *Facebook* group, "Rayne Remembered." Founded in May 2013 by Rayne native Monique Domingue Moreland, this group virtually exploded overnight and is credited with a renaissance of interest in Rayne's history. If I had a question about a business or a person, one simple post usually gave me my answer, literally within minutes.

I would be remiss if I did not mention our predecessor in preserving Rayne's history, Emile Daboval Jr., known as Milo. Mr. Milo preserved so much of Rayne's early history and was able to do tremendous research without the help of a computer or the Internet. I would like to thank his daughter, Margo Daboval Goertz, for sharing his research and treasured items with me.

I would like to recognize the keepers of our history who have come before me, especially Mary Alice Fontenot, who was able to preserve so much of Rayne and Acadia Parish's early history. Rayne's own Dr. Lauren Post's "Cajun Sketches" documented the Cajun way of life so many years ago.

Today, Rayne is fortunate to have so many people interested in keeping our history alive, like Gene Thibodeaux, who wrote a history of Rayne titled *Rice, Railroads, and Frogs*; and Jim Bradshaw and William Thibodeaux, who write articles on our history for the local newspapers. With so many people interested in our history, it will be documented and preserved forever.

I would like to thank Judy Chatelain Devalcourt, daughter of Wiltz and Eloise Chatelain, for the historic artifacts from her parents' home. Her gifts have expanded my collection of Rayne treasures.

I would like to thank Kevin Meche of Rayne Sign Company, who has given his time and equipment to help me with this project to preserve Rayne's history. No matter the size of the project, he was always willing to help. I would also like to thank Angie Broussard for letting me use photography equipment for this book.

I appreciate the help of Paul Kedinger, Lisa S. Soileaux, and Josie Henry of the *Rayne Acadian-Tribune*, who allowed me access to their archives to conduct research.

I would also like to extend thanks to Trudy Thevis Ronkartz and her staff at the Rayne Branch Library for their help in researching information and the use of their microfilm machine. Also Ann Mire of the Acadia Parish Library in Crowley for assistance she has given in this project.

Lost Rayne is a collection of buildings and businesses that, for whatever reason, left our local landscape. A giant was lost when the *Rayne Independent* newspaper printed its last edition on May 31, 2013. It was founded in 1967 by Robert and Lillian "Jo" Cart, whom I affectionately called Uncle Robert and Aunt Jo. They will never be forgotten. Thanks to the efforts of Scott Cart and Becky Boudreaux, I was able to preserve the *Independent's* pictures and negatives for future generations after its closing.

I would also like to thank the following people for allowing me to use their precious pictures for this book: Denald Beslin, Phyllis Besse, Mary Helen Broussard Reed, Andrus Fontenot, Gene Guidry, Fair Craig Hash, Lou Hoffpauir, Marguerite Kahn Hoskin, Carl Jennings, Clyde Leger, Delores Daigle Lagneaux, Tony Laperous (with pictures from his father, Leonard J. Laperous), "The Photo Shop" Collection, Louisiana Digital Library, Thomas Marcotte, Julie Anna Ousse and Butch Ousse, Eddie and Ann Palmer, Donald Petitjean, Steve Raymond, *Rayne Acadian-Tribune*, Rayne High School, *Rayne Independent*, Ronnie Richard, Chuck Robichaux, William "Kootsie" Simoneaux, Rose Marie R. Stelly, Sidney Stutes, and Melba Olinger.

I would like to thank Andrus Fontenot, Melba Olinger, Fair Craig Hash, Tom Johnson, Josie Henry, Ron Sonnier, Rhonda Olinger Broussard, Lisa S. Soileaux, and Sidney Stutes for proofing the draft and helping with additional information and corrections.

Finally, I would especially like to thank my wife, Verna Begnaud Olinger, and my children, Nolan Anthony and Mackenzie Claire, for sharing their family time so I could work on this project. I would also like to thank my mother, Melba Roy Olinger, for helping secure pictures, and my sister Rhonda Olinger Broussard, for helping to identify and sort pictures.

I am dedicating this book to my father, Hilary Anthony Olinger Sr., who passed away in 2010. Going through years and years of newspapers, I was amazed at the number of times he appeared in the paper. Whether it was being in charge of local American bicentennial celebrations, working on the Rayne Centennial Celebration, being a member of the Rayne Chamber of Commerce, Rayne Recreation Board, Rayne Lions Club, and Knights of Columbus, or coaching Bronco League baseball, he was my inspiration and taught me to work hard and volunteer to help others. Thanks Dad. You are with me always.

INTRODUCTION

It has been said that a photograph is taken "for the future," serving as something that will live on beyond the moment—a record, so to speak, of times that all too quickly escape. Unfortunately, once taken, a photograph is nothing but a reflection on paper, unless a memory is recorded with it—a name, a date, an event—that serves as a peg in our lives.

One wonders how much of a person's life history is lost when an old photograph of them lies unclaimed, unidentified in an attic, drawer, or closet, fading in color and relevance to younger generations who draw no connection or significance to it. As a result, these young people are left with little or no past with which to understand how they came to be.

The same holds true for photographs of old buildings that once had biographies of their own and a reason for being—as a home for a family, a building for a business, a church for prayer. Buildings are made venerable over time by reason of age, dignity, or location, and come to symbolize the character of the builder or owner. Within these buildings, occupants breathed and rooms filled with sounds. Photographs of them reach into the future and serve as treasured keepsakes. But, once demolished without record, these buildings fade into memory, denied of their symbolic place in the history of a community and of their viability as landmarks that once housed souls and a special purpose.

With *Lost Rayne*, Rayne's young collector of the past, Tony Olinger, attempts a resurrection of sorts, bringing to light and life photographs of these lost buildings and businesses, in hopes of giving them identity again as visual evidence of a past we all share.

—Charles Sidney Stutes

One

Going Downtown

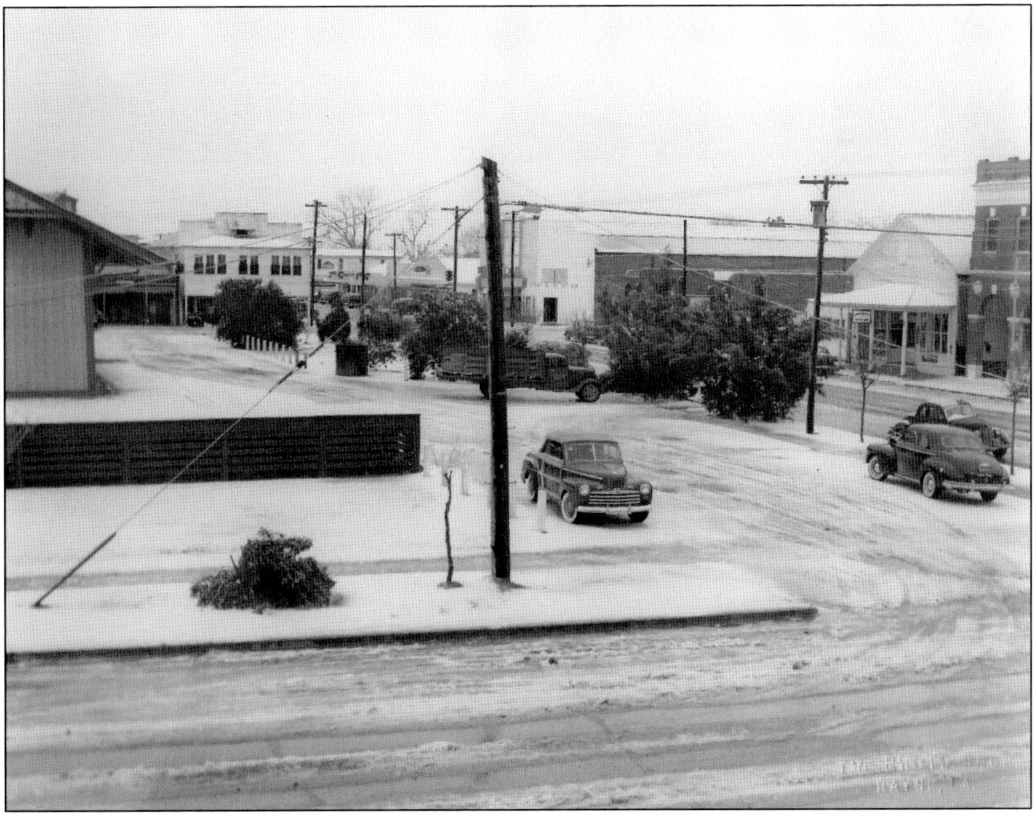

Snow in Rayne is a fairly unusual occurrence. On January 31, 1948, Leonard J. Laperous, owner of The Photo Shop, captured downtown Rayne from the second floor of O. Broussard's Pharmacy. At far right is the Commercial Bank Building, and to its immediate left is Simoneaux's Coffee Shop. Across the Depot Square is the two-story Besse Restaurant and Hotel. At far left is the freight depot. As indicated by the tire tracks in the snow, the depot was a very busy place. Most people do not know that Rayne holds the Louisiana record for snowfall, 24 inches, in February 1895. (Courtesy of Leonard J. Laperous, The Photo Shop.)

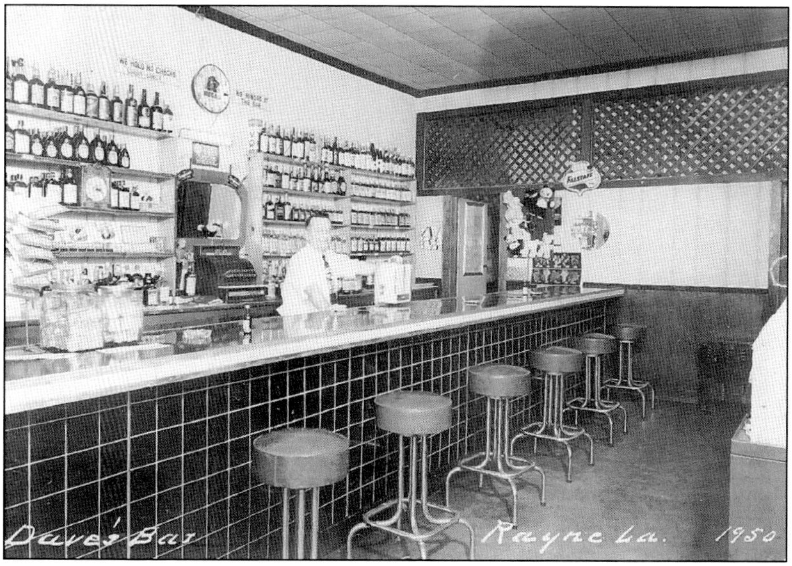

Dave's Bar was owned by Dave Besse, who is seen here behind the bar in 1950. Dave later managed the Hollywood Club, owned by Albert Besse. The bar was located on East Texas Avenue near the Joy Theater. George Boudreaux, among others, later operated bars in this location. (Courtesy of Phyllis Besse.)

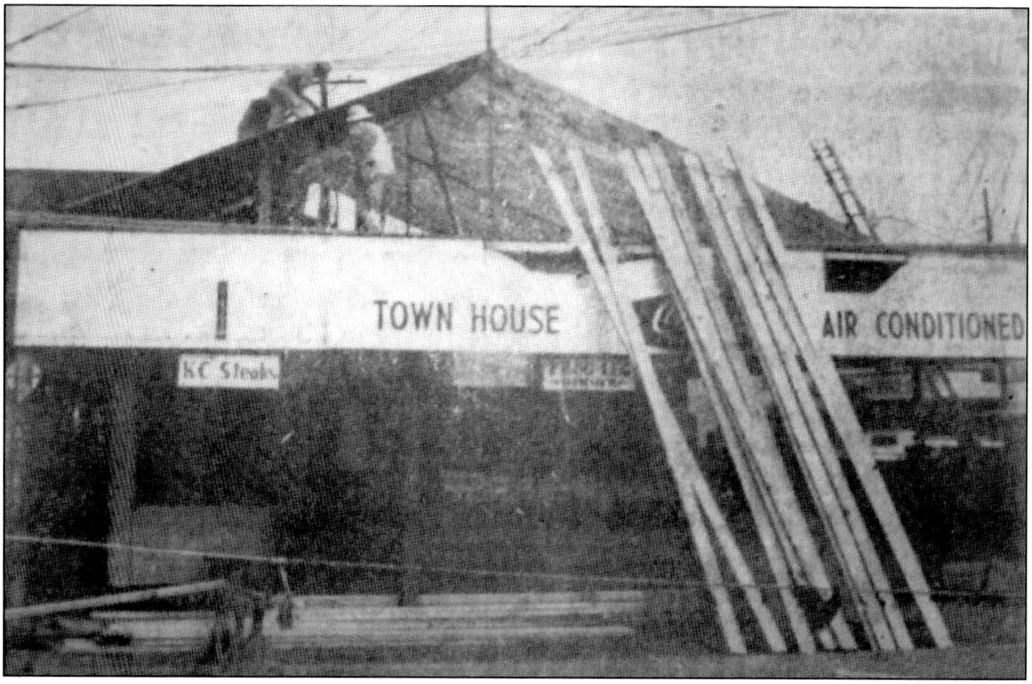

The Town House Restaurant, owned by Edmond Stelly, had eight boarding rooms on the second floor when it caught fire in 1962. This photograph was taken when the decision was made not to rebuild the top floor, but instead put a roof over the restaurant. At the time of the fire, Ron Sonnier was waiting for a bus to go to trade school in Crowley when waitresses came running out of the restaurant carrying dishes and utensils. Edmond Stelly ran out with the cash register and went across the street to the Joy Theater. He told Sonnier that perhaps he should come meet him because the building was on fire. The Town House was located on the corner of South Polk Street and East Texas Avenue, across from the Depot Square. It was later Michael & Suns Restaurant and, most recently, the Rayne Diner. (Courtesy of *Rayne Acadian-Tribune*.)

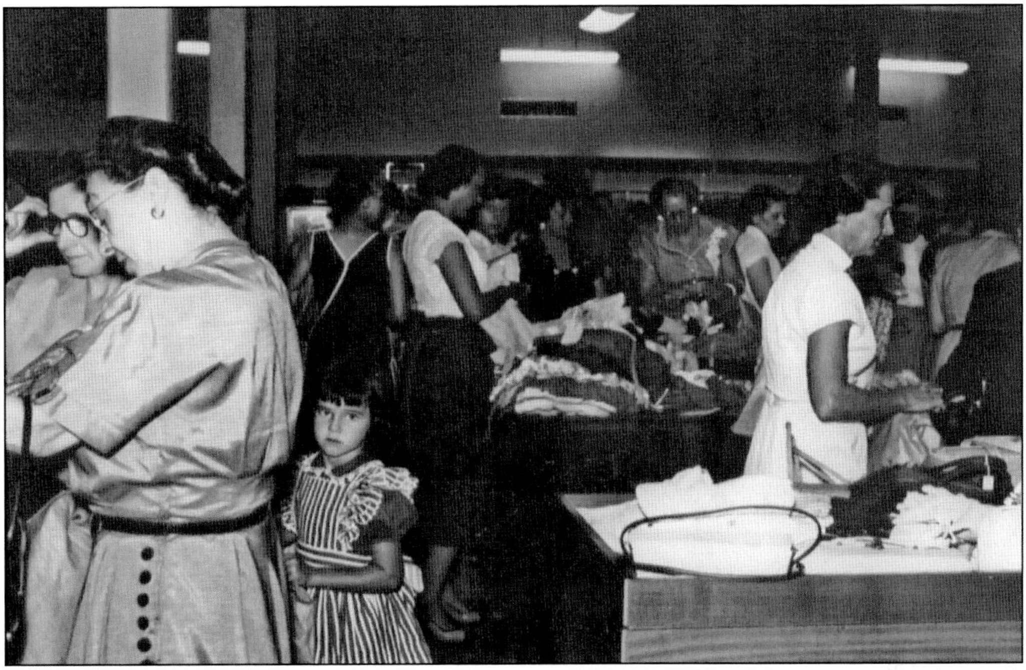

After the Mervine Kahn Company Store was remodeled in 1953, it was reopened with much anticipation. The doors had to be locked periodically to leave enough room in the store for shoppers to examine the goods. A large crowd is shown at this very popular shopping destination. With over 3,000 charge accounts, it is easy to understand why it was said that "Mervine's was the biggest store between Houston and New Orleans." (Courtesy of Donald Petitjean.)

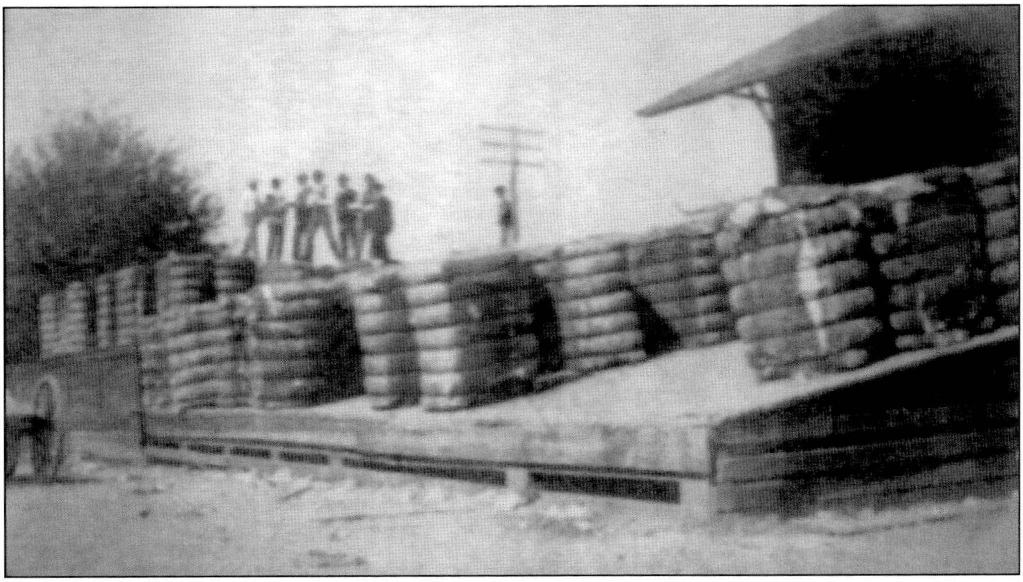

Cotton was king, even in Rayne. These large bales, weighing 500 pounds each, were off-loaded from wagons, then moved up the ramp to the loading dock, which was at the same level as the train. This ramp was on the south side of the freight depot. Visible at center is the telegraph pole that ran along the railroad tracks. There were several cotton gins in Rayne, but the majority of the harvested cotton was shipped to other markets. (Courtesy of Sidney Stutes.)

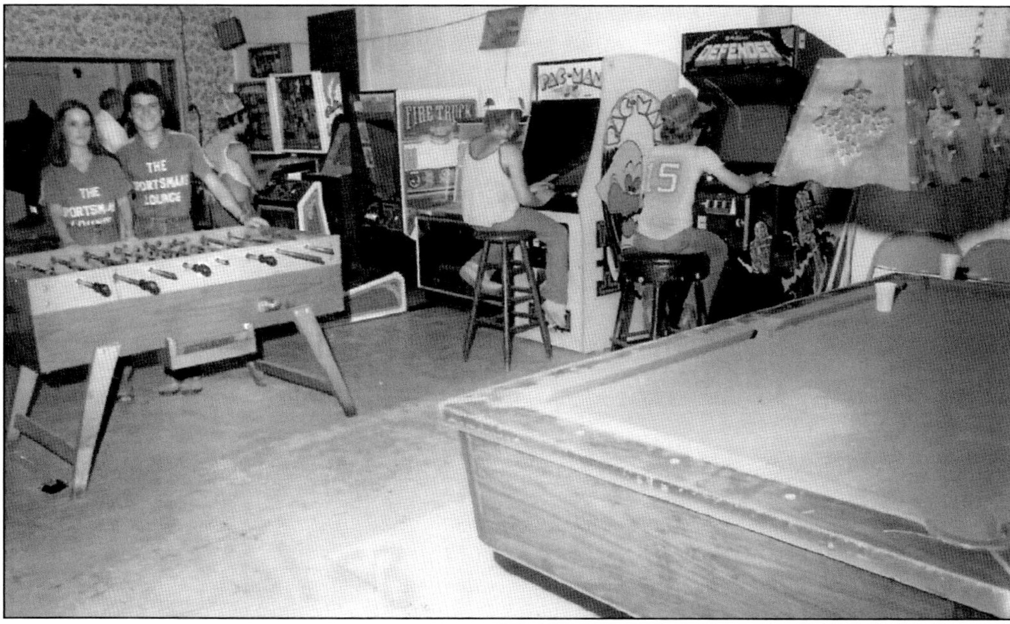

This is a mid-1980s view of the Sportsman's Lounge, located at 206 East Texas Avenue. Among the games are a pool table, foosball, Defender, and Pac-Man. At the time, it was not unusual to see teenagers playing video games in a bar. (Courtesy of *Rayne Independent*.)

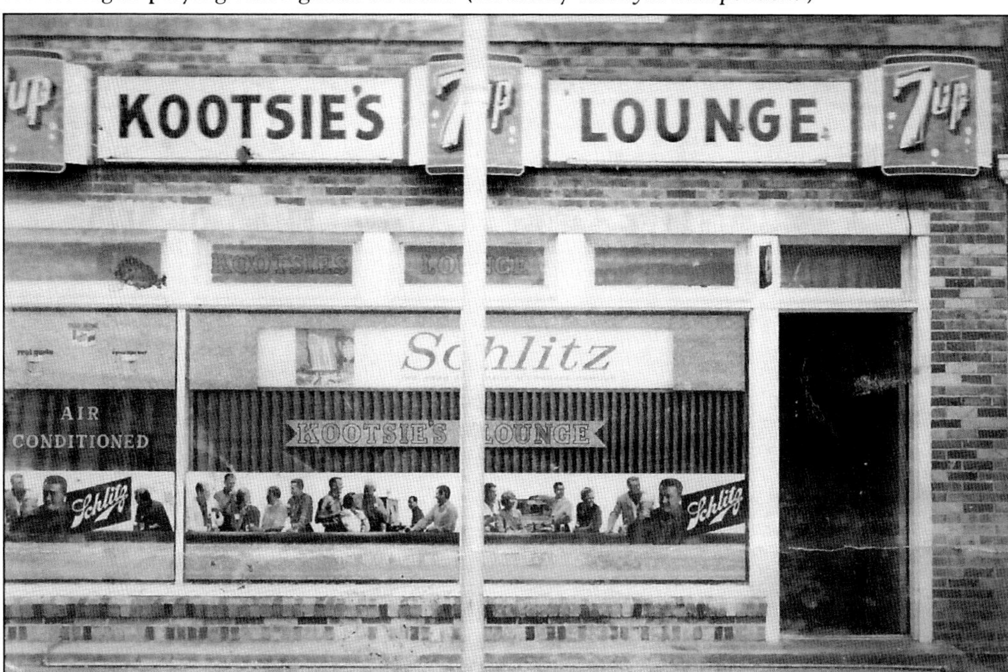

This legendary bar Kootsie's Lounge was initially owned by Wallace Simoneaux and his son William "Kootsie" Simoneaux. Later, Kootsie was the sole proprietor. It stood on East Texas Avenue where Fontenot Insurance is now located. Kootsie Simoneaux counted the bars along Highway 90 in its heyday, and came up with an astonishing total of 39. (Courtesy of William "Kootsie" Simoneaux.)

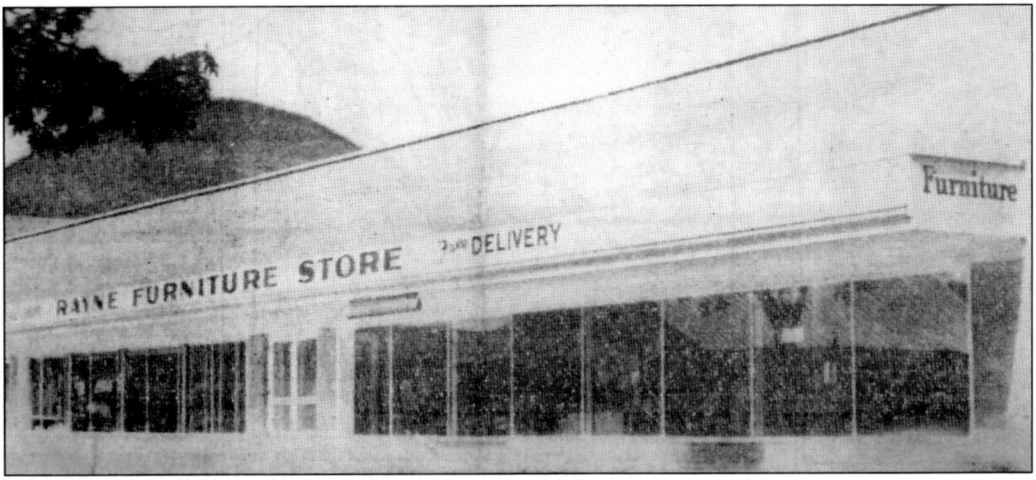

Rayne Furniture Store is pictured during its grand opening in May 1950. It was located on South Polk Street, behind the Joy Theater (the round building in the background). The store was owned by Nick Dischler and Nolan Albarado. The building later served as a Romero's Tire Store and even housed the Brief Encounter Bar, owned by Ed Hoffpauir. (Courtesy of *Rayne Acadian-Tribune*.)

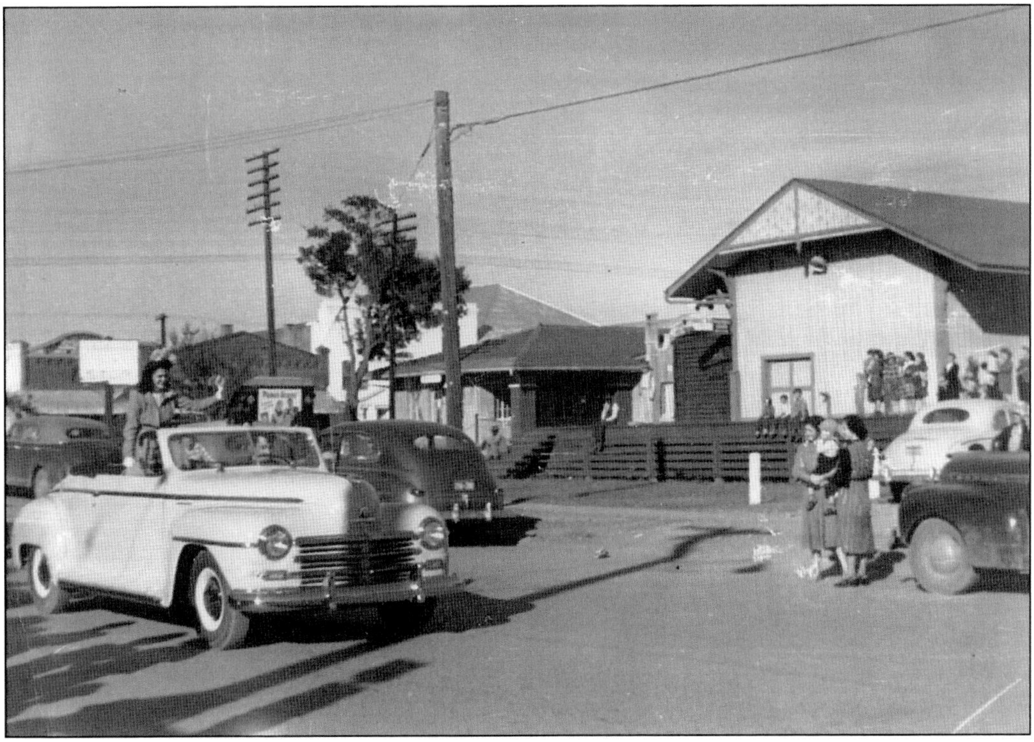

A homecoming parade rolls through the streets of Rayne in the late 1940s. Note the German influence on the structure of the freight depot. The more modern, stucco passenger depot was on the north side of the tracks. (Courtesy of Sidney Stutes.)

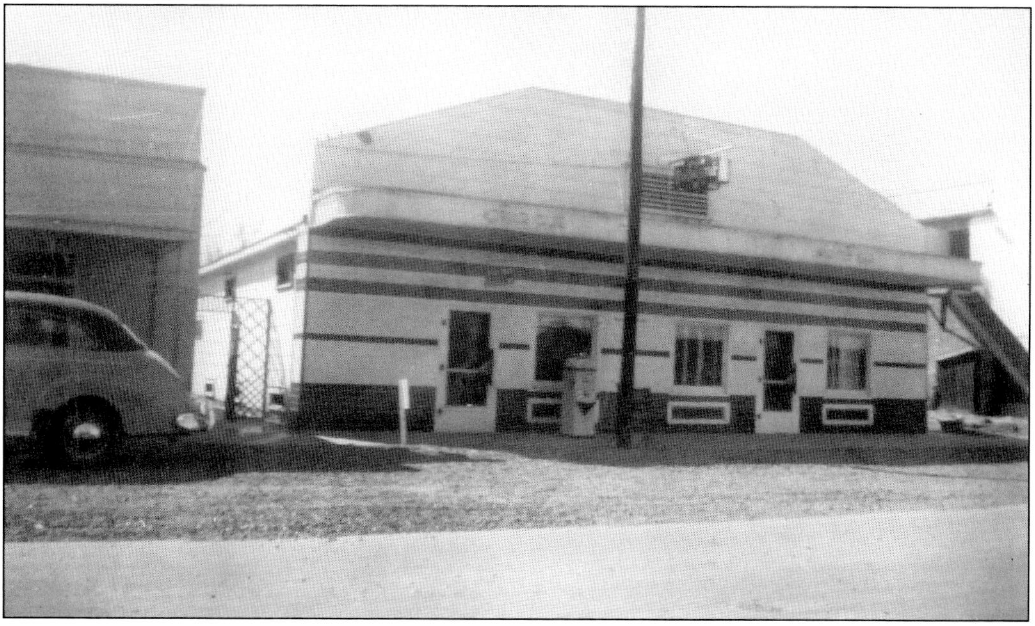

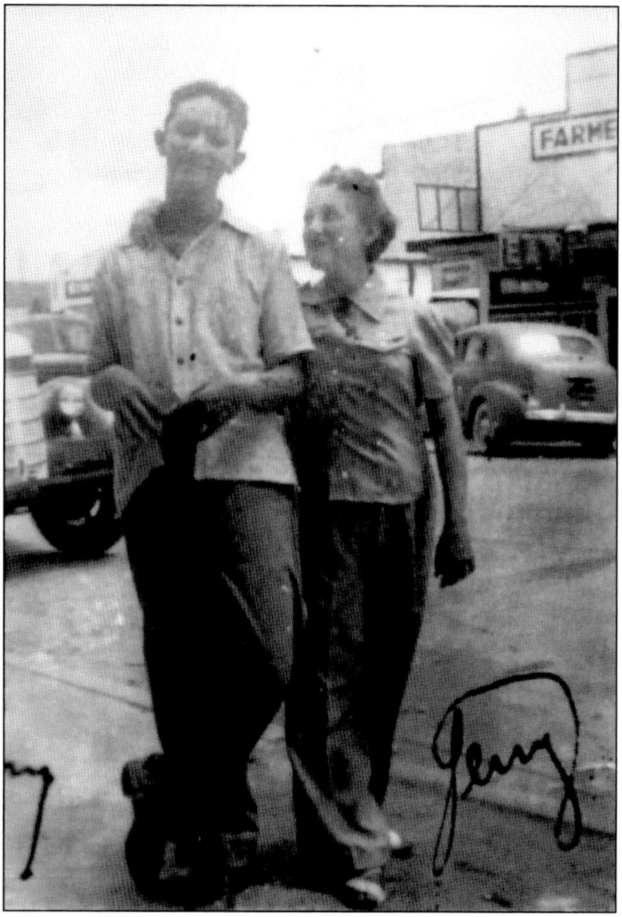

East Texas Avenue was home to many businesses, including this building, which was divided into two sections. On the left side was a pool hall owned by Jimmy Ancelet; on the right was Boudreaux's Bar, owned by George Boudreaux. Andrus Fontenot recalls drinking his first beer there at age 15, a Regal Beer that cost 25¢. On the far left is the Craig Printing Company, owned by Bill Craig. It was later the home of the *Rayne Tribune* and McBride's Office Supply. At far right are the stairs entering the second floor of the first Joy-Acadia Theater. (Courtesy of *Rayne Acadian-Tribune*.)

Anthony "Tony" Privat and Jeraldine "Jerry" McBride are on South Adams Avenue in front of McBride's Pharmacy in the early 1940s. Farmers Cafe is in the background on the right, and to the far left is the Sinclair gas station. It was later a Canal station for many years and is now Cal's Electric. Jeraldine McBride later married A.E. "Shorty" Raymond and Tony Privat ran Privat's Bakery. (Courtesy of Julie Anna Ousse and Butch Ousse.)

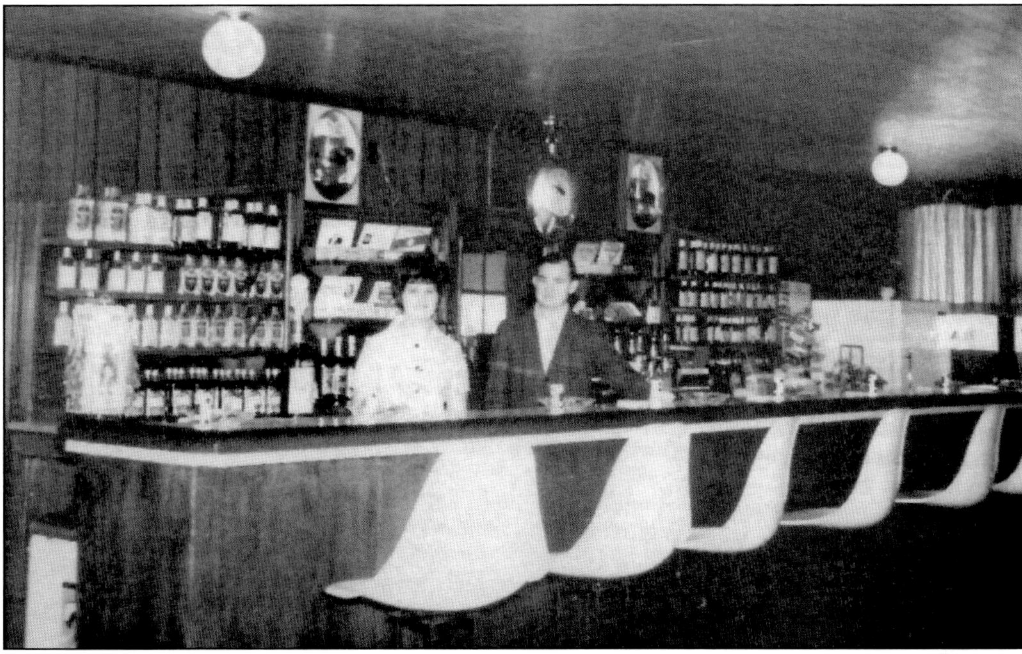

Gene and Martha Royer, owners of Gene's City Bar, pose in their newly remodeled barroom in April 1969. The bar featured new paneling, flooring, light fixtures, bar stools, and table and chair groupings. A free barbecue was held to celebrate the opening. The building was home to many drinking establishments, including, originally, Pop & Herbs, and various versions of the City Bar. It was on West Texas Avenue, behind the old location of Bank of Commerce. The building was torn down many years ago, and the lot is now vacant. (Courtesy of *Rayne Acadian-Tribune*.)

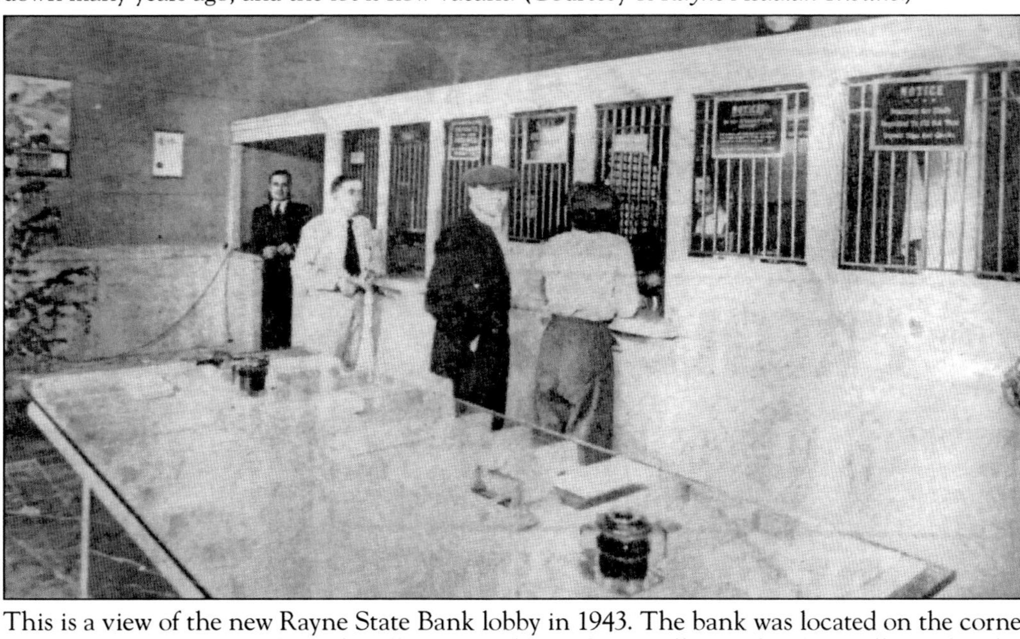

This is a view of the new Rayne State Bank lobby in 1943. The bank was located on the corner of East Texas Avenue and South Polk Street, where Cline, Miller, Richard & Miller had its law offices. Bercier Family Dentistry is currently housed in the building. Here, Oscar "Paco" Borne (second from left) conducts banking business for his café. (Courtesy of *Rayne Acadian-Tribune*.)

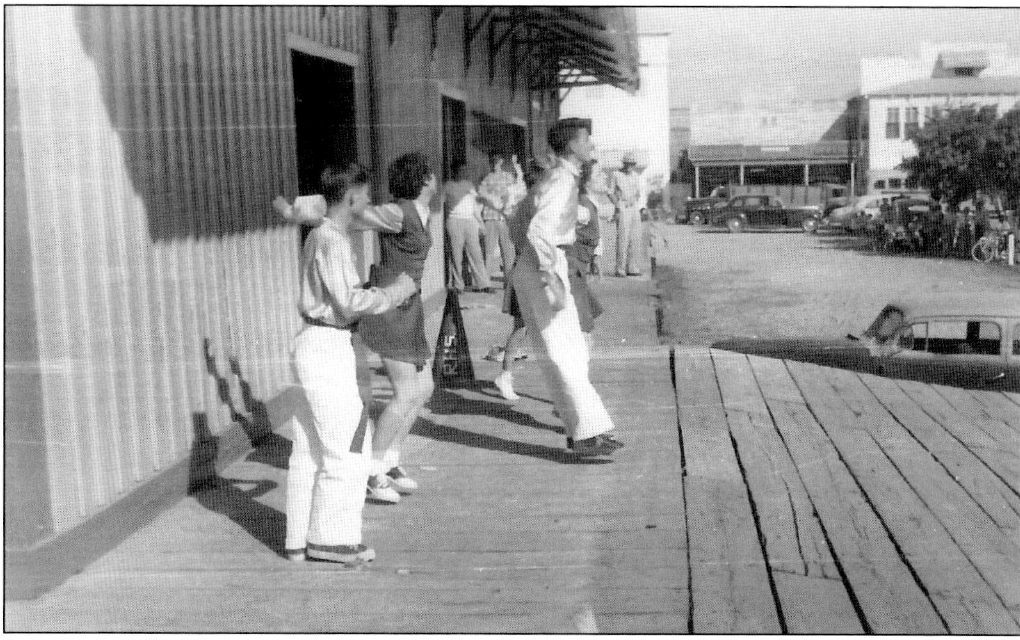

A homecoming pep rally conducted by the Rayne High School cheerleaders is being held on the loading dock of the freight depot. A parade before the big game started at Rayne High and marched down Polk Street to the depot. Visible in the background are Orton Besse's Firestone (center) and the Town House Restaurant (right). (Courtesy of Sidney Stutes.)

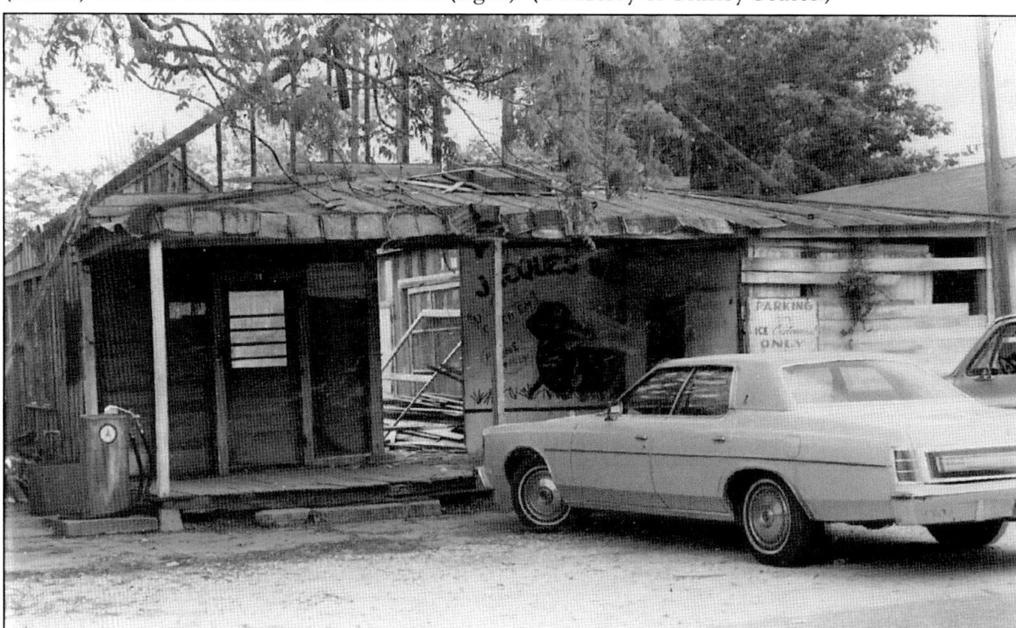

The historic Jacques Weil building, located in the 200 block of South Polk Street, is seen being torn down in 1976. The author lived next door to Wiltz and Eloise Chatelain, the owners, and helped move office furniture and equipment into storage. Many years later, the estate donated these important artifacts to the City of Rayne, and they are now on display at the J.D. Bernard Home on The Boulevard. (Courtesy of Melba Olinger.)

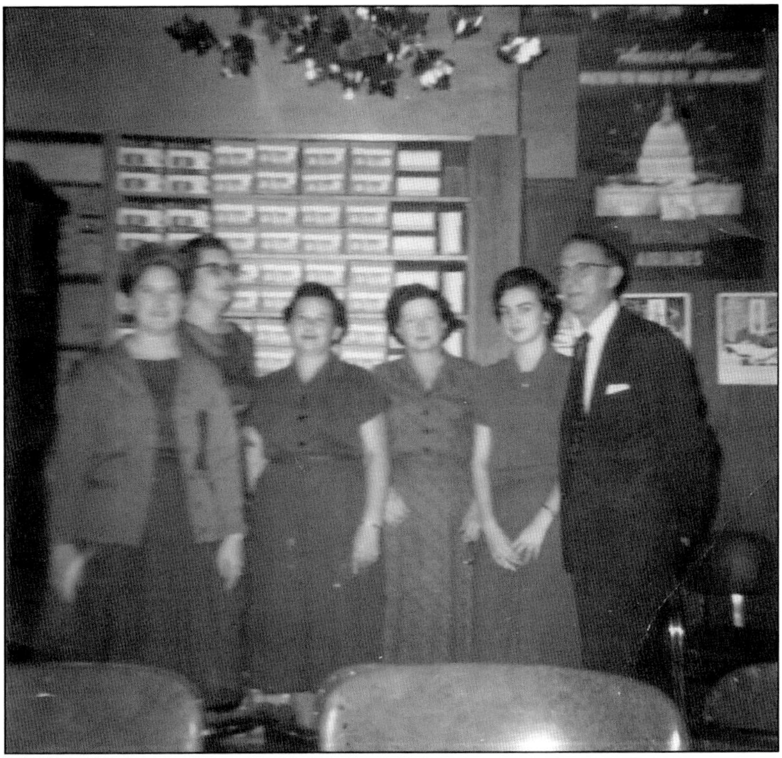

The staff of the Mervine Kahn Company shoe department poses on December 25, 1959. From left to right are Mary Nell Smith, Effi Hebert, Hazel Trahan, Eva Guidry, Bertha Doucet, and manager Walter Beslin. Beslin went to work at Mervine's in 1928 and was employed there for over 50 years. He set a retail record for fitting over 300,000 pairs of shoes in his career. (Courtesy of Denald Beslin.)

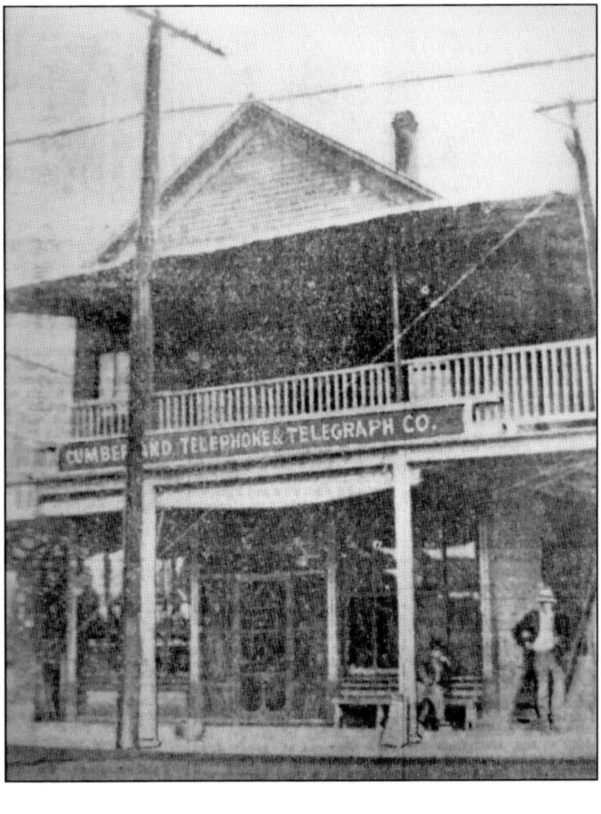

The Cumberland Telephone & Telegraph Company is seen here at the corner of East Texas Avenue and South Polk Street, facing East Texas Avenue in the early 1900s. It was later bought out by Bell Systems. On this corner, the Besse Hotel & Restaurant was built many years later. (Courtesy of *Rayne Acadian-Tribune*.)

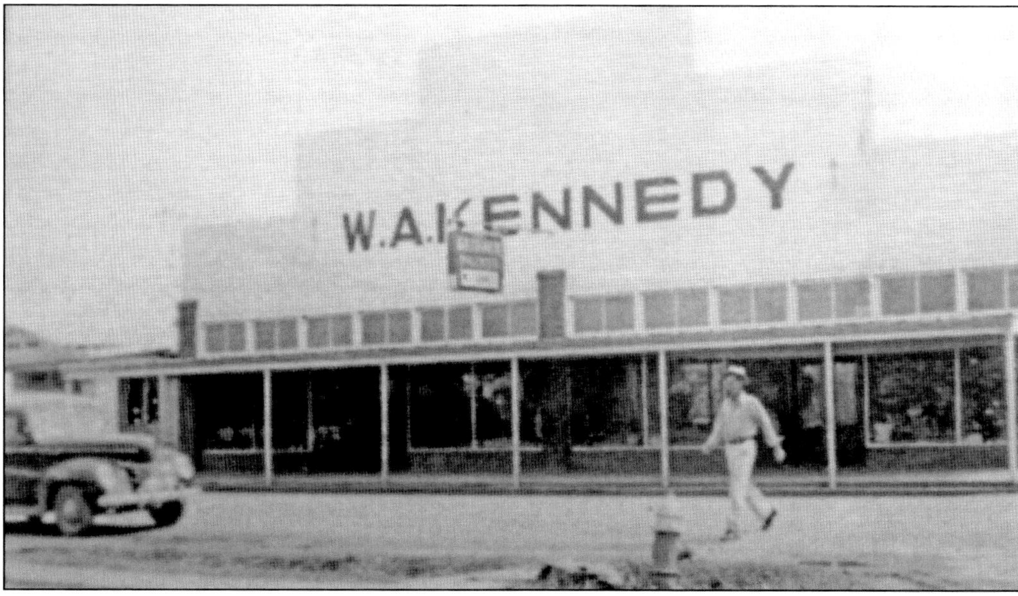

The W.A. Kennedy Store was located in the 200 block of North Polk Street. It was founded by Gustavus Kennedy as the G.A. Kennedy Store. He later partnered with his brother Wilbur Kennedy. After the deaths of the Kennedy brothers, Walter, Bertha, Myrtle, and Helena "Honey" Kennedy then co-owned the business until it closed in 1968. It was known as the "Complete Store," offering anything that was needed. The store competed with Mervine Kahn Company for many years, being only a block away. (Courtesy of *Rayne Independent.*)

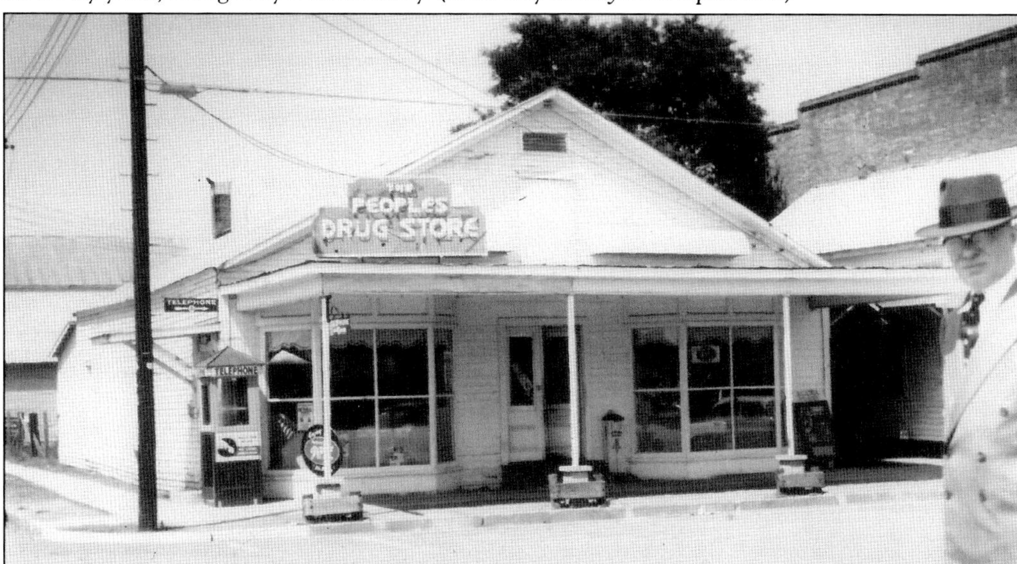

Arnold Kahn poses in front of his People's Drug Store on the corner of East Louisiana Avenue and North Polk Street. It was the first commercial building in Rayne to offer a new feature to customers—air-conditioning. It also had a soda fountain, with nectars being a local favorite. On the immediate right is the medical office of Dr. J.P. Mauboules. The Mervine Kahn Warehouse is on the far right. The drugstore was torn down in 1956, and a modern brick building was erected in its place. (Courtesy of Marguerite Kahn Hoskin.)

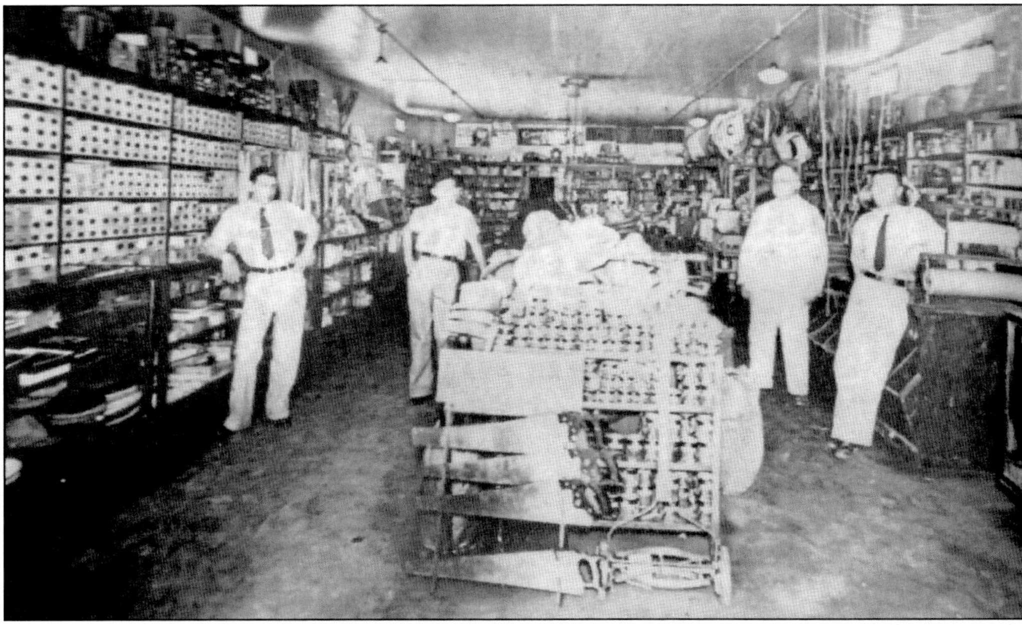

This interior photograph of the McDonald-Johnston Store shows its wares in the early 1900s. The men are, from left to right, Wilbert Laine, Guy Johnston, W.G. McDonald, and Louis Arceneaux. Located at the corner of North Adams Avenue and Edwards Street, the building was later the home of many establishments, including the post office. J&J Cleaners now occupies the building. (Courtesy of *Rayne Acadian-Tribune*.)

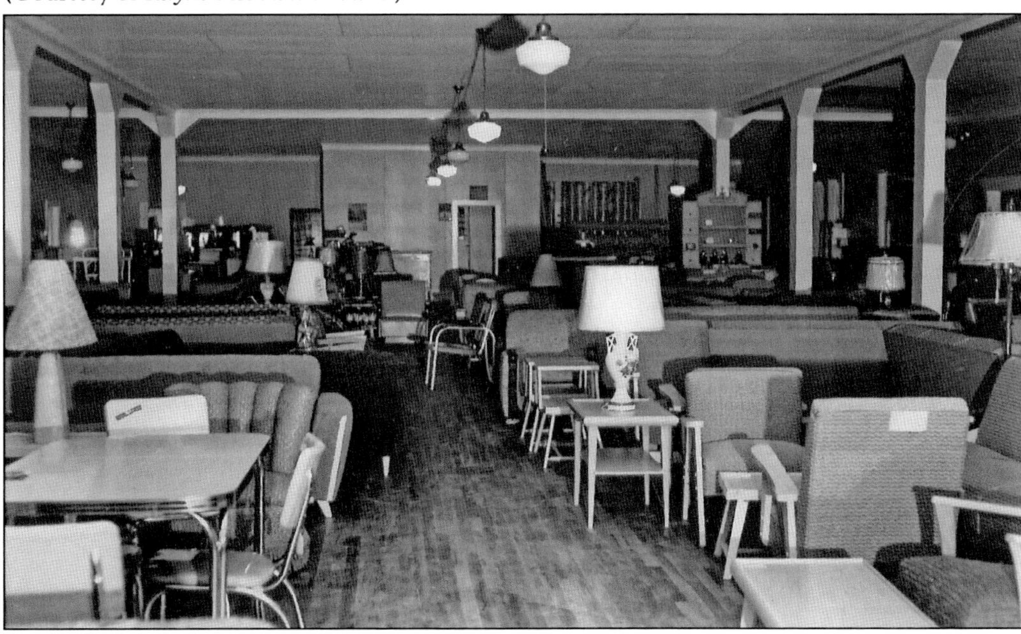

For many years, about the only place to buy furniture in Rayne was the Acadia Furniture Store, located on South Adams Avenue across from St. Joseph Catholic Church. It was founded in 1946 by a partnership between Pete Devillier, August Chappuis, and Jimmy Venable. Here, the showroom displays dinette sets and assorted furniture. The building now houses the Family Life Center for St. Joseph Catholic Church. (Courtesy of *Rayne Independent*.)

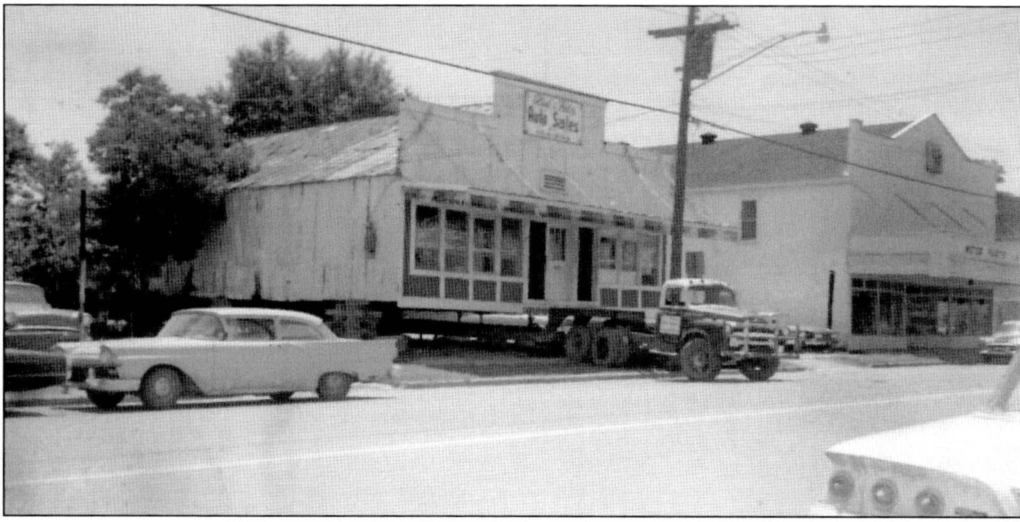

Customers could call Red & Fats Used Cars at ED4-5169. Opened in 1956, the dealership was owned by Walter "Red" Hebert and managed by Wallace "Fats" LeBlanc. The building was moved back on its South Adams Avenue lot to display cars in front. It was moved by Trahan House Moving for $380. Originally housing Bailey Radio Company in 1936, this building was home to many businesses over the years. At right is NAPA Motor Parts, where Farmers True Value is today. (Courtesy of Sidney Stutes.)

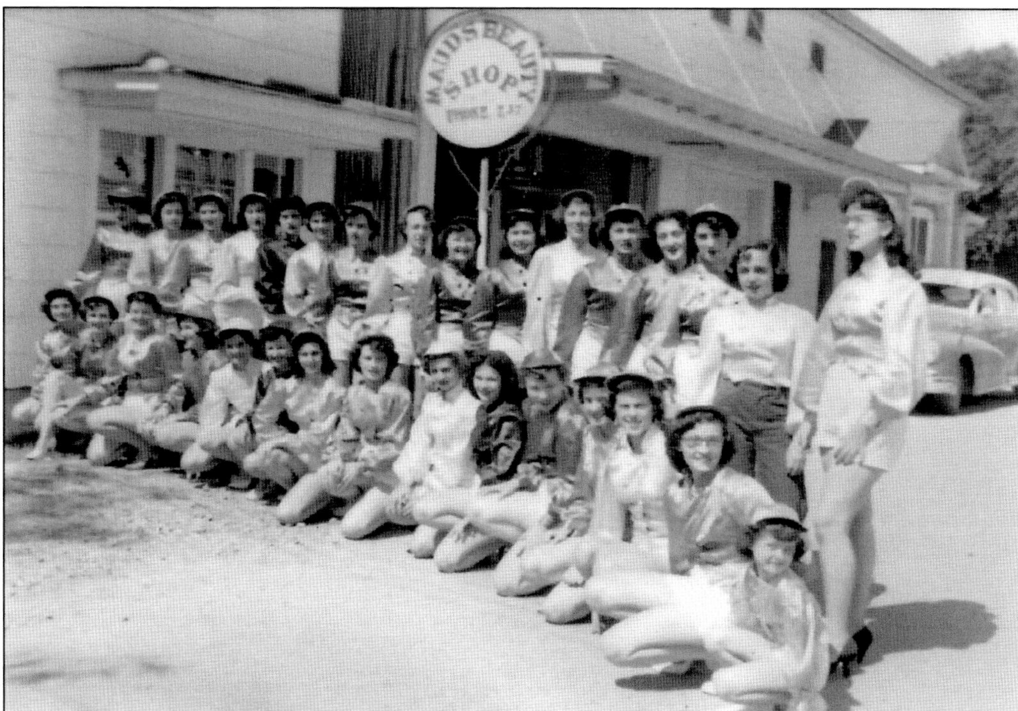

These Rayne Lions Club Frog Jockeys pose for a publicity photograph wearing their "silks" uniforms. The photograph was taken on Devil's Alley (now Gabriel's Alley), probably in the early 1950s. The Rayne fire station is in the background. At left is Maud's Beauty Shop (call 237 to make an appointment). (Courtesy of *Rayne Independent*.)

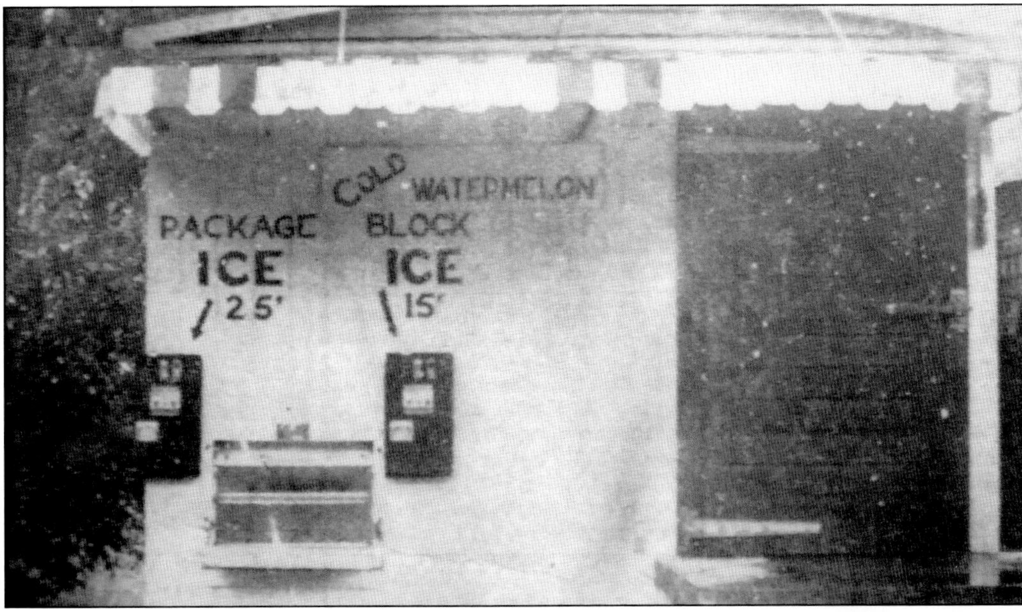

The Jacques Weil Produce Iceteria is shown here in 1954 on its first day of business. It advertised packaged crushed ice for 25¢ or block ice for 15¢, any time of day or night. Owned by Wiltz J. Chatelain, it had the coldest watermelon at the lowest prices in town. The author went to buy ice with his dad, and knew to keep his hand away from the chute when the block ice came down. The Jacque Weil building was located on South Polk Street, behind what is now Bercier Family Dentistry. (Courtesy of *Rayne Acadian-Tribune*.)

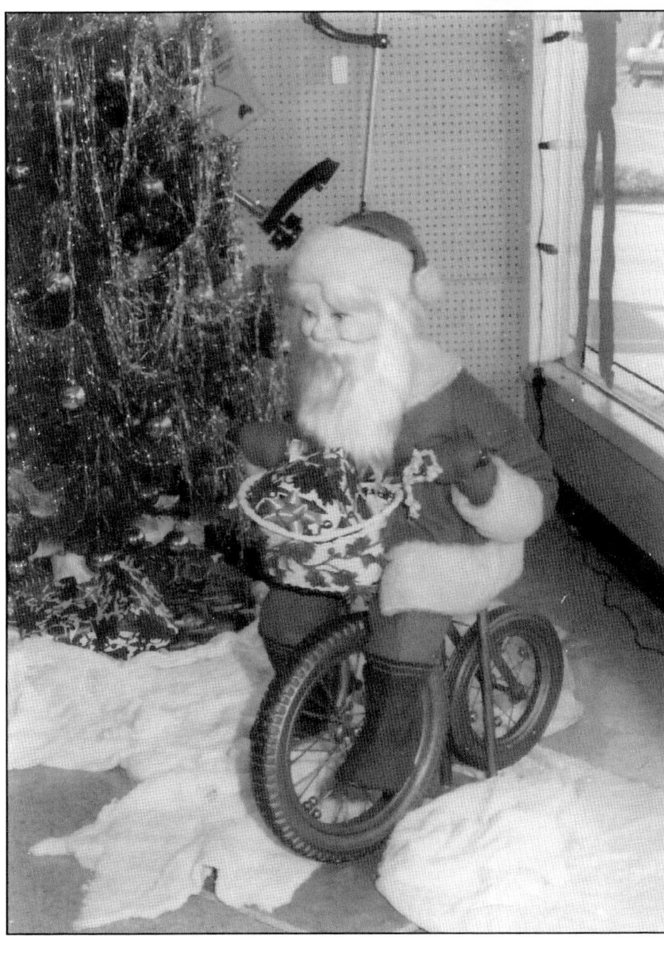

Not all things lost in Rayne were buildings or businesses. Certain items or events will always hold a special part of the past. One such item was this Santa Claus riding a motorized bicycle in the large picture-glass window at E.C. Fremaux's every Christmas season. (Courtesy of *Rayne Independent*.)

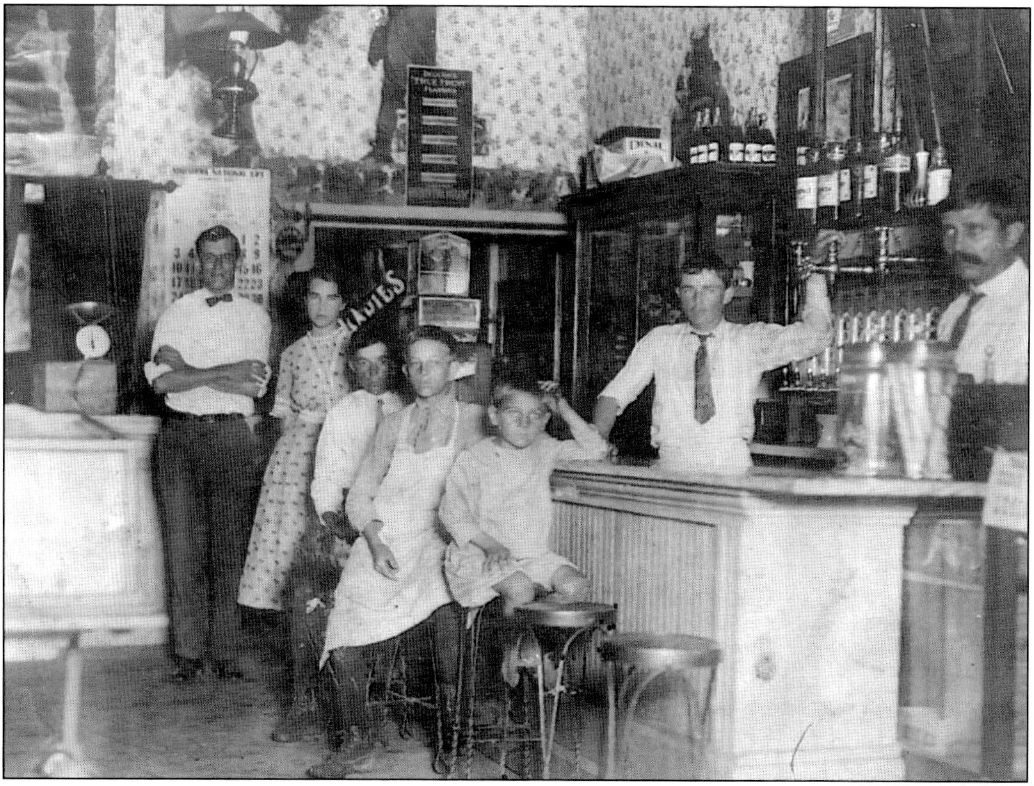

This early photograph of O. Broussard's Pharmacy apparently was taken at the newly installed soda fountain. The photograph predates electricity, as evidenced by the oil lantern hanging from the ceiling at left. (Courtesy of Sidney Stutes.)

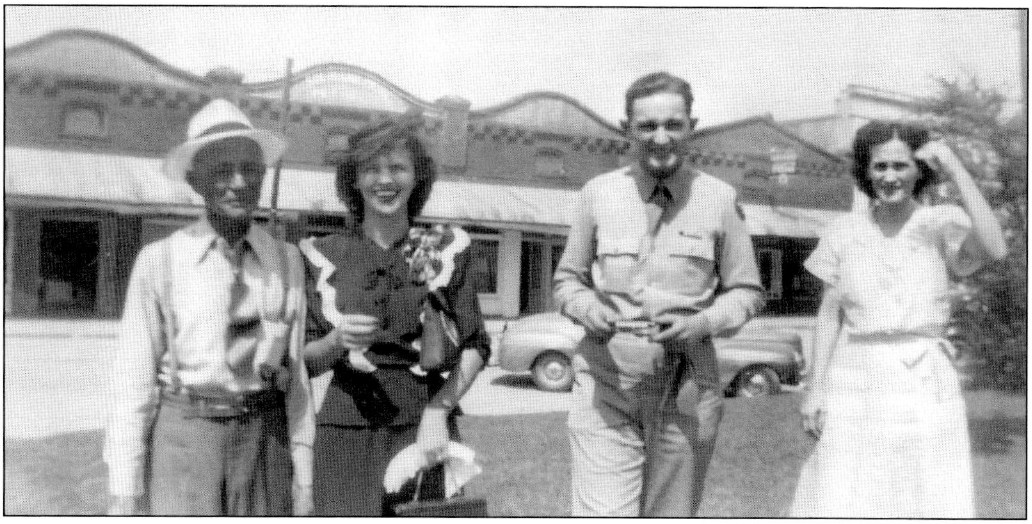

This late 1940s photograph shows the downtown business area of East Louisiana Avenue in the background. The establishments include, from left to right, Sol Kahn general merchandise, T-Mier's bar, a café, and Mervine Kahn Company. The persons seen here are, from left to right, Joe Privat, Rita Privat, Tony Privat (Rita's husband), and Julie Privat (Joe's wife). Note the Sol Kahn sign painted at the top of the building. (Courtesy of Julie Anna and Butch Ousse.)

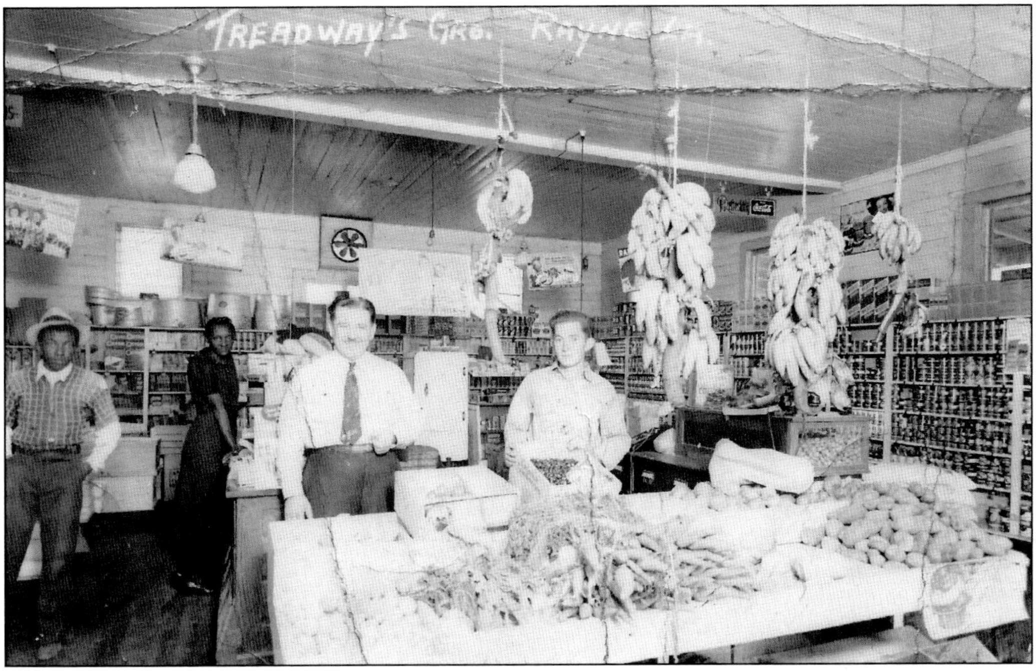

This is a rare view of the inside of Treadway's Grocery Store in the mid-1940s. From left to right are two unidentified, Batson Richard, and Otis Hoffpauir. James "Tie" Treadway bought the Red and White Grocery in 1940. It was originally the Matt Rimmer & Herbert J. Sills Grocery Store. Treadway then sold the business to Batson Richard in 1949, and it became Batson's Grocery. It was on the corner of North Adams and East Edwards Avenues. The building was torn down and Rayne Building & Loan currently occupies the corner. (Courtesy of Lou Hoffpauir.)

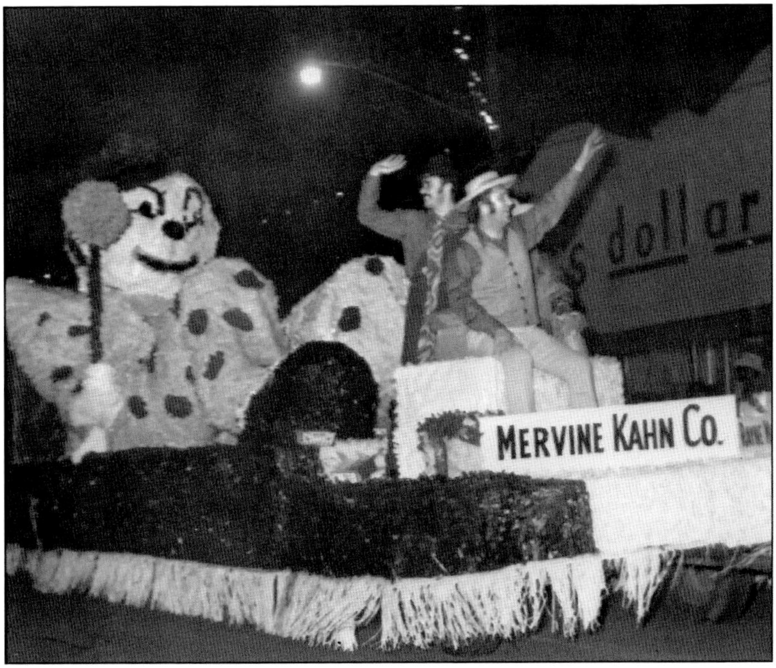

Downtown Rayne was the scene of many parades over the years, including this one, the annual Christmas Parade. Riding on a Mervine Kahn Company float is a familiar face, Polycarp Philip Pecot II (in straw hat), beloved morning host of *Polycarp* on KATC-TV 3. To his left is the Crazy Professor, "VJ" Boulet, from Rayne. (Courtesy of Rayne Independent.)

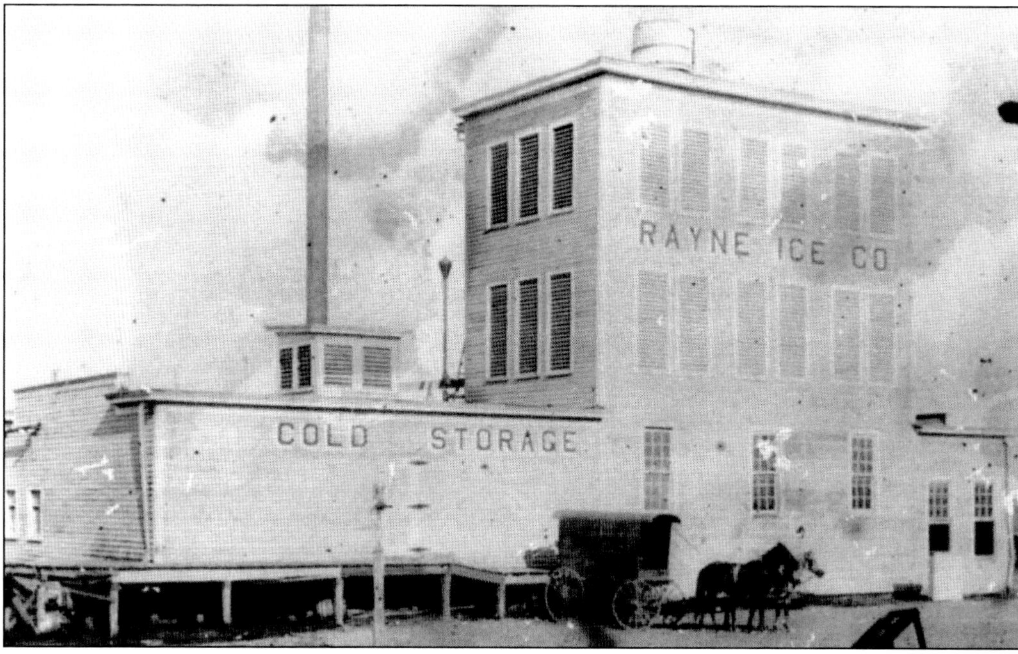

Before electricity and refrigerators were widespread, iceboxes kept food cold. This is the Rayne Ice Company, located on West Texas Avenue across from the Rayne Power Plant and along the railroad tracks. Large blocks of ice would come out of the freezer and were cut in 5¢, 10¢, or 25¢ blocks. The blocks were then delivered in a horse-drawn wagon such as the one shown here. The cold storage was used to store perishable goods. (Courtesy of Sidney Stutes.)

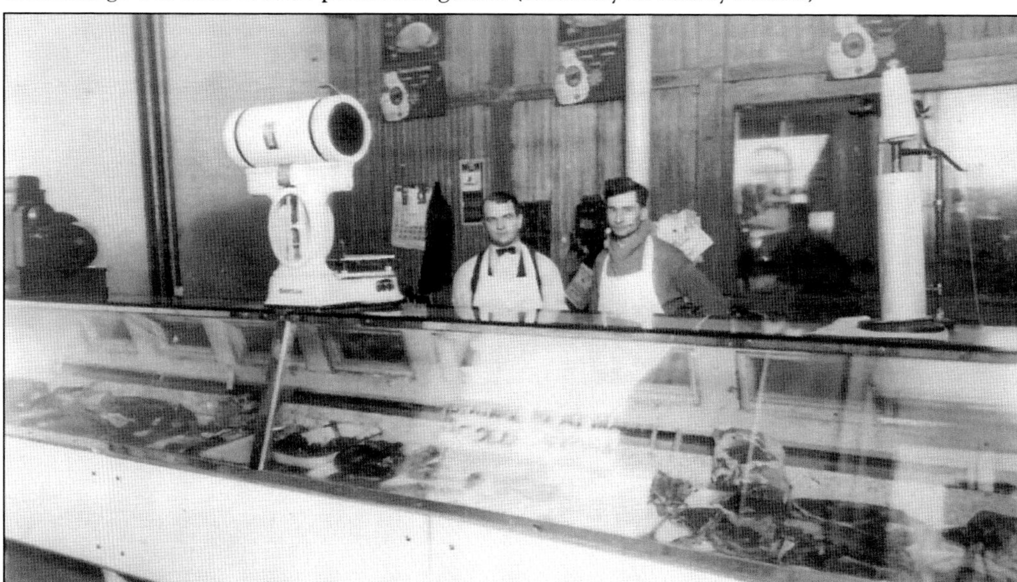
Robichaux's Meat Market was a landmark business in Rayne for many years. Behind the counter is Lauless Robichaux (left) and Emile Dumesnil. Robichaux's was located on the bottom floor of the two-story LaCroix Building on the corner of South Adams and West Texas Avenues. Rayne State Bank purchased the property and built its present building on the corner. (Courtesy of Rose Marie R. Stelly.)

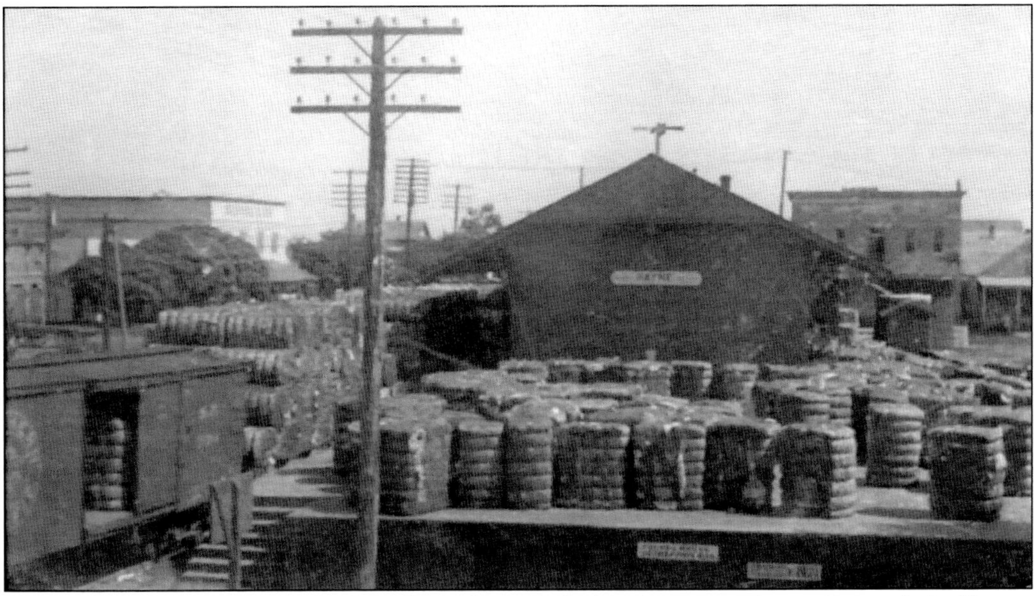

This postcard shows the sheer number of cotton bales that were shipped out of the Rayne depot during the harvesting season. The photograph was taken from the second floor of the O. Broussard Pharmacy in 1905. Many familiar landmarks around town are visible here. (Courtesy of Melba Olinger.)

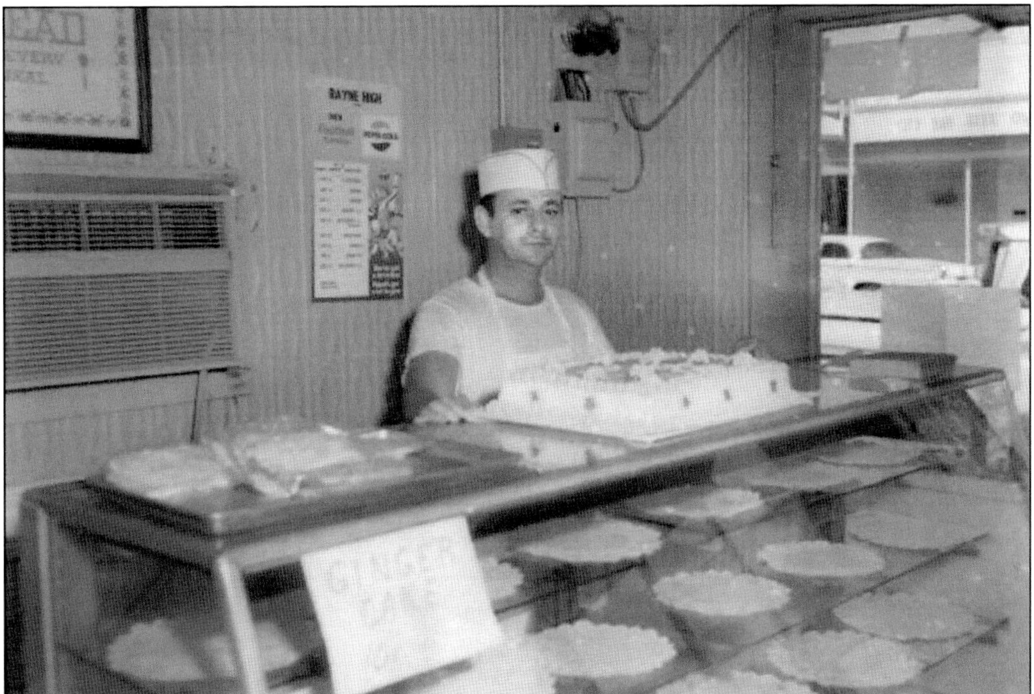

Charlie Arceneaux is behind the counter of his business, Charlie's Bakery, in 1969. This was another bakery operating in the old Privat building on West Texas Avenue, behind Rayne State Bank. Visible on the back wall is the 1969 Rayne High School basketball schedule. Seen through the window is the City Bar. (Courtesy of *Rayne Independent.*)

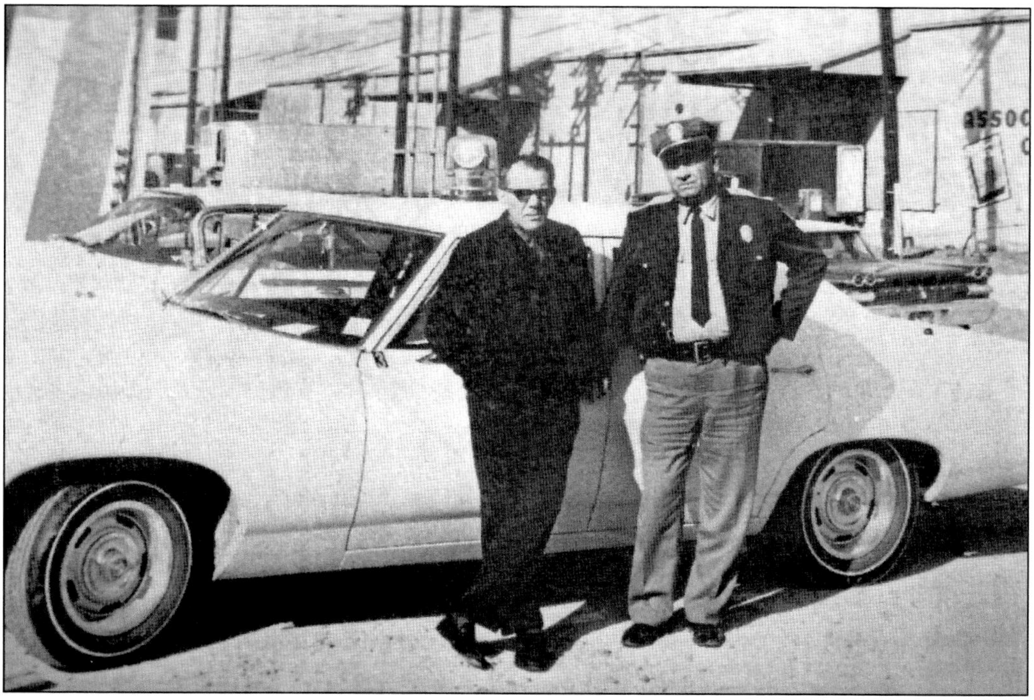

The city purchased a 1967 Chevrolet Biscayne from Bernard Brothers as its newest police unit. Pictured next to the car are Raleigh Bernard (left) and officer Asa Touchet. At that time, the police station was located on West Texas Avenue, next to the power plant. Rayne Wholesale's massive buildings can be seen in the background, including a mural indicating that Associated Brands products were packaged there. (Courtesy of *Rayne Acadian-Tribune*.)

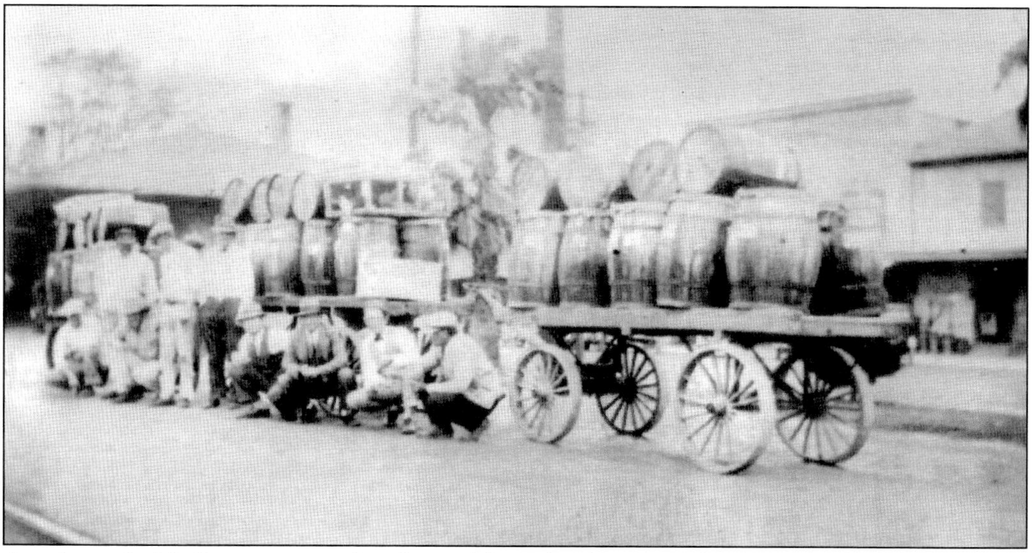

Another valuable Rayne commodity shipped from the depot was the *Rana catesbeiana*, Louisiana bullfrog. This photograph, taken on the north side of the tracks, shows barrels full of frog legs destined for restaurants. This photograph was used in producing the mural painted by Robert Dafford on the side of Koury's Jewelry Store on North Adams Avenue and West Edwards Street. (Courtesy of Fair Craig Hash.)

Two

Old Spanish Trail

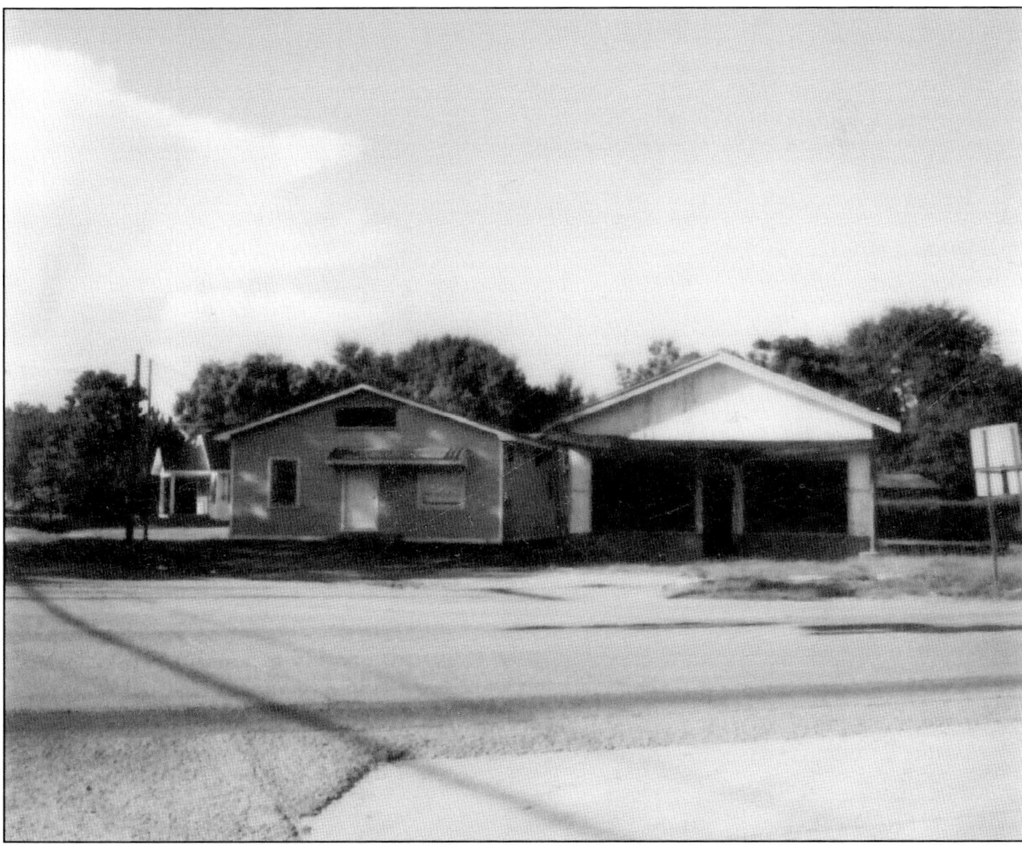

The Old Spanish Trail, or the OST, as it is better known, connected St. Augustine, Florida, to San Diego, California, and passed through Rayne. Later named Highway 90, it brought prosperity until Interstate 10 was opened in 1966. This corner of Highway 90 and Abbeville Highway shows a Sinclair station (right) and "Papa George" Saloom's grocery store. The gas station was torn down, and the store was sold and moved away in 1976. Hilary and Melba Olinger built Olinger's TV & Radio Shack on the corner. (Courtesy Melba Olinger.)

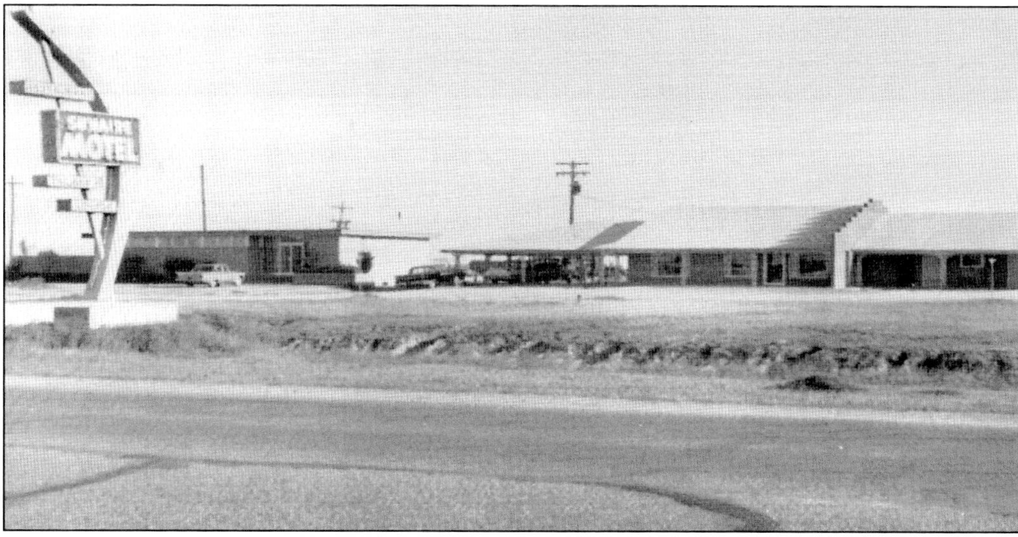

In 1958, the Sunaire Motel was opened by Lloyd Nickel of Crowley. It offered a state-of-the-art restaurant, cocktail lounge, and 12 rooms. Located just outside of Rayne on East Highway 90, the motel was closed and reopened several times for many years after. It was a popular place for drinking and for playing dominos and high-stakes poker. (Courtesy of *Rayne Acadian-Tribune.*)

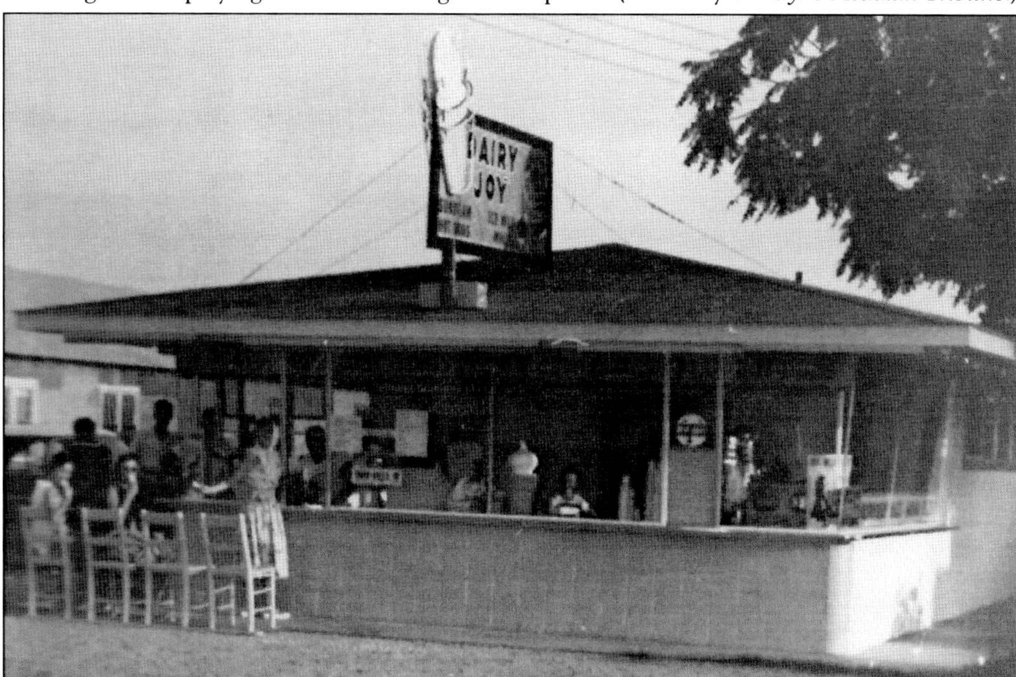

This business originally opened as Dairy Maid in September 1953, with Earl "T-Ring" Bolnar as manager. It was located next to Builder's (Babineaux's) Lumber Yard and across from Rayne Economy Motors on Highway 90 West. It offered Polar Pies, Nutty Bears, malts, shakes, and sundaes. Its name was later changed to Dairy Joy and was owned by a doctor. Clet Richard managed it then, and he eventually bought out the business. Dairy Joy was known for its hot dogs and dip cones in a cup. (Courtesy of Sidney Stutes.)

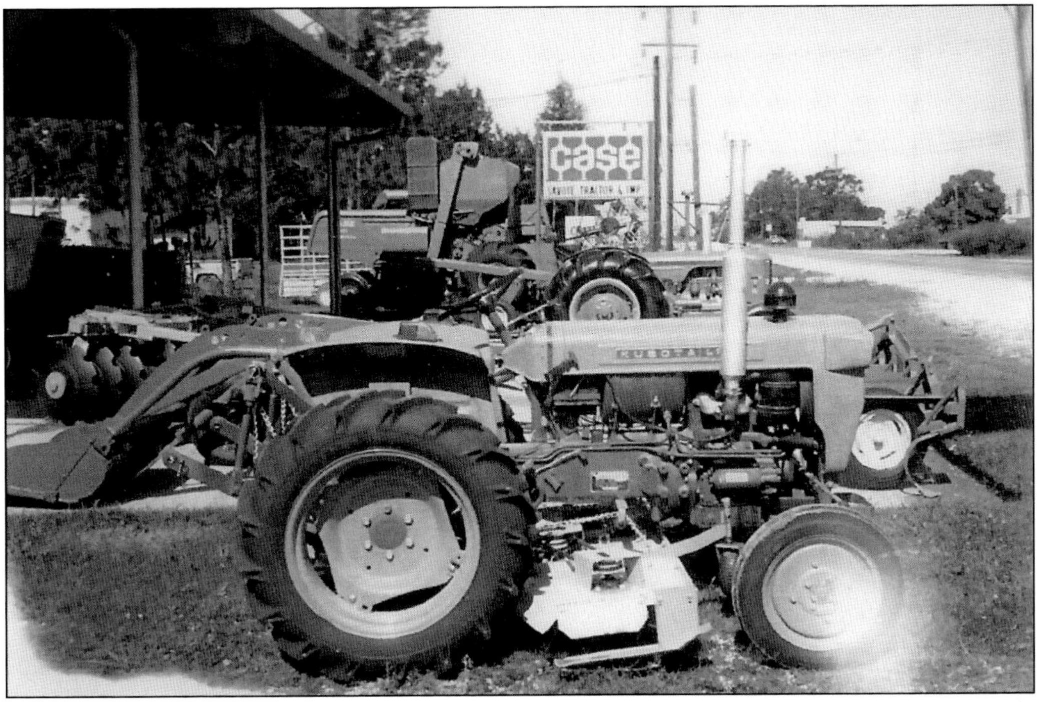

Savoie Tractor & Implement Company had a Rayne branch business on West Highway 90 and Hilda Street, with the main office in Crowley. Kids loved to see the tractors and combines in front of the building. There was also a large loading dock in front of Stamm-Scheele to unload equipment from the trains. Venable Fabricators now occupies the building. (Courtesy of *Rayne Independent*.)

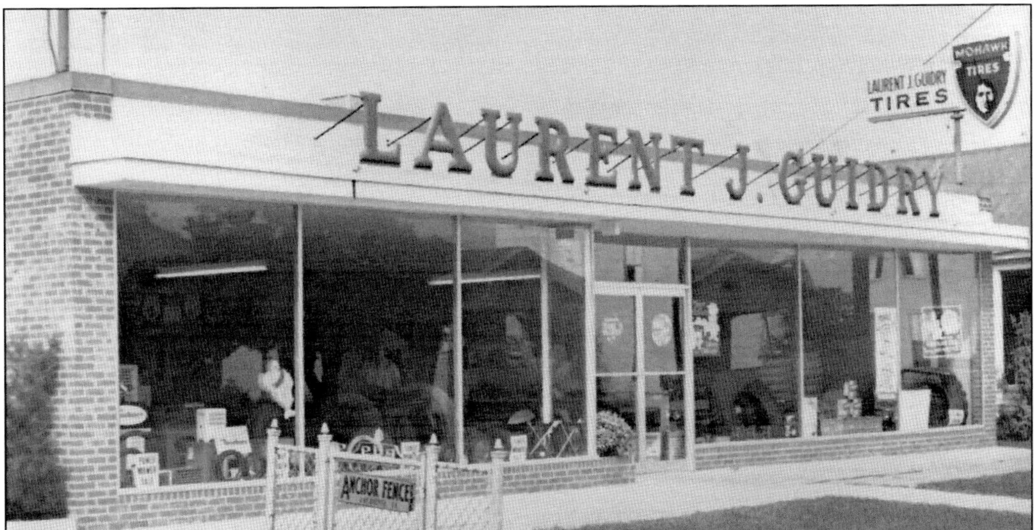

These are the picture windows of Laurent J. Guidry Tires, founded in July 1947 at 310 South Adams Avenue. The business grew, and to keep up with demand, additions were made in 1957. In 1967, the company moved to Highway 90 East to expand its service department and warehouse. It offered a large line of tires, including Dunlop, tire recapping, and alignments. The picture windows have since been bricked in, and this is now the Gilbert Building. (Courtesy of *Rayne Acadian-Tribune*.)

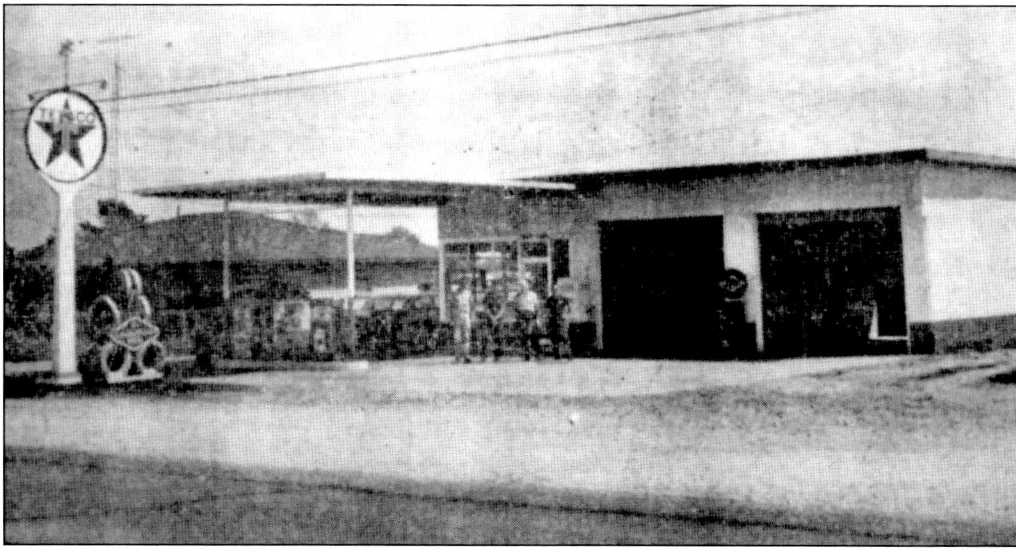

This 1961 photograph was taken before Lester J. Richard held the grand opening for his new gas station. Posing here are, from left to right, Anatole Thibodeaux, Willie Foreman Jr., Lester J. Richard, and Willie Foreman Sr. The Texaco service station was located on Highway 90 West and Live Oak Street, where C.J.'s Garage is now located. (Courtesy of *Rayne Acadian-Tribune.*)

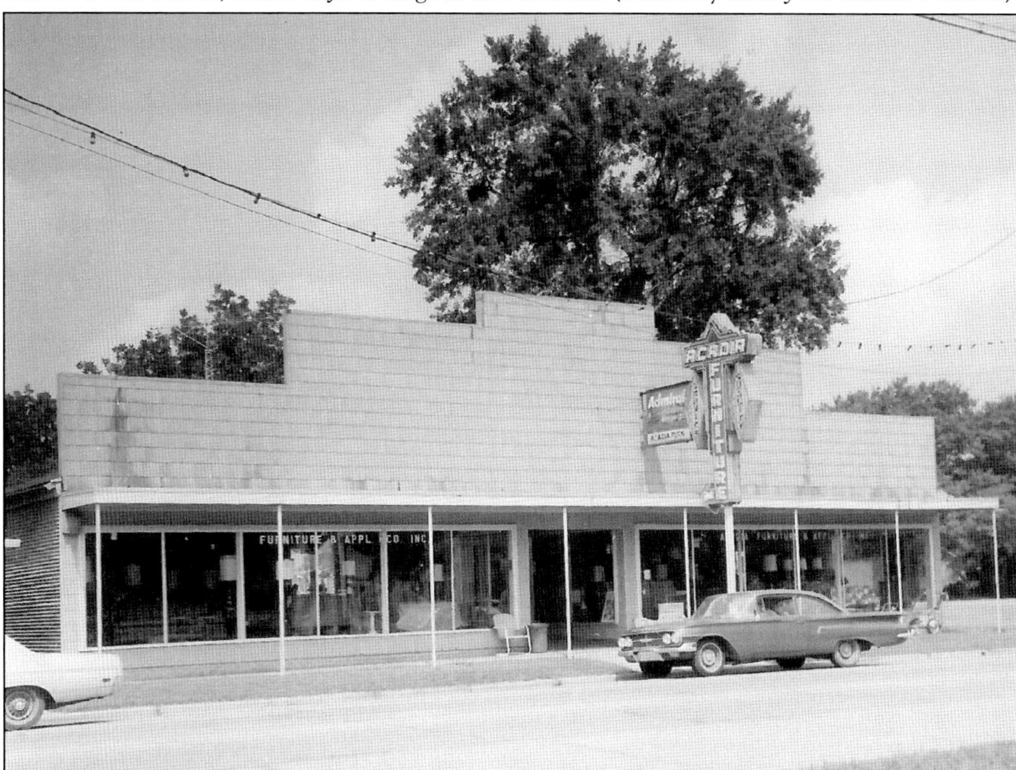

The Acadia Furniture Store operated at this location, in front of St. Joseph Catholic Church on South Adams Avenue. The company had a large warehouse in the back, on Devil's Alley (renamed Gabriel's Alley). (Courtesy of *Rayne Independent.*)

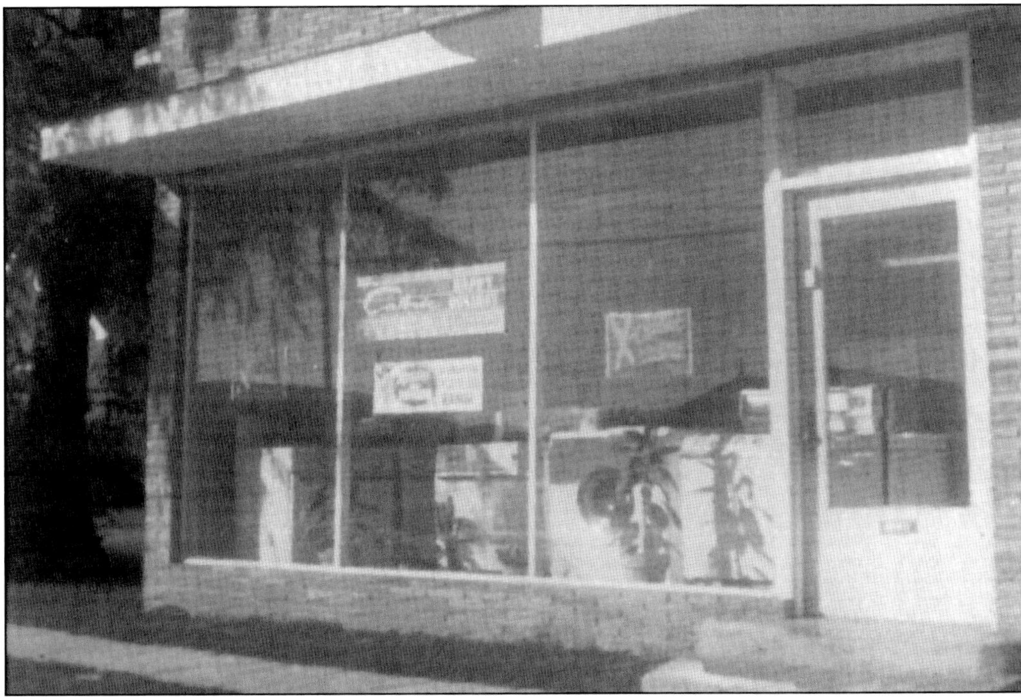

This is the United Gas Company Building on South Adams Avenue in 1953. With the discovery of natural gas in the Bosco fields, cities like Rayne had access to affordable gas service. This building later housed Entex Gas and then was used by Josie Henry for her trophy shop. It eventually was torn down to make room for the expansion of the Piggly Wiggly grocery store. (Courtesy of *Rayne Acadian-Tribune*.)

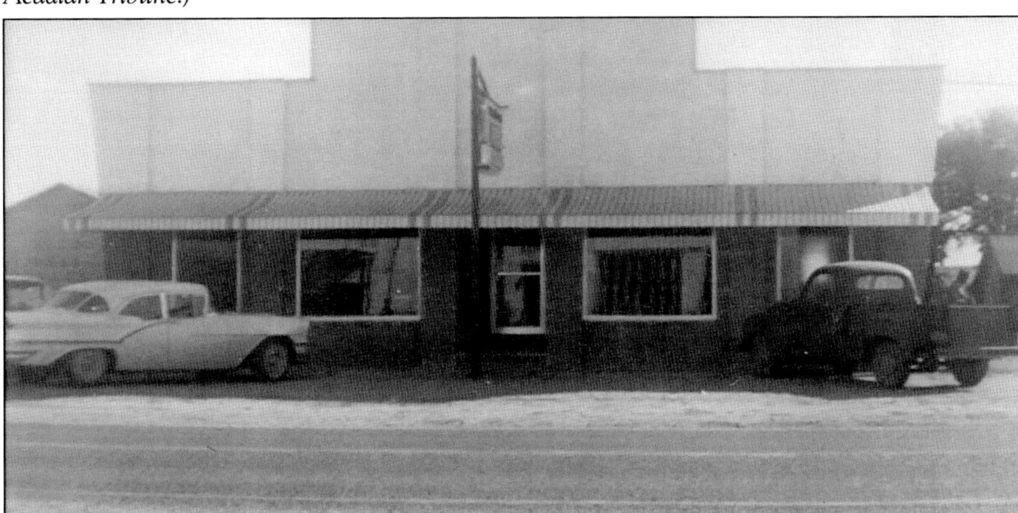

Originally Builder's Lumber Yard, then renamed Babineaux Brothers Lumber Yard, this business was owned by Lionel, Pete, and Desire' Babineaux. In the rear of the property, Babineaux Brothers also ran the Louisiana Frog Company, where they had a large frog pen. As a young boy, the author remembers taking a field trip to see the frogs while attending Rayne Catholic Elementary. In 1974, this location became Guidry Lumber Yard, owned by Douglas "Bee" Guidry. (Courtesy of *Rayne Independent*.)

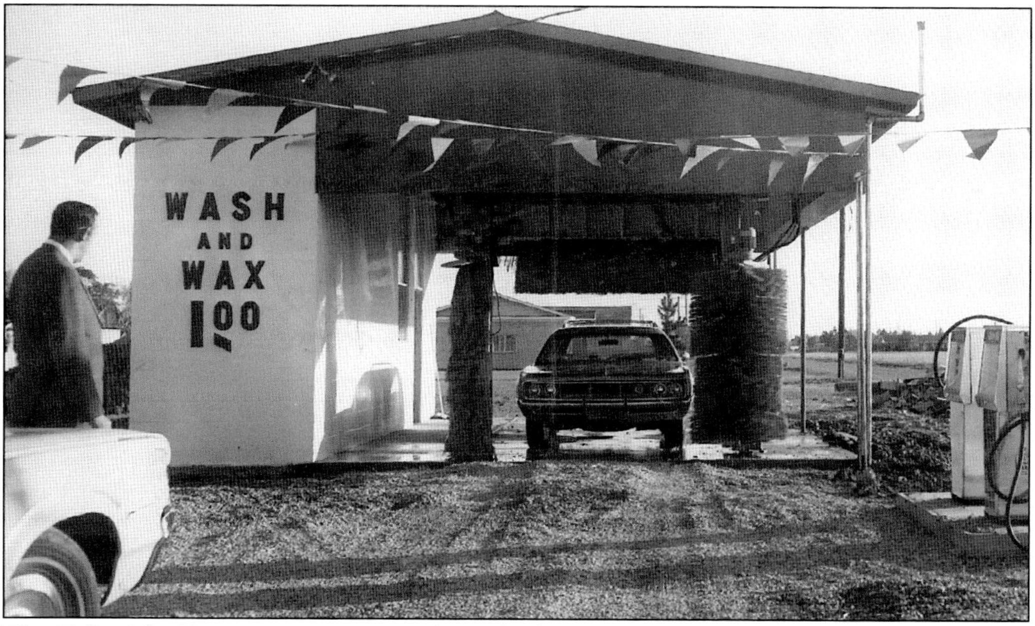

This Talk of the Town automatic car wash was built in 1969 by Dr. Benny Thibodeaux, seen here watching a car being washed. Located on the corner of Comeaux Street and West Highway 90, it was reported to be the first automatic car wash, not only in Rayne, but in Louisiana. The facility had gas pumps (right) and employed a full-time attendant. (Courtesy of *Rayne Independent.*)

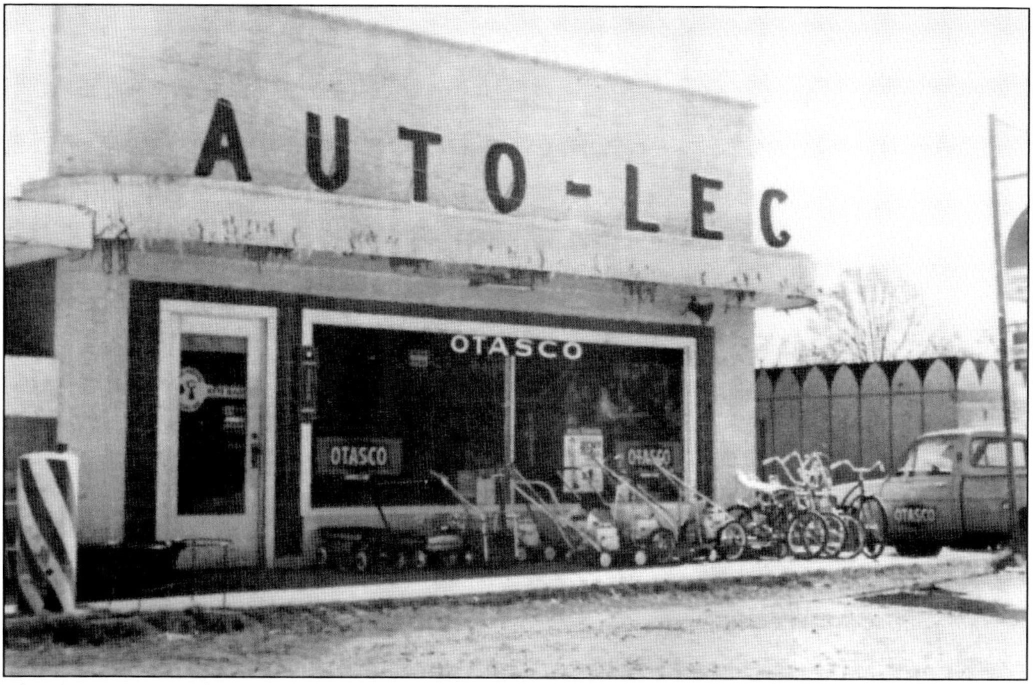

The Auto-Lec Hardware Store was located at 705 South Adams Avenue, where Gautreaux's Donut Kitchen now operates. Auto-Lec was originally owned by J. Glady Johnson. G.B "Brad" Thomas purchased the business in 1969 and changed it to an Otasco, which offered a larger variety of hardware products. (Courtesy of *Rayne Acadian-Tribune.*)

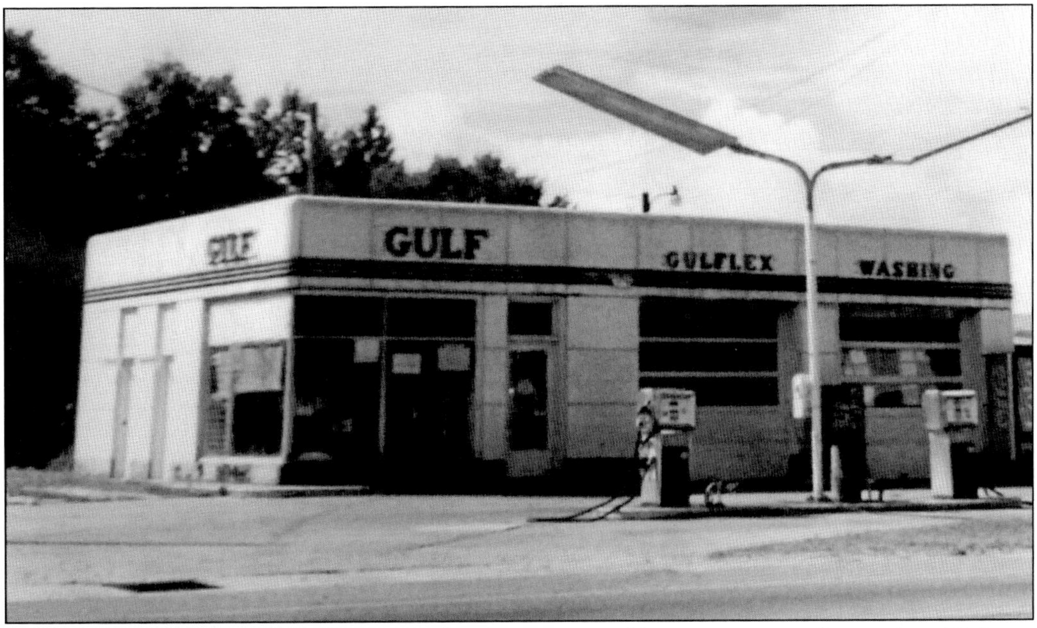

This Gulf gas station, still standing today, has been operated by many owners. Located on Highway 90 next to Olinger's Radio Shack, it is the home of a construction company as of 2015. (Courtesy of Thomas Marcotte.)

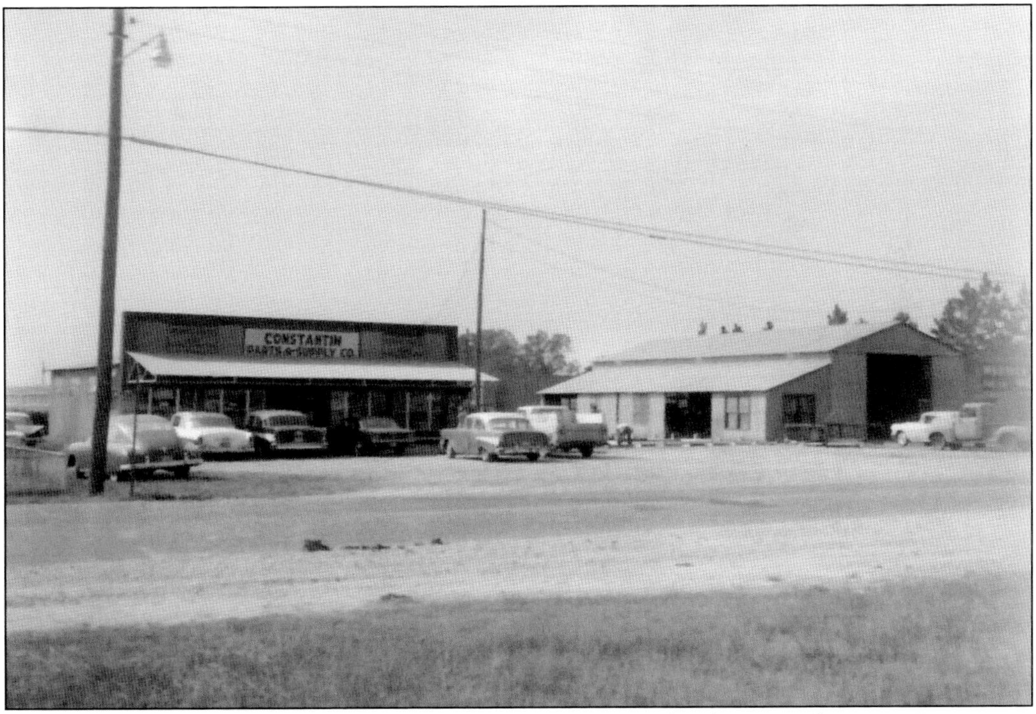

A staple along Highway 90 East for many years was the ever-expanding business of Maurice Constantin. At left is Constantin Parts & Supply, and on the right is a welding shop. Eventually, the business evolved into Rayne Plane, which developed a unique land-leveling implement. It also manufactured other implements such as Rayne Grain and Rayne Drain. (Courtesy of *Rayne Independent*.)

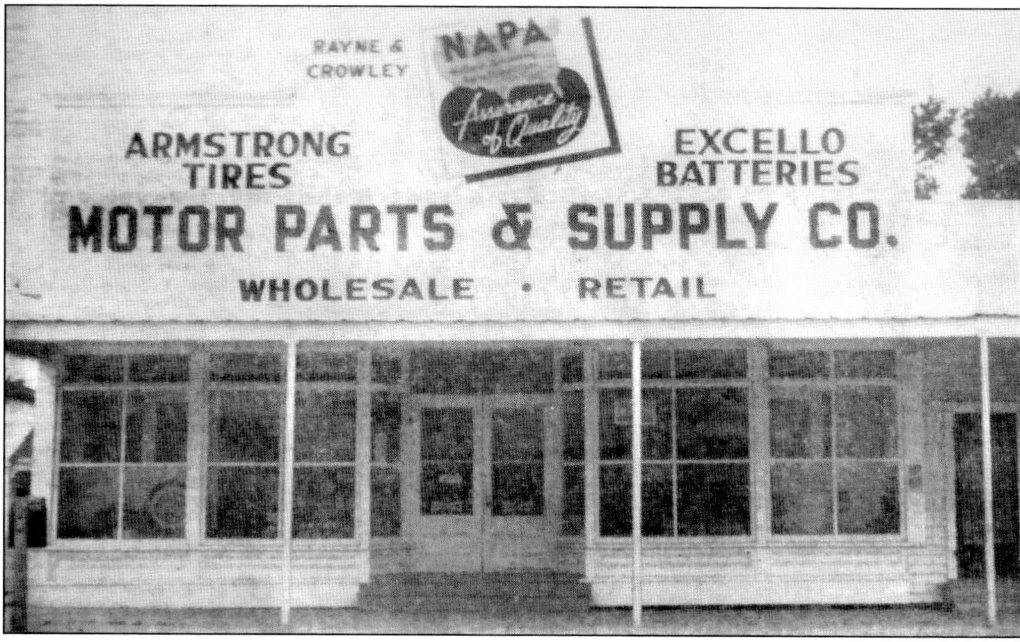

Motor Parts & Supply Co., also known as NAPA, was located in the Plattsmier-Hulin Grocery Building in the 200 block of South Adams Avenue when this photograph was taken in 1955. The company sold automotive, truck, tractor, and implement parts. It later moved across the street to the Farmer's Hardware Store building. The building is currently abandoned. (Courtesy of *Rayne Acadian-Tribune*.)

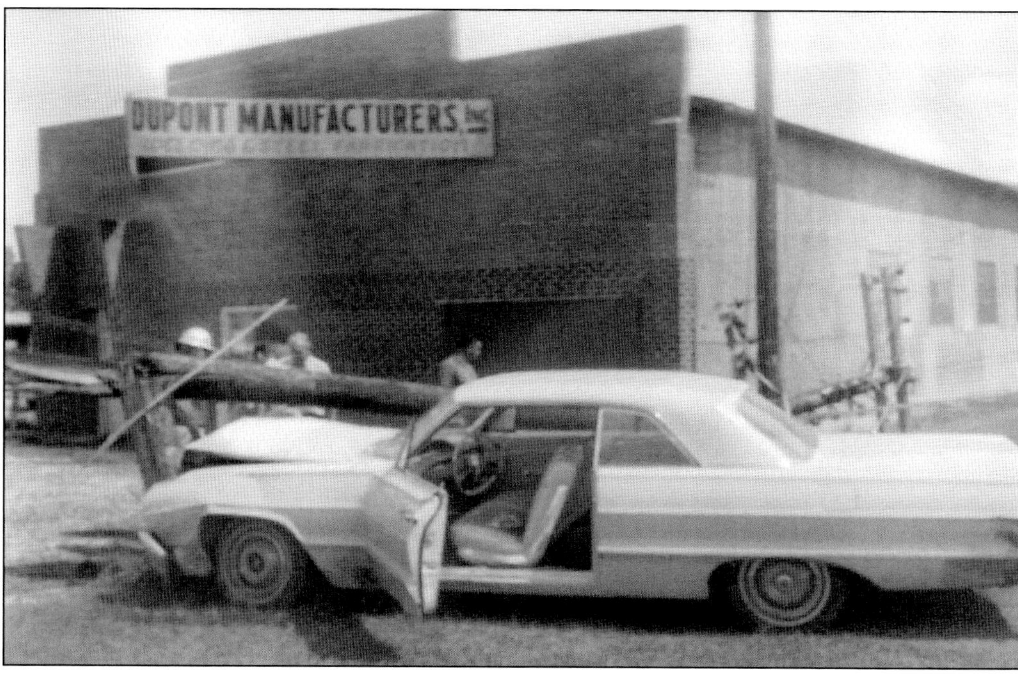

This crash occurred in front of Dupont Manufacturers Inc. on East Highway 90. Owned by Cliff Dupont, the firm built hatches for boats and was one of the first in the area to design and manufacture steel grain bins. (Courtesy of *Rayne Acadian-Tribune*.)

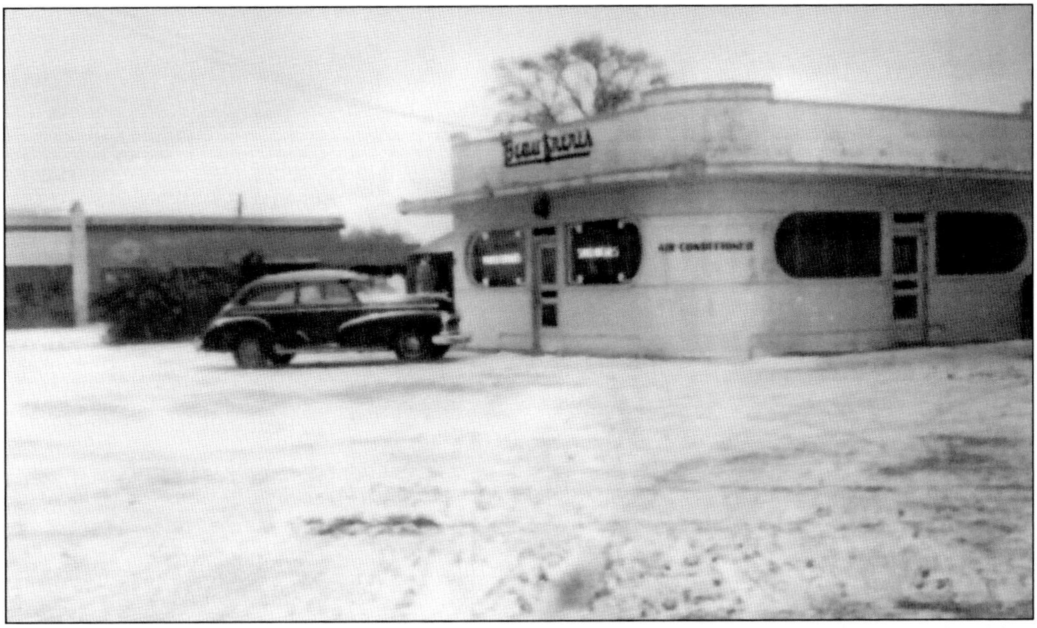

This Art Deco building was a first for Rayne when Joe Wright originally opened his cocktail bar and lounge. Aubrey Leger purchased the business in January 1947 and had a contest to rename it. Mrs. Louis Butaud submitted the name Beau Frere's and was awarded $25. This photograph shows two unusual sights for the era—snow on the ground and air-conditioning at an establishment. This building was in the 600 block of South Adams Avenue. A self-storage locker was later built on this site. (Courtesy of Clyde Leger.)

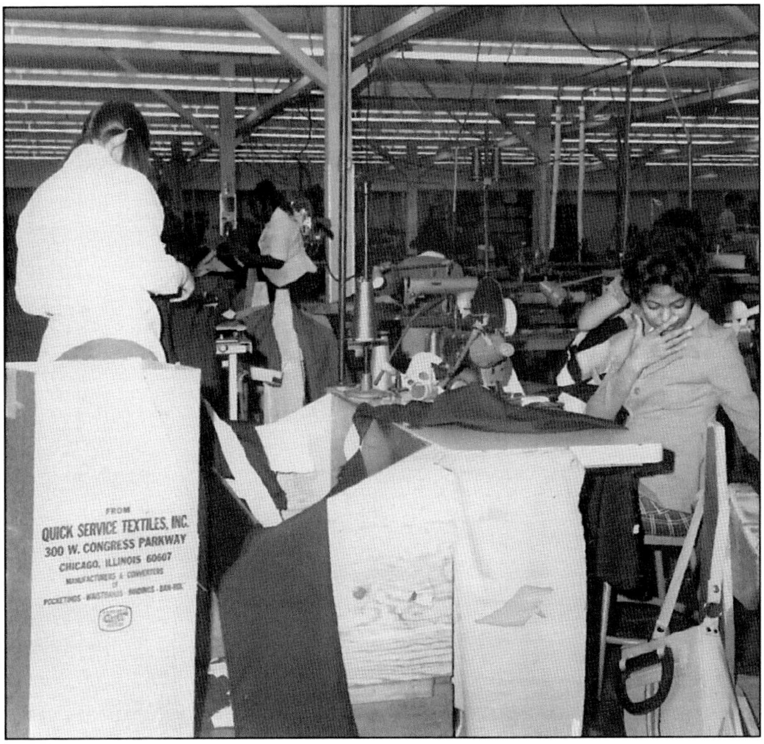

Employees of Glen Oaks Manufacturing are shown sewing pants in the plant established in the old Mervine Kahn Rice Warehouse in 1976. It was located across from the post office on Highway 90 East. This is the current site of the Doug Ashy Warehouse. (Courtesy of *Rayne Independent*.)

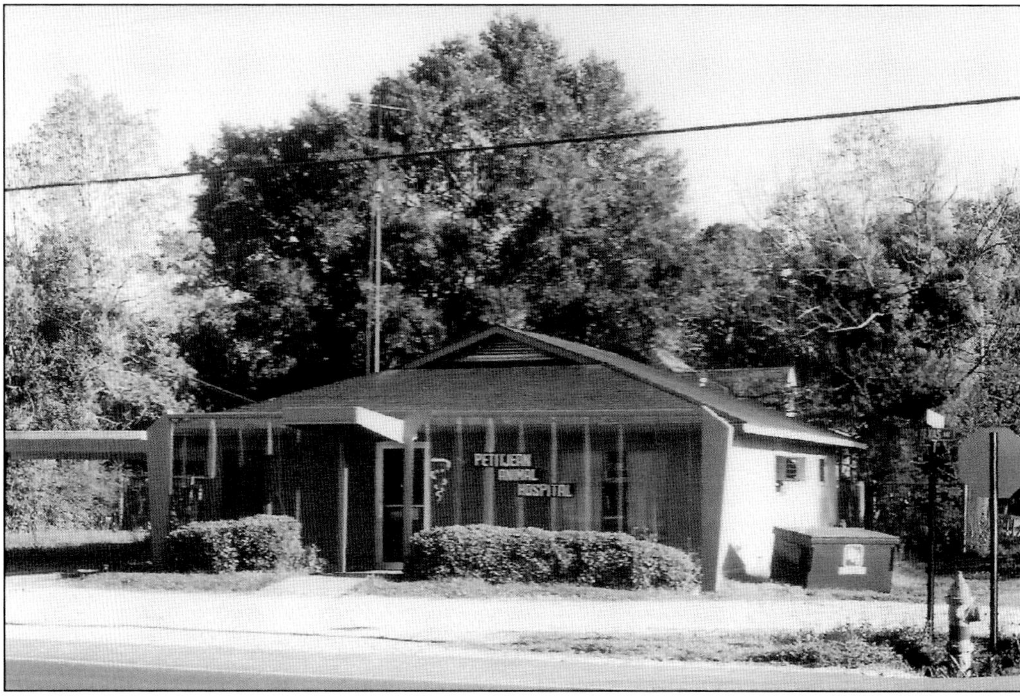

Dr. Elmo Petitjean practiced veterinary medicine at the Petitjean Animal Hospital, on East Highway 90 and South Cunningham Street. The building was subsequently used by many businesses, including a hair salon in 2015. (Courtesy of *Rayne Independent*.)

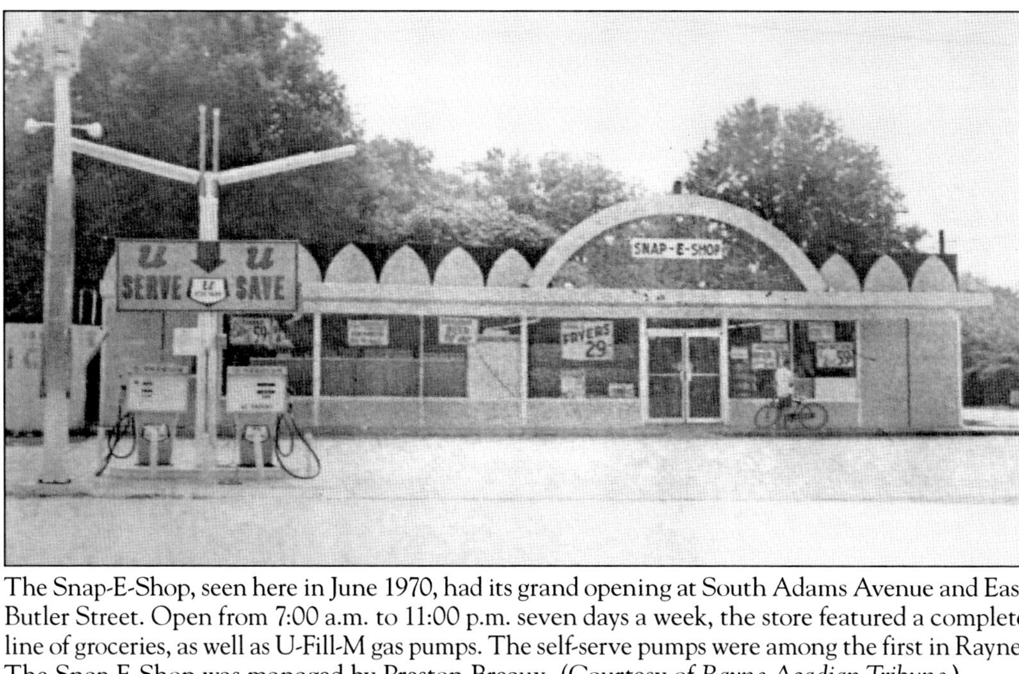

The Snap-E-Shop, seen here in June 1970, had its grand opening at South Adams Avenue and East Butler Street. Open from 7:00 a.m. to 11:00 p.m. seven days a week, the store featured a complete line of groceries, as well as U-Fill-M gas pumps. The self-serve pumps were among the first in Rayne. The Snap-E-Shop was managed by Preston Breaux. (Courtesy of *Rayne Acadian-Tribune*.)

This is the showroom and front entrance of Rayne Motors Inc., owned by Lewis Cook Sr. The building, originally a service station, was built in 1937 and was home to another car dealership, Bickham Lincoln Mercury. (Courtesy of *Rayne Independent.*)

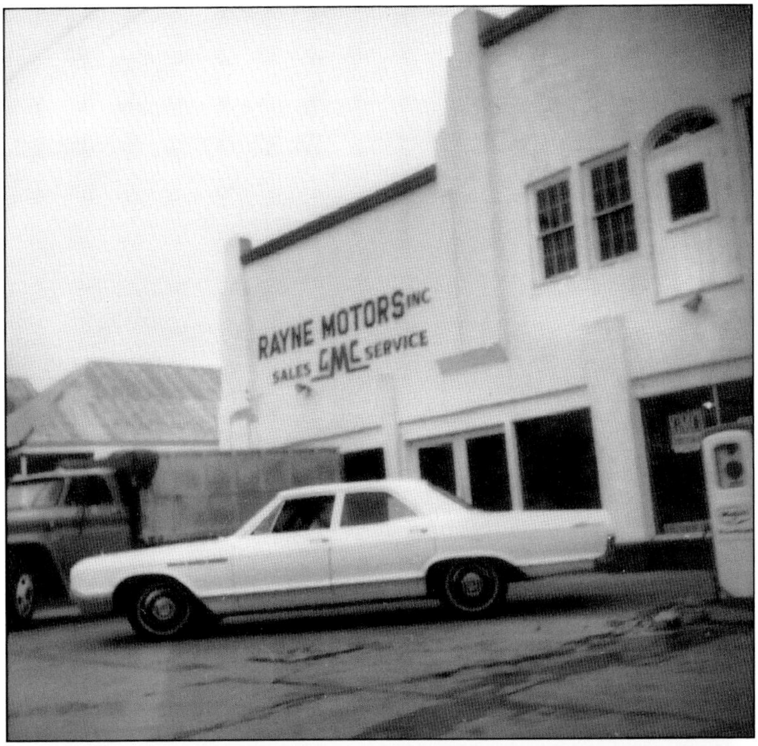

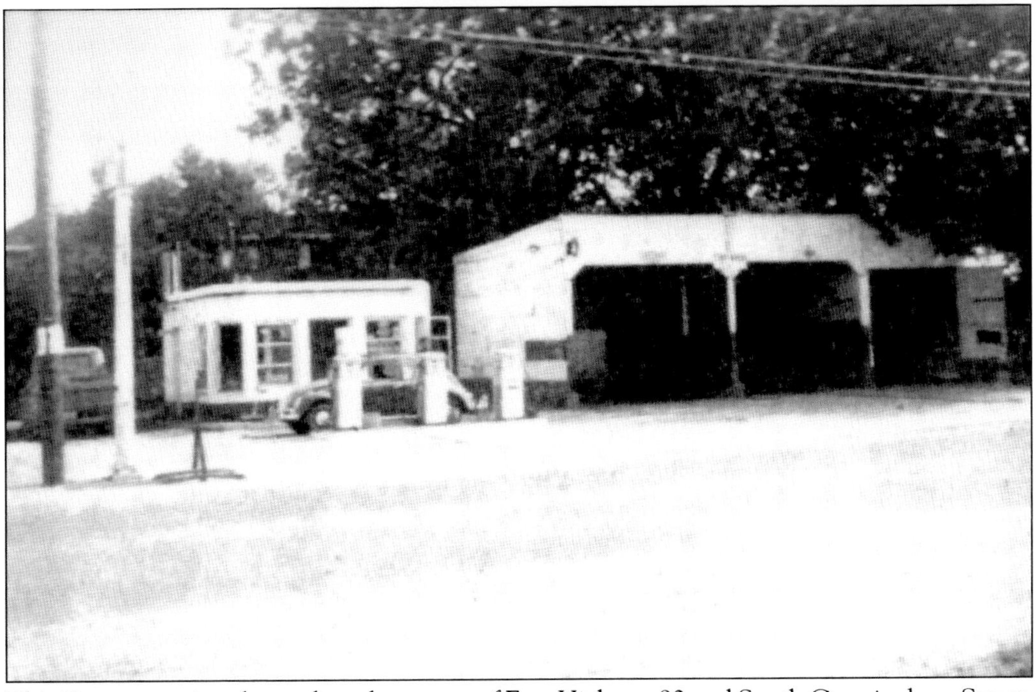

This Esso gas station, located on the corner of East Highway 90 and South Cunningham Street, was owned by Elton Blanchard. Ron Sonnier worked his first job there for $2 a day and later got a raise to $3 a day. Today, Doug Ashy has its lumberyard at this location. (Courtesy of *Rayne Acadian-Tribune.*)

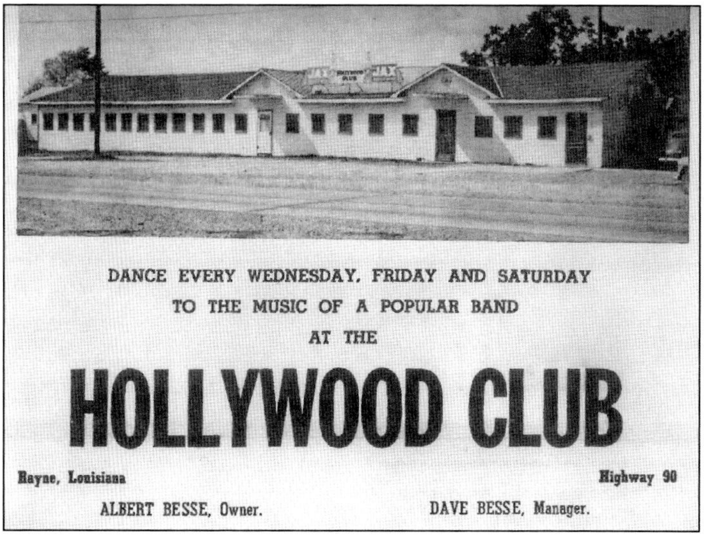

The fabulous Hollywood Club was a landmark for many years on West Highway 90. Owned by Albert Besse, the establishment's interior had a tropical theme, including palm trees blowing in the wind. This business took up most of the city block. It was a popular spot for newlyweds, who paid up to $100 to have their wedding dance there, which brought in additional business. This advertisement is from 1948. (Courtesy of *Rayne Acadian-Tribune*.)

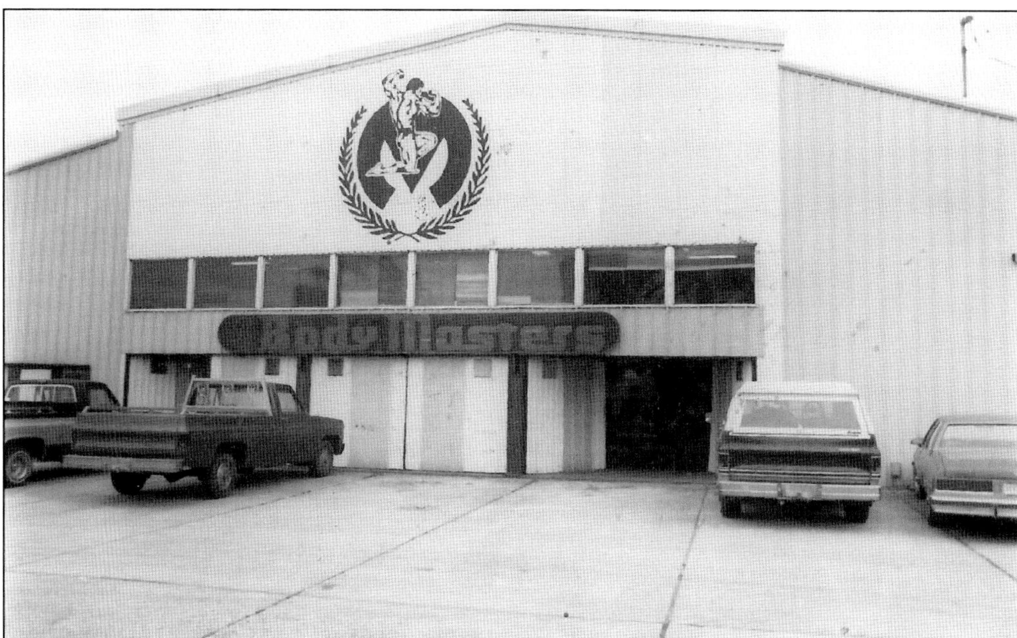

Body Masters, owned by local attorney Robert Cline, was housed in the largest building along Highway 90, taking up an entire city block. The company was renowned for exercise equipment, which was shipped throughout the world and was the preferred equipment for many military bases, colleges, and professional teams. The equipment was also used in the Olympics and at world championships. At its peak of operation, the plant was producing equipment 24 hours a day and had several 18-wheelers traveling the country making deliveries. Originally owned by Constantin Welding, Knight Oil Tools operates in this building today. (Courtesy of *Rayne Independent*.)

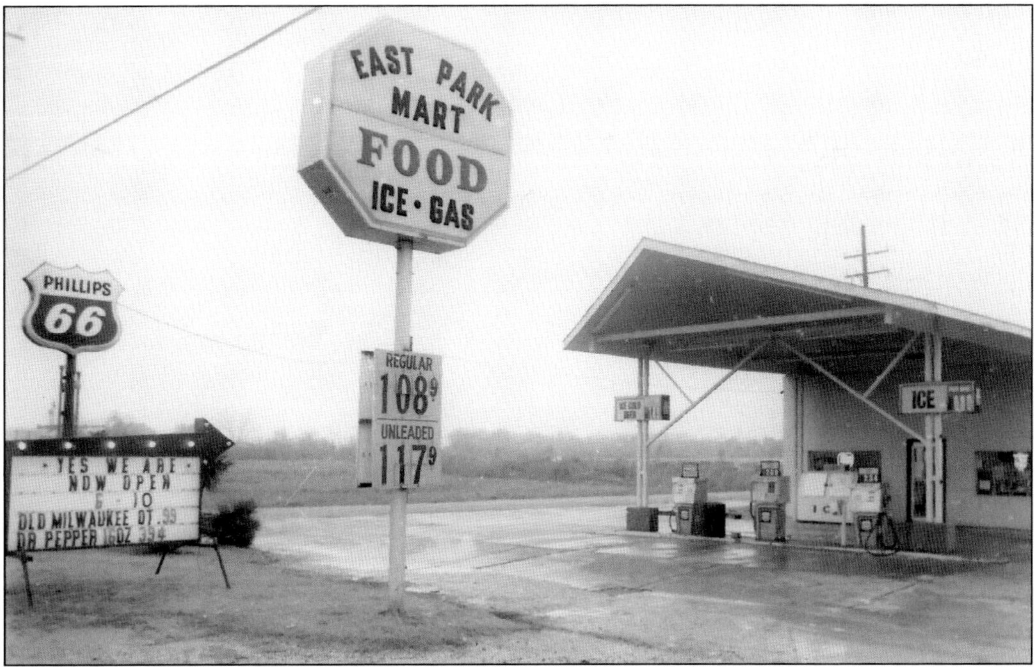

This Phillips 66 station was owned and operated by Kelly LeBlanc as East Park Mart. The first gas station a traveler encountered coming into Rayne on Highway 90 East, it was a popular stop and had many operators over the years. The building still stands at the corner of South Eastern Avenue and East Highway 90. (Courtesy of *Rayne Independent*.)

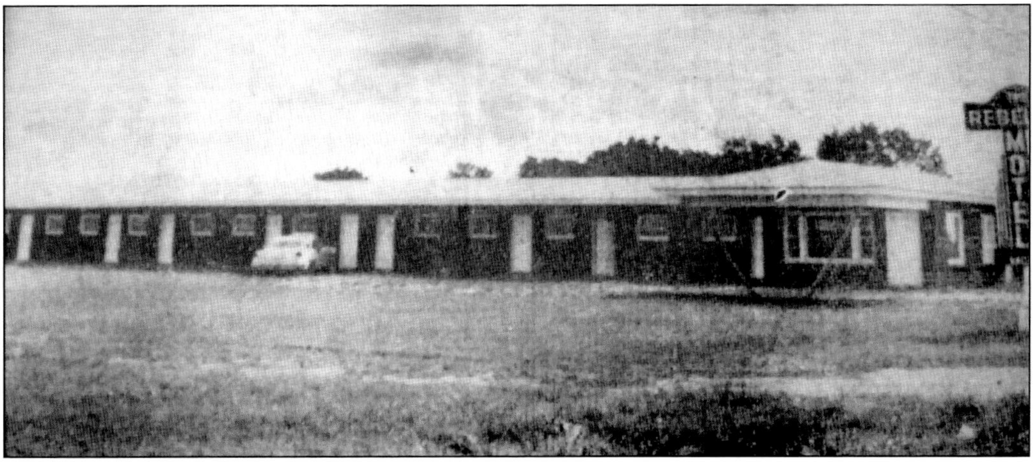

The Rebel Motel, built at a cost of $40,000 in 1953, included a bar and restaurant and offered its occupants 10 rooms. It was owned by Iris Daigle and was a popular stop on the OST. Much later, under different ownership and after I-10 opened and traffic stopped flowing on Highway 90, the Rebel gained an unflattering reputation. It was said that a room could be rented for three hours for around $60 with the room already occupied by a female guest, or $15 if one brought their own date. The author has no immediate knowledge if this story is true. (Courtesy of *Rayne Acadian-Tribune*.)

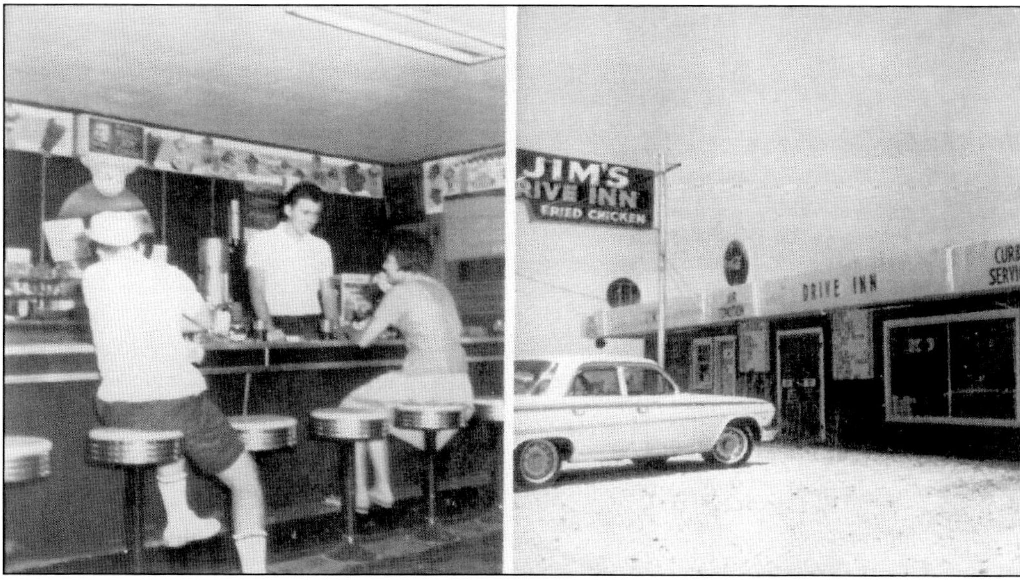

Jim's Drive Inn, located on West Highway 90, is seen here in 1963. Owned by Jimmy Ancelet, it was one of the many drive-ins that popped up along the OST, providing the traveling public a place to rest and eat. It was later the site of the Oua Oua Ron Bar. (Courtesy of Rayne High School.)

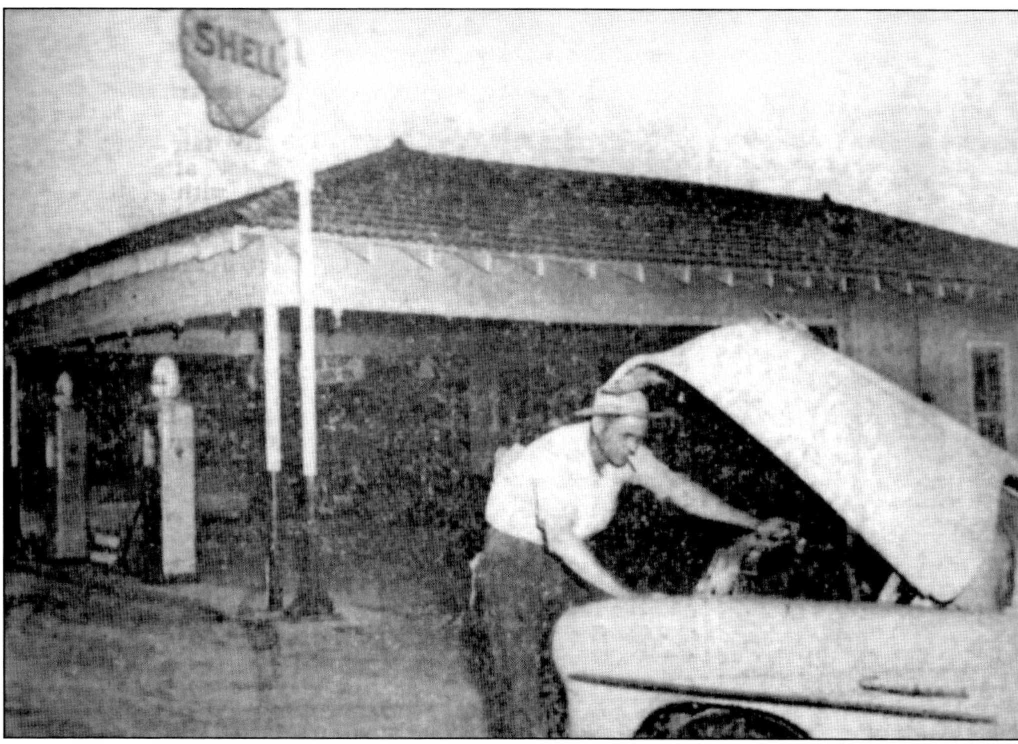

This 1952 photograph shows Sweeny Gary checking under the hood of a Chevrolet at his newly opened Shell gas station. This and many other photographs were taken to celebrate Oil Progress Week in Rayne. The station stood on the corner of West Highway 90 and Highway 35 South (Abbeville Highway). (Courtesy of *Rayne Acadian-Tribune*.)

Patrons line up to buy tickets for the reopening of the Joy Theater in 1972. It was owned by the chief of police, George Melancon, and his wife, Ruby. The building, owned by Knight Oil Tools, is now used for storage. (Courtesy of *Rayne Independent*.)

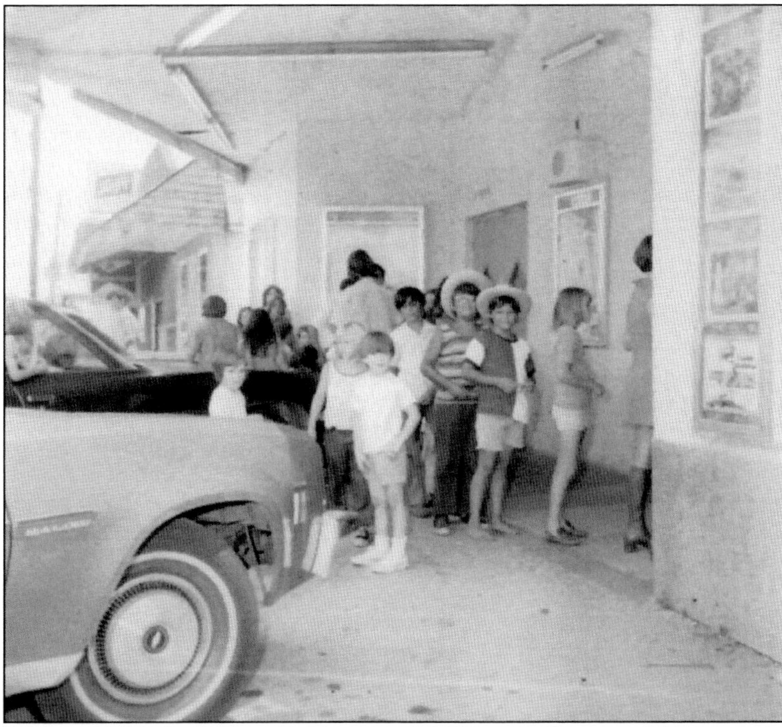

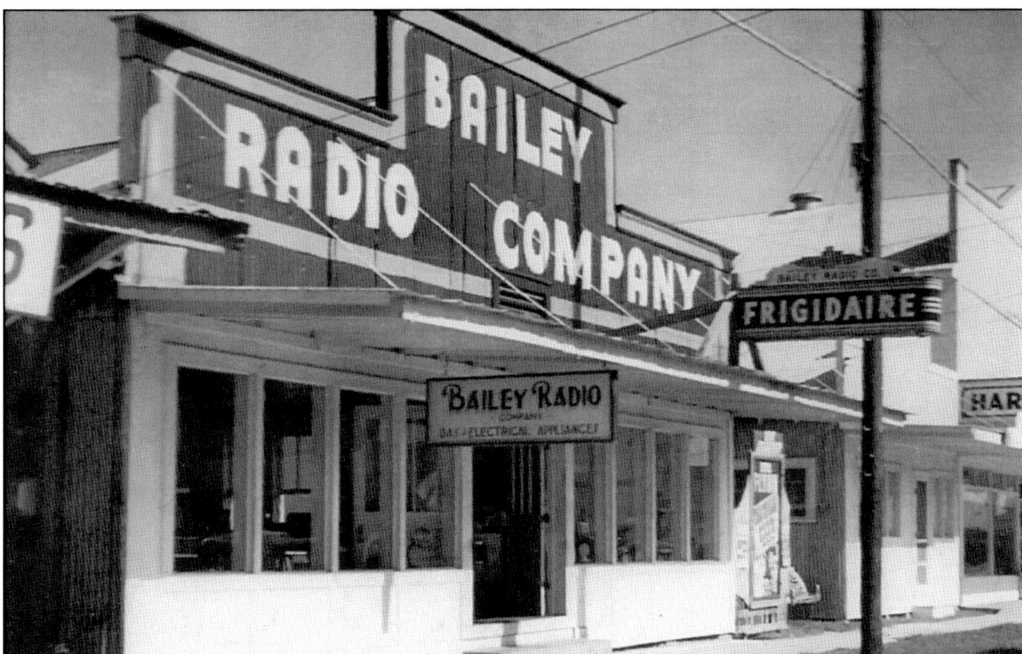

The Bailey Radio Company opened in 1936 and was located on South Adams Avenue. Hilman Bailey, who received his radio knowledge in the Army, put it to good use selling and repairing radios. At the time, radio was the only source of home mass entertainment. To the immediate right is a Joy Theater movie display, a beauty shop, and, at far right, Farmers Hardware. (Courtesy of Donald Petitjean.)

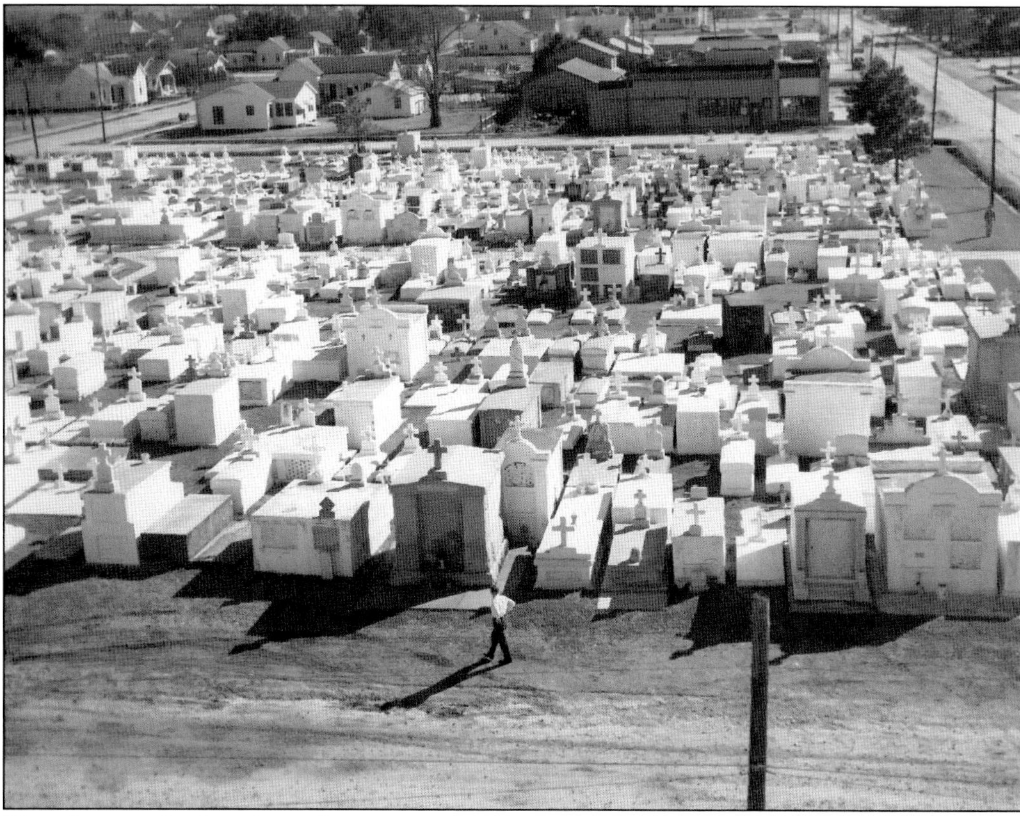

This photograph of southeast Rayne was taken from the bell tower at St. Joseph Catholic Church. Among the visible businesses along South Adams Avenue, beyond the graveyard, are Gulf and Texaco gas stations. (Courtesy of Leonard J. Laperous, The Photo Shop.)

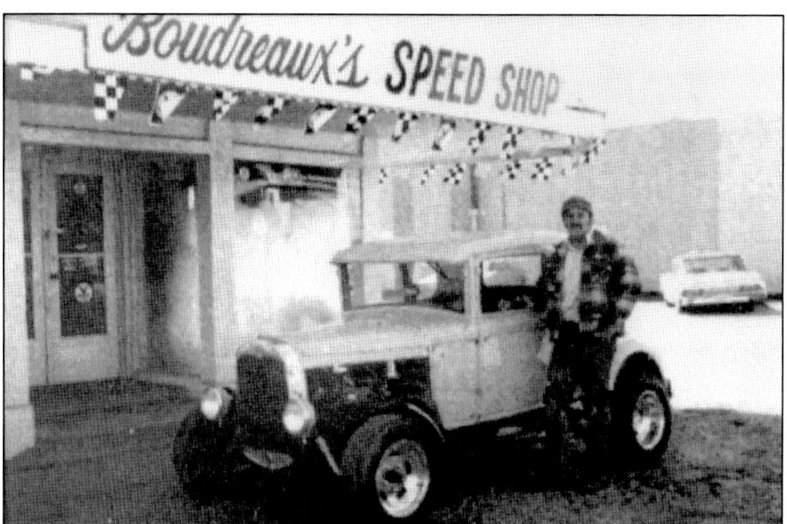

Larry Boudreaux stands next to his 1932 Ford Coupe as he promotes his new business, Boudreaux's Speed Shop, in 1973. Located in a two-story building at 300 East Texas Avenue, next to Privat Lumber Yard, it was the first place in Rayne offering to "soup up your hot rod." (Courtesy of *Rayne Acadian-Tribune*.)

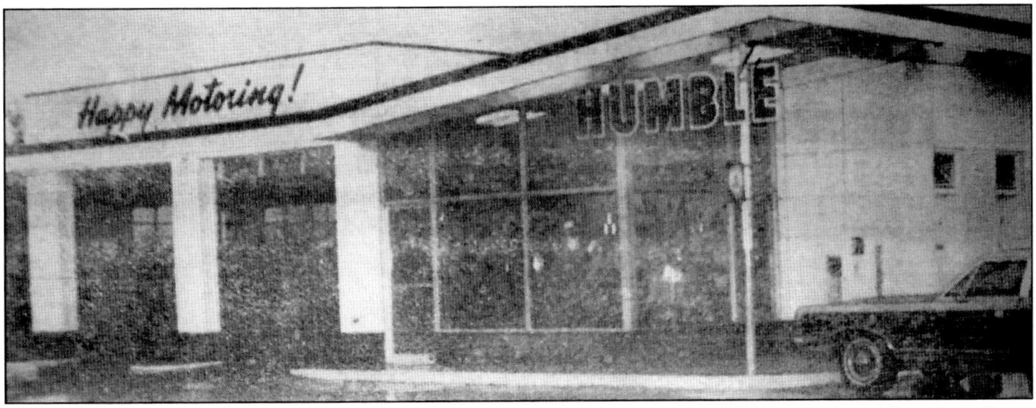

This Southside service station was located on the corner of East Branche Street and South Adams Avenue. It was owned by Peter Comeaux and managed by James Lavergne at the time of this 1969 photograph. The building was bought by Hilman Meche and Vernal Daigle, who erected a metal building next to it as part of Rayne Plastic Signs. The service station building is used for storage and is still standing, although it is covered in sheet metal. It is still intact, although hidden from passersby. This corner was the original location of the OST Dancehall before it was moved to South Arenas Street in 1927. (Courtesy of *Rayne Acadian-Tribune*.)

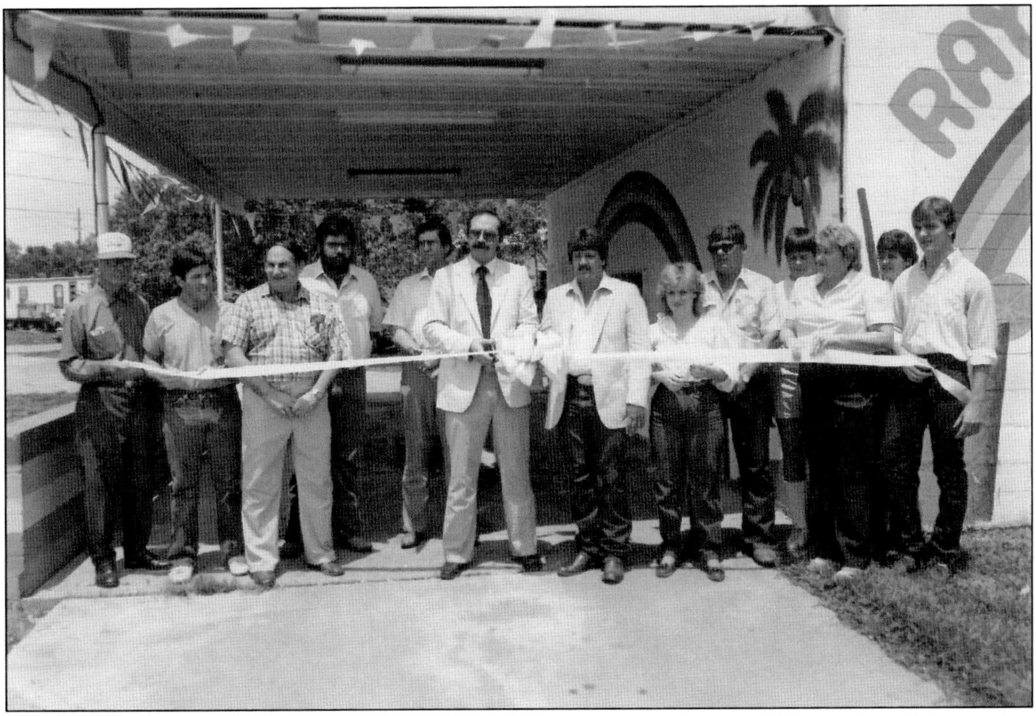

Shown here at the Rayne-Bo Daiquiri Outlet ribbon cutting in August 1983 are, from left to right, R.F. "Pop" Morgan, Bobby Robichaux (building owner), John "Piggy" Arceneaux (police chief), Chuck Robichaux (building owner), Preston Venable, Marty Melancon, Ricky Morgan (owner), Vicky Labbe, Freddie Morgan, John Morgan, Mrs. Freddie Morgan, Daphne Morgan, and Kevin Morgan. The drive-through business offered 25 daiquiri flavors. (Courtesy of *Rayne Independent*.)

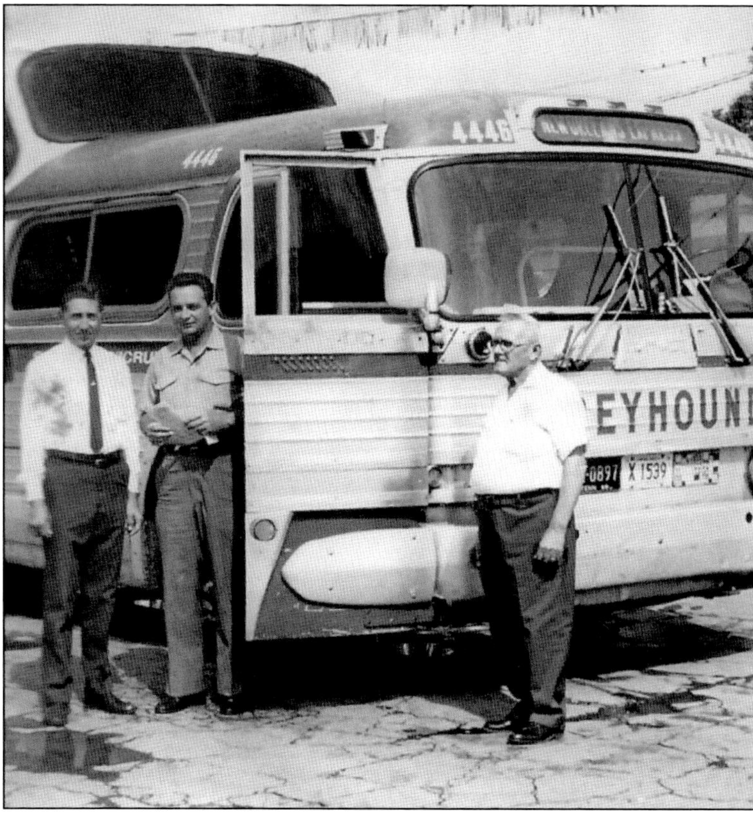

This Greyhound bus has stopped at Roy's Used Car Sales, owned by Roy Ancelet (left). An unidentified bus driver is in the doorway, and Andrew "G" Hebert is on the right. The dealership was located on the corner of West Highway 90 and South Adams Avenue. A car wash is now located on the corner. (Courtesy of *Rayne Independent*.)

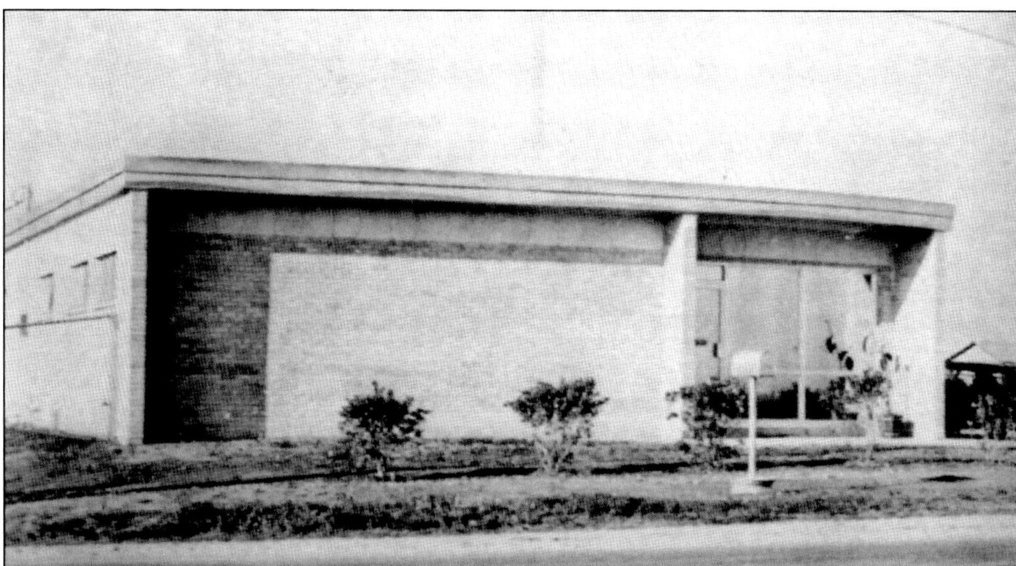

The new offices of Rimmer & Garrett, a widely known contracting firm, were located on Highway 90 West just outside of Rayne. Started by Tom Garrett and Henry Rimmer, the company was awarded dirt foundation work for the new Interstate 10 construction project near Rayne in the mid-1960s. There were several large equipment barns at the rear of the property. (Courtesy of *Rayne Acadian-Tribune*.)

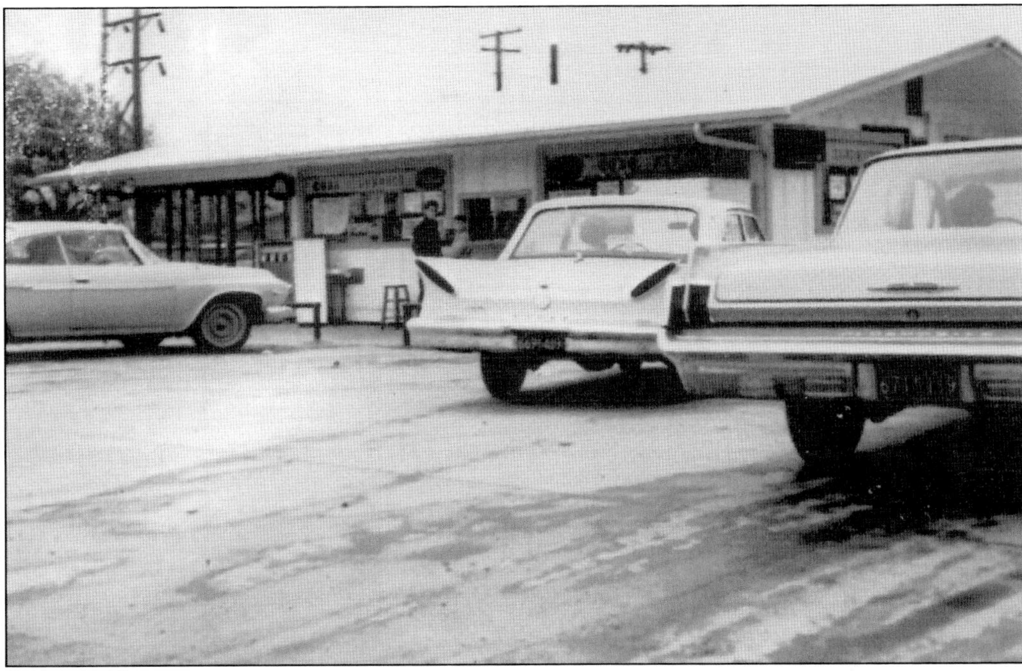

A familiar sight on the OST, Johnson's Drive Inn is seen here in 1963. Originally, Johnson's was located on the east side of South Adams Avenue and later moved to the west side. (Courtesy of Rayne High School.)

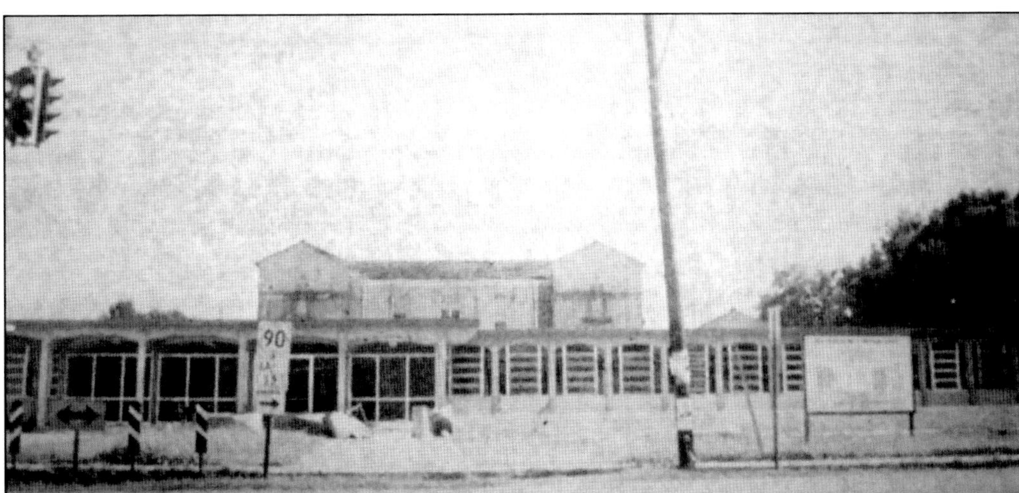

This photograph shows construction progress for the South Rayne Elementary School on the corner of East Branche Street and Highway 35 South. The old pink stucco building is in the background. Seen here in August 1963, this major intersection was controlled at the time by a stoplight. (Courtesy of *Rayne Acadian-Tribune*.)

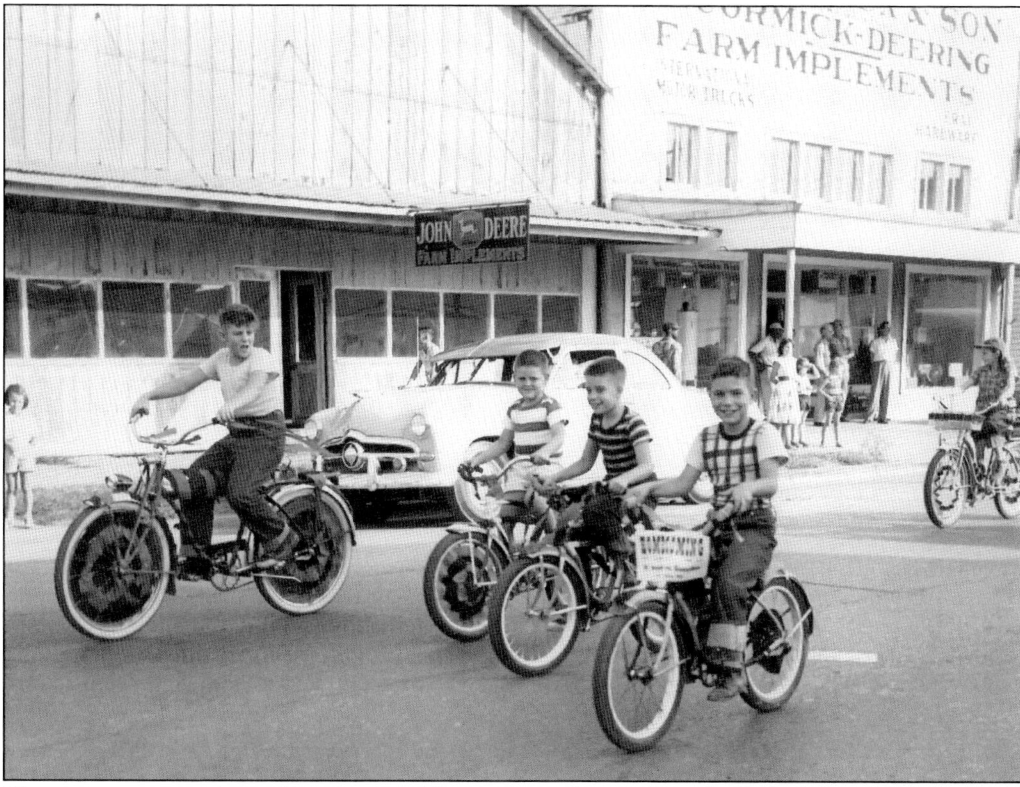

These young men show their spirit as they ride in the St. Joseph High School Homecoming Parade in October 1953. The big game featured the St. Joe Tigers and the Gueydan Bears. In the background is E.C. Fremaux Farm Implements on South Adams Avenue. The building at left was later torn down. The site is now occupied by Mouton Pharmacy. (Courtesy of Leonard J. Laperous, The Photo Shop.)

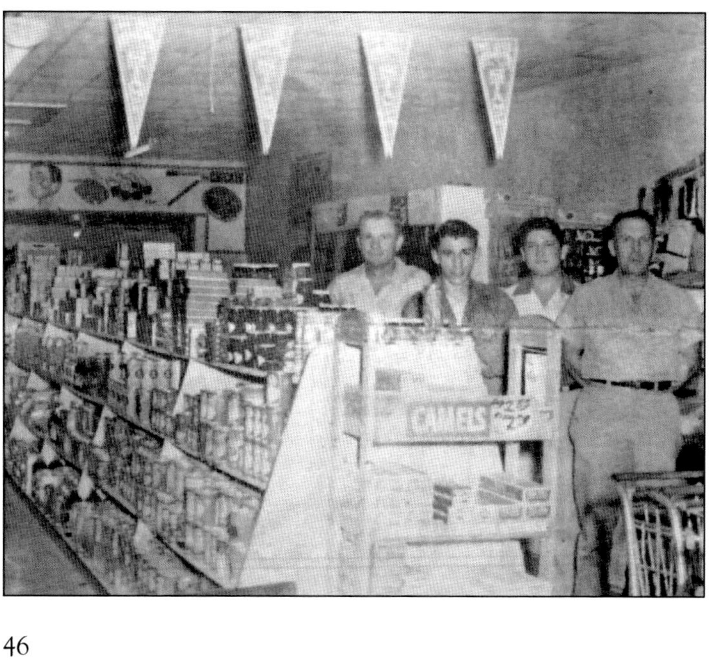

This is a rare look inside a local grocery store in 1956. The Rayne Food Center is ready for its first day of business on South Adams Avenue. Members of the staff are, from left to right, Frank Choate, Horace Broussard, Jeff Choate (Frank's son), and Francis Robichaux. At the time, Frank was giving out Lucky Stamps (later Quality Stamps). Note the Camel Cigarette display in the front, advertising regular size for $2.35 per carton and king size for $2.70. (Courtesy of *Rayne Acadian-Tribune*.)

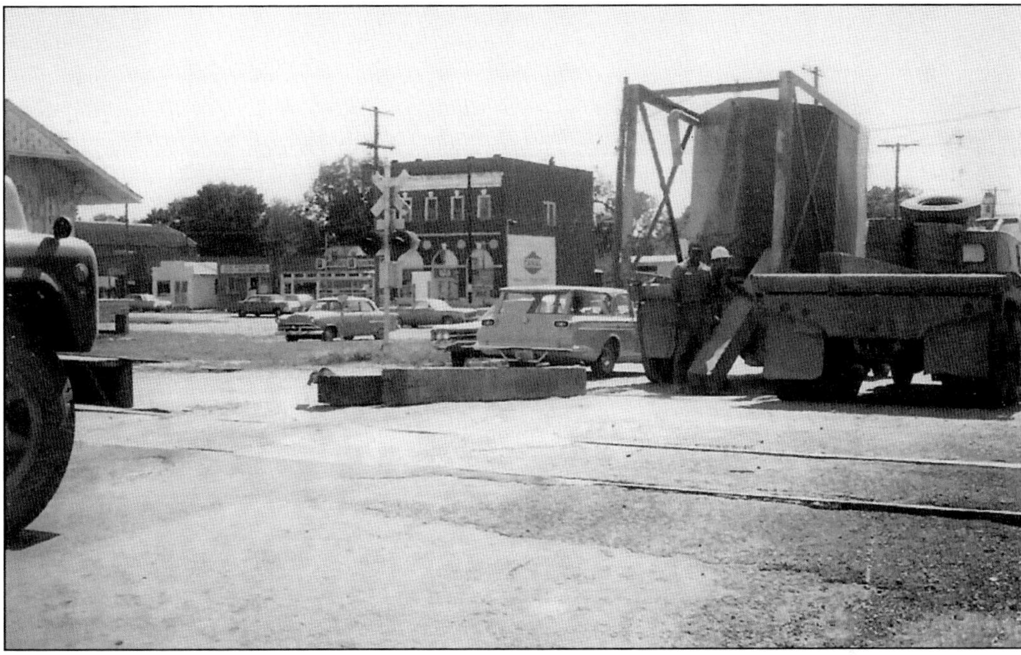

This photograph of the Depot Square area was taken when repair work was being completed on the railroad crossing. In the background are the two-story Commercial Bank Building and, to its immediate left, Kootsie's Lounge. On the far left is the freight depot. (Courtesy of *Rayne Independent*.)

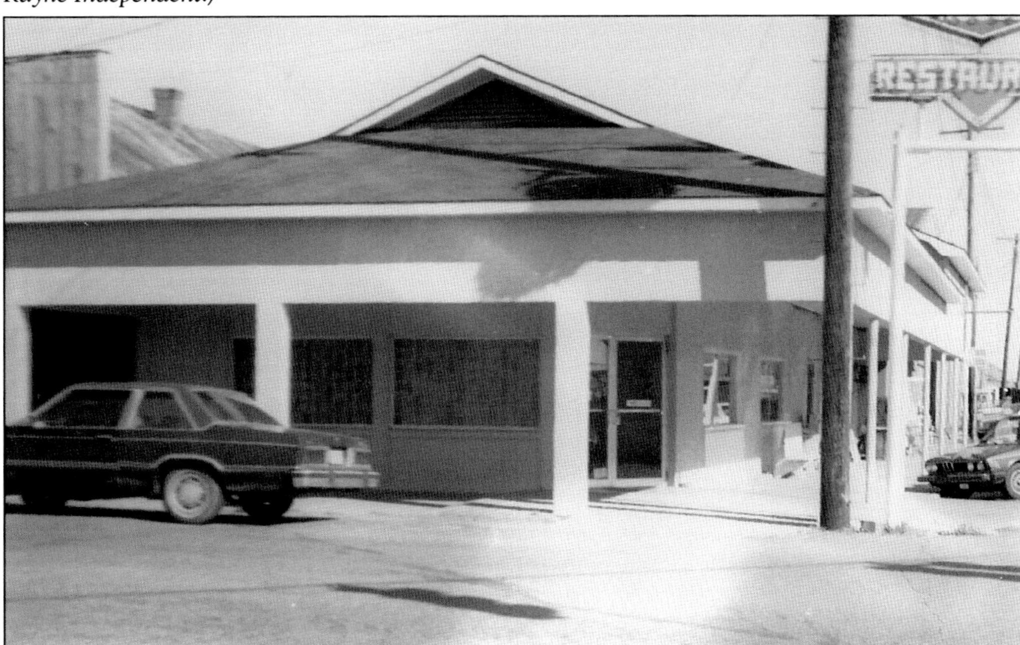

A familiar landmark on the OST was the Town House Restaurant, located at the corner of East Texas Avenue and South Polk Street. The establishment was owned by several people, with Edmond Stelly operating it the longest. It was open 24 hours a day and was a stop for the Greyhound Bus Lines. (Courtesy of *Rayne Independent*.)

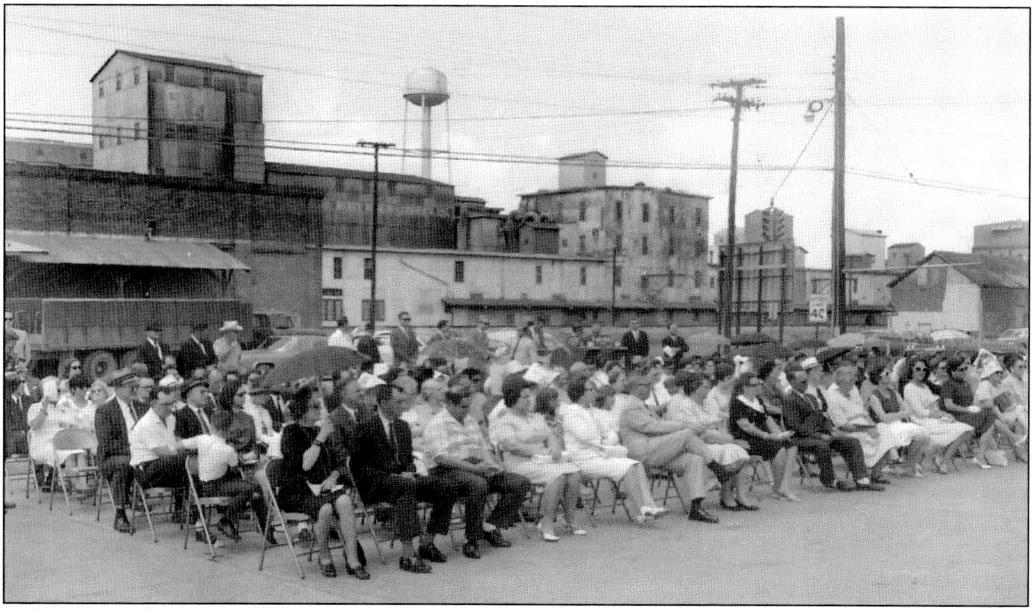

A large crowd was on hand for the grand opening of the new Rayne Post Office in June 1967. Gone from today's Rayne landscape are the numerous rice mills seen in the background. (Courtesy of *Rayne Independent*.)

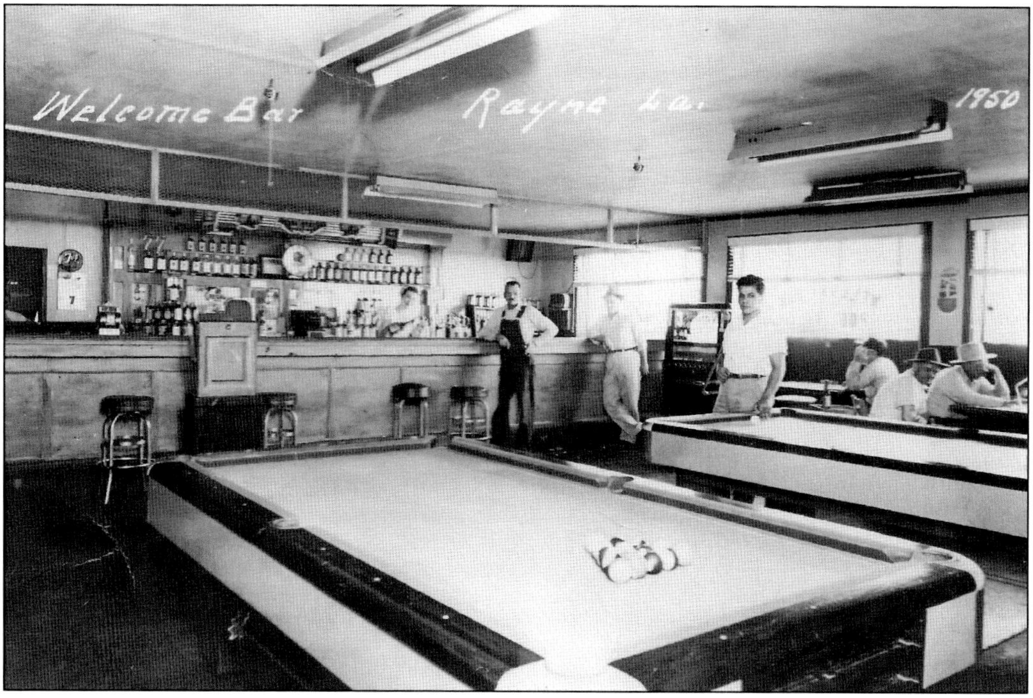

This inside view of the Welcome Bar shows entertainment of the day—billiards and, at right, what are likely games of pitch dominos. This 1950 photograph shows the back of a slot machine at the bar and a cigarette machine on the right. The bar, owned by "Papa" George Broussard, was on East Texas Avenue across from Hank's Warehouse on Highway 90. The building later became Robichaux's 5 & 10 Variety Store and is now a dance studio. (Courtesy of Chuck Robichaux.)

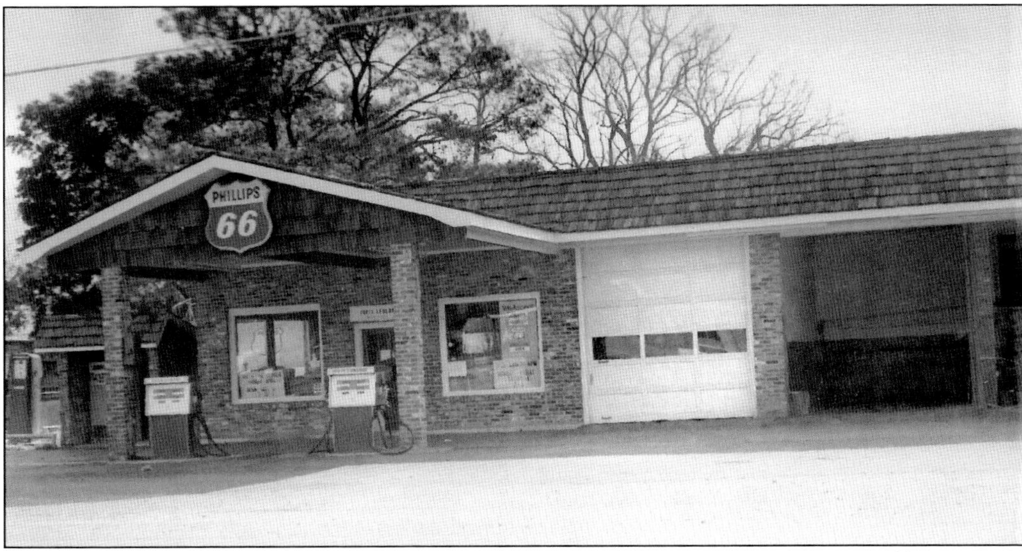

A familiar sight along South Adams Avenue was the Phillips 66 service station owned by Augustus LeBlanc and his heirs. Young drivers "dragging The Boulevard" would make a U-turn in the station's parking lot and head north again. This business was on the corner of East Bull Street and South Adams Avenue, where Acadia Climate Control Self Storage is located. (Courtesy of *Rayne Independent.*)

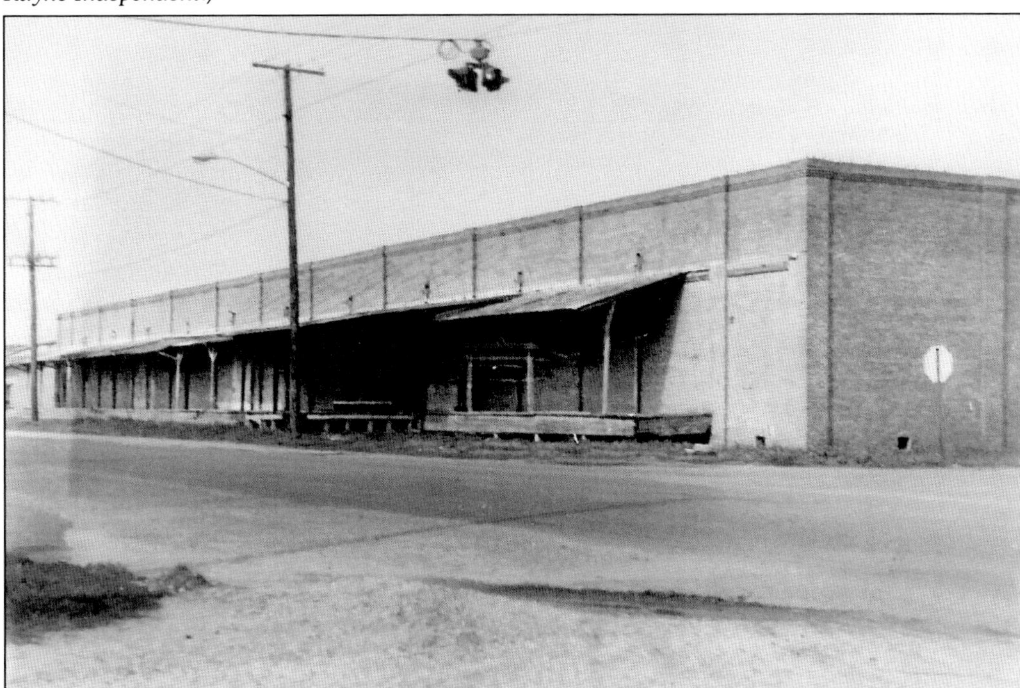

The Mervine Kahn Rice Warehouse was located on East Texas Avenue, across from the post office. Rice was stored until it could be loaded onto a train on a side rail. The warehouse was abandoned until Glen Oaks Manufacturing converted it into a garment plant. It later was used as a flea market. Damaged by Hurricane Lily, the facility was purchased by Doug Ashy, who tore it down to build a new warehouse. (Courtesy of *Rayne Independent.*)

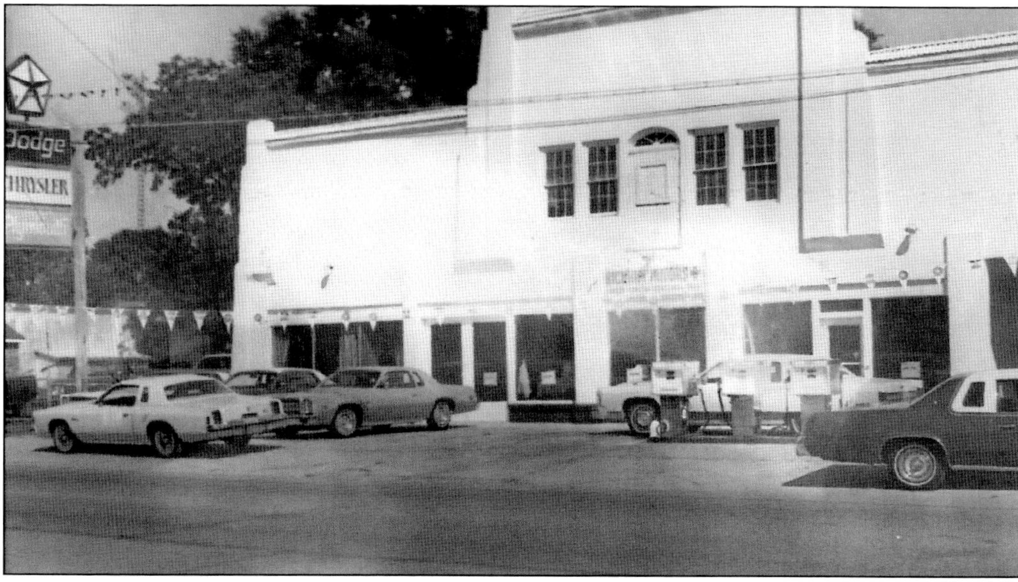

In 1977, Bickham Motors, a Dodge, Chrysler, and Plymouth dealer, was located on South Adams Avenue. It was the only dealership in Rayne for many years. Originally a garage owned by Benton Mauboules, it was later Rayne Motors, owned by Lewis Cook Sr. (Courtesy of *Rayne Independent*.)

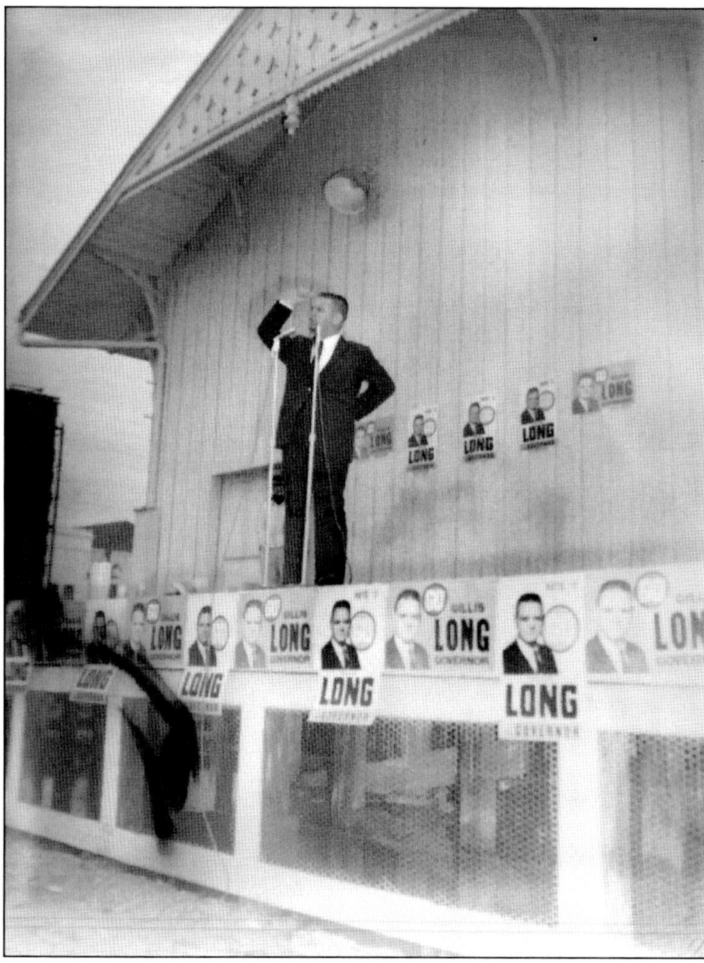

Rayne was a stop on the campaign trail for any candidate running for office in the state. Gillis Long, Democratic primary candidate for Louisiana governor in 1963, is shown speaking at the depot. He lost his bid for governor, as well as his representative seat near Alexandria. (Courtesy of Sidney Stutes.)

Manager Tommy Adams (far left) watches a pool game in 1966 at the neighborhood Youth Corps Recreation Center. It was located in the old St. Joseph Church parish hall on South Adams Avenue. The center included a pool table, record player, and ping-pong table. (Courtesy of *Rayne Acadian-Tribune*.)

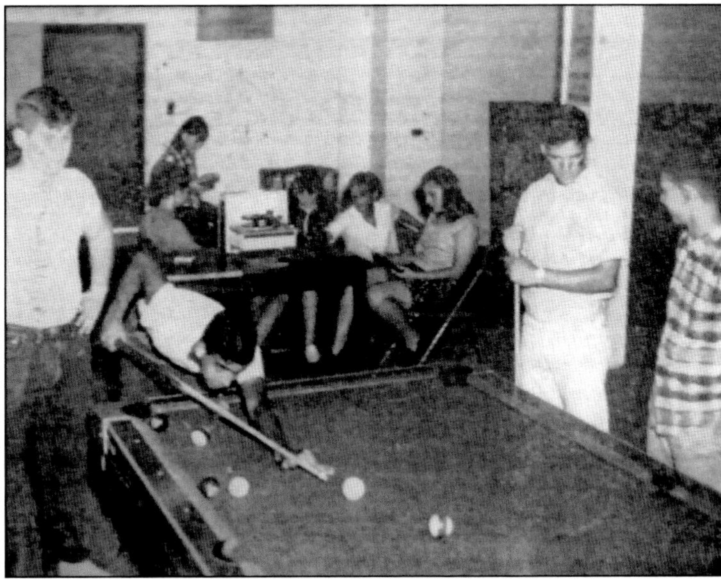

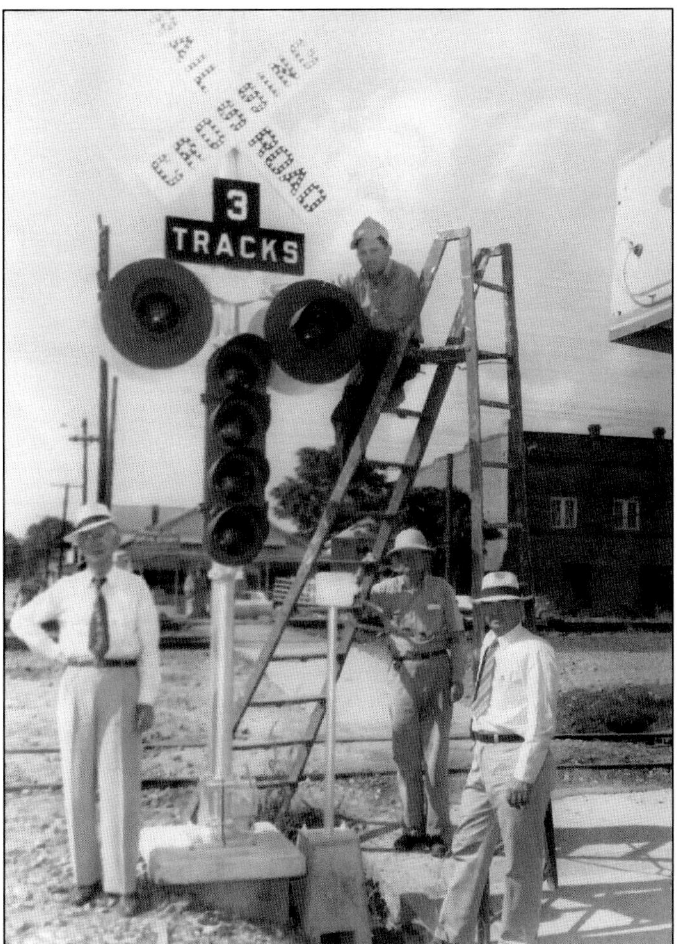

In 1952, Southern Pacific Railroad updated the warning system at the Polk Street crossing. Wallace Begnaud (on ladder) is making the final adjustments, while local agent Edward Poimboeuf (left), foreman E.G. Stone (center), and R.J. Nesler look on. The cost of the project was $15,300, and it took six weeks to complete. The corner of the Bruce Theater building is at top right. People's Drug Store and the Mervine Kahn Warehouse are in the background. (Courtesy of Donald Petitjean.)

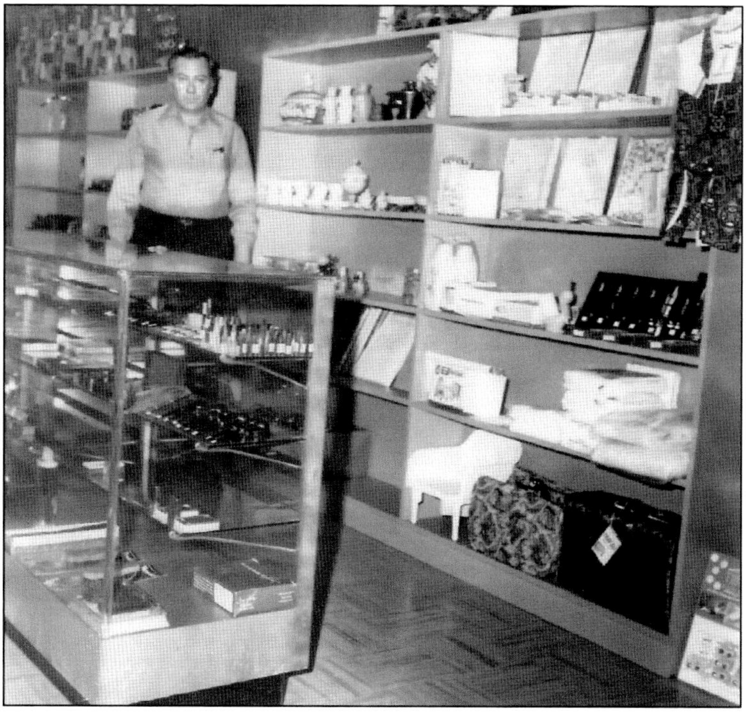

Adley Boyer, originally from Henderson, is shown behind the counter of Boyer's Pharmacy, located across from St. Joseph Catholic Church on South Adams Avenue. Adley began his career working for Lasseigne's Pharmacy before opening his own pharmacy. He served as mayor of Rayne from 1974 to 1978. (Courtesy of *Rayne Independent*.)

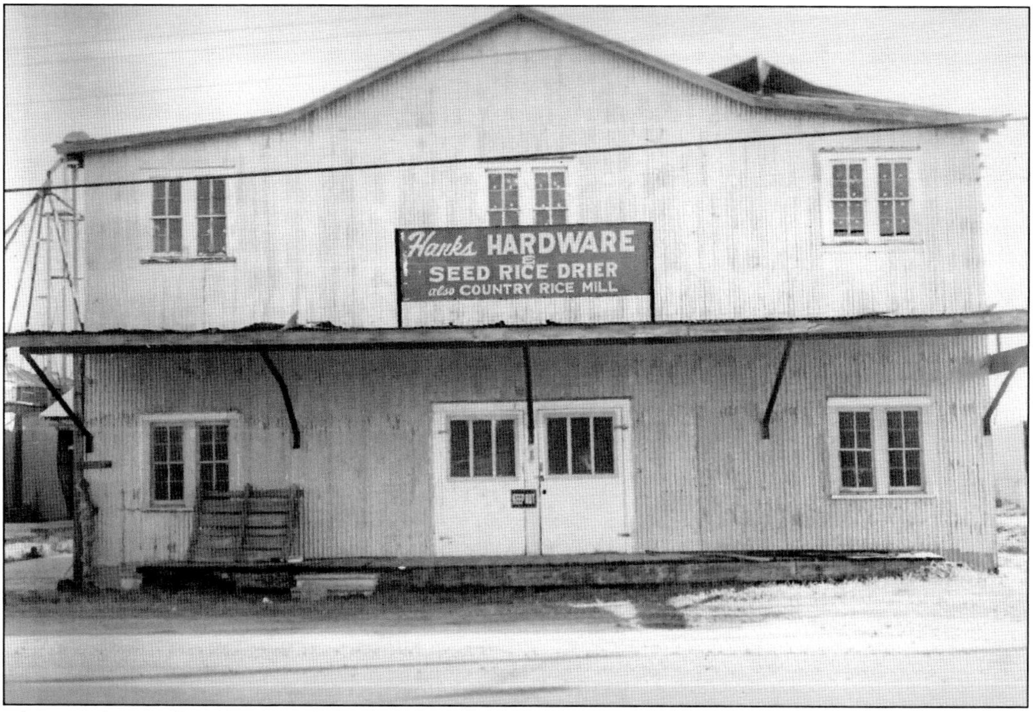

The Hanks Hardware & Seed Rice Drier was originally the Lernes J. Labry Rice Mill. The Hanks family operated a hardware store for a while and milled rice. This building was torn down in the late 1970s, and a new, metal Hanks Warehouse building was erected in its place on Highway 90 East. (Courtesy of *Rayne Acadian-Tribune*.)

Three

DRAG THE BOULEVARD

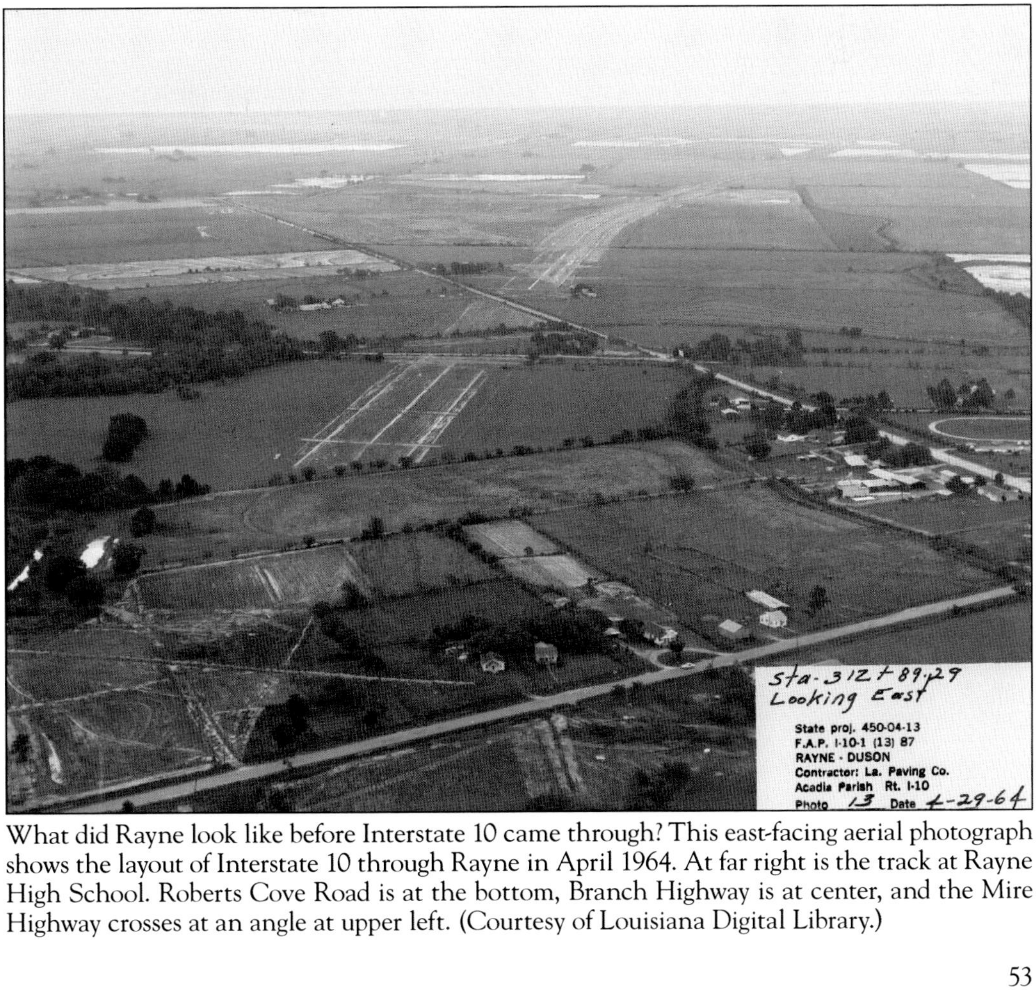

What did Rayne look like before Interstate 10 came through? This east-facing aerial photograph shows the layout of Interstate 10 through Rayne in April 1964. At far right is the track at Rayne High School. Roberts Cove Road is at the bottom, Branch Highway is at center, and the Mire Highway crosses at an angle at upper left. (Courtesy of Louisiana Digital Library.)

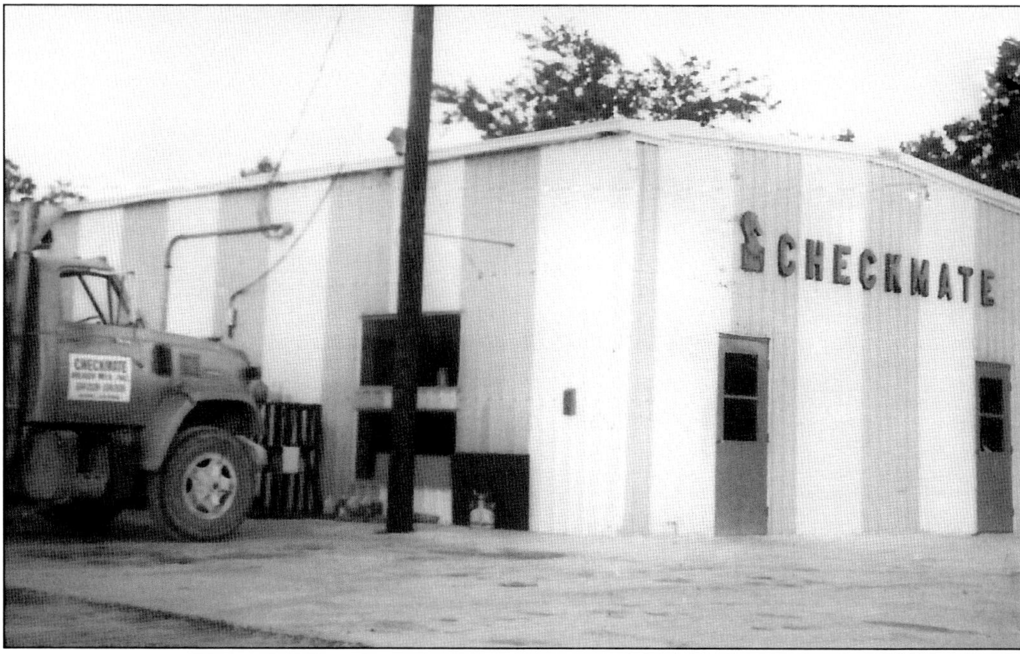

This familiar blue-and-white building housed the offices of Checkmate Concrete Company. It was located across from the Rayne police station. Walgreens is now located on that corner. Being the only concrete business in Rayne, Checkmate poured most of the foundations for homes and businesses for many years. (Courtesy of *Rayne Independent*.)

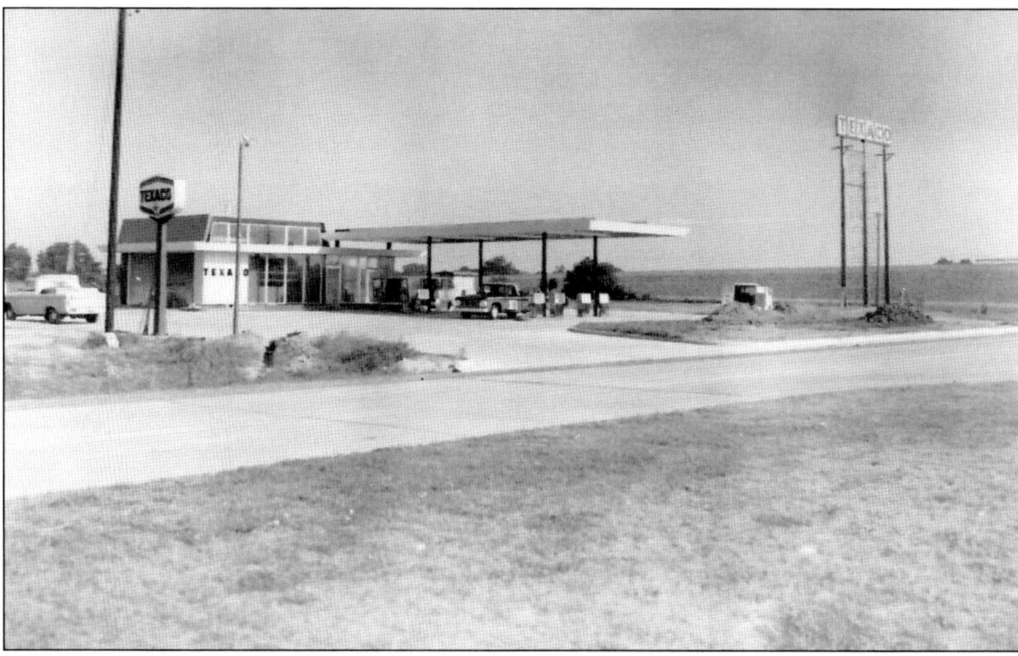

The Acadian Texaco service station prepares for its grand opening in June 1967. It was advertised as "Rayne's Newest Service Station," located at the Interstate 10 interchange in North Rayne. Owned by Elton A. Arceneaux Jr., it was open daily from 6:00 a.m. to 10:00 p.m. (Courtesy of *Rayne Independent*.)

The Rayne Kiddie Swimming Pool was a popular spot for young mothers to get out of the summer heat. It was on the south side of the main pool at the end of the parking area. There was no charge to use the pool, but mothers had to stay with their toddlers. With the water being six inches deep, everyone climbed on the fountain, like this young swimmer. (Courtesy of *Rayne Independent*.)

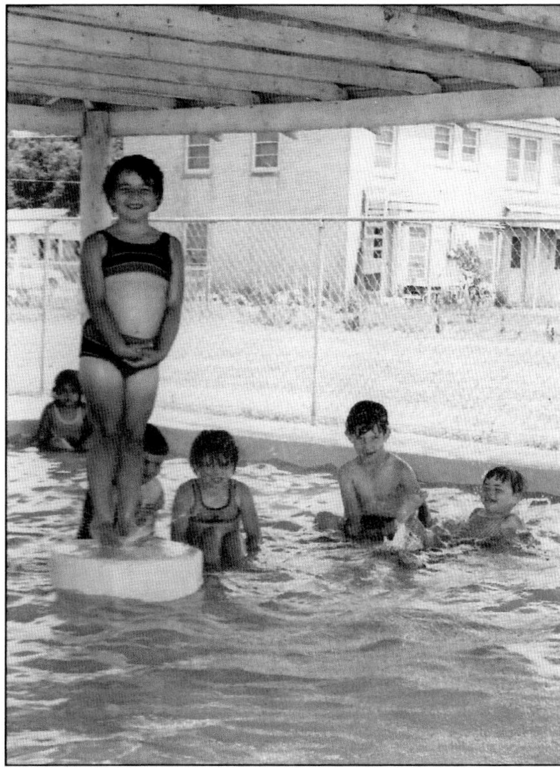

When the interstate was opened in 1967, businesses sprung up in the area. One such service station was Foot's Gulf Station, owned by Foot Nolan. He proudly advertised S&H Green Stamps. A new Chevron station is now located on this corner, across from Burger King. (Courtesy of *Rayne Acadian-Tribune*.)

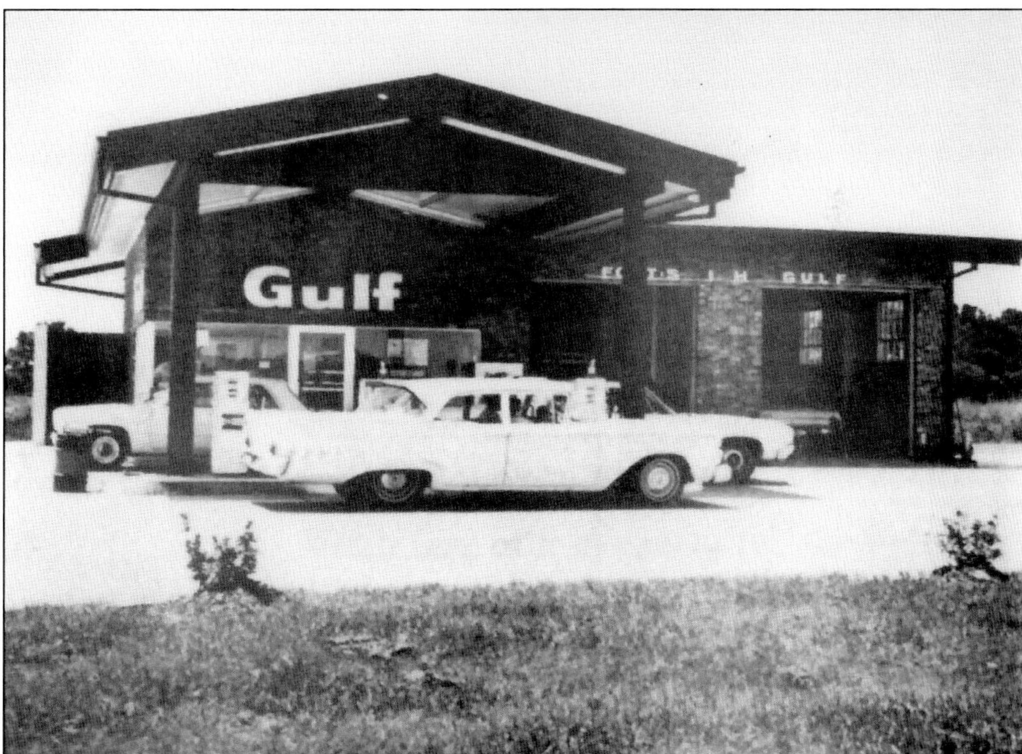

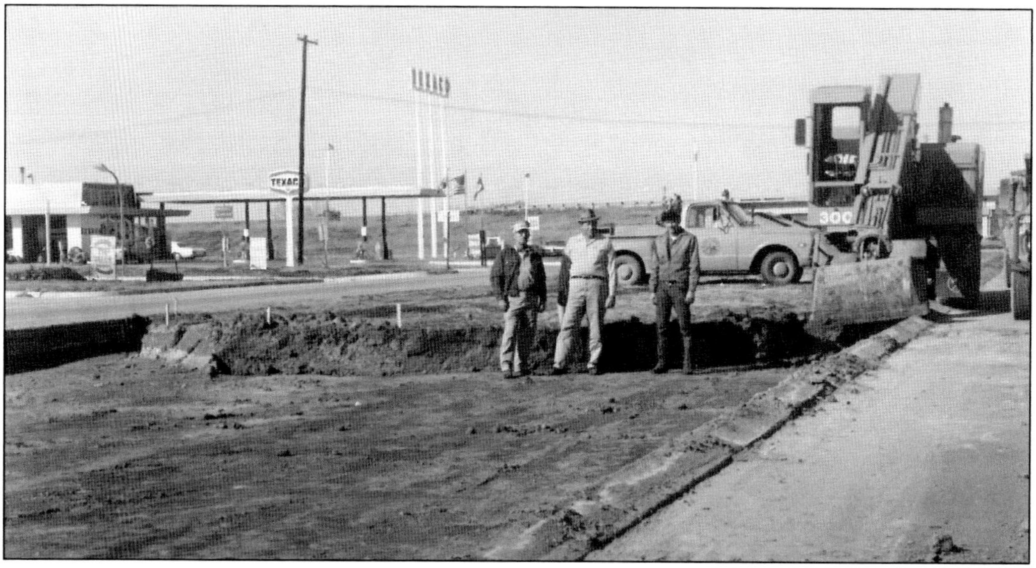

This turnaround on The Boulevard was obtained by state representative John N. John in 1973 to help develop business in Rayne, and it did much more. Any teenager in Rayne with a driver's license and access to the family car had to drag The Boulevard. A typical dragger would drive through Sonic, Burger Plaza, Burger Chef, or Mr. Cook (depending on the era). Drivers would then head south and usually turn around in LeBlanc's Phillips 66 gas station, then head north again, looking to see who was at the Side Pocket or Pizza Palace. Any night would do, but Friday and Saturday nights were the most popular. (Courtesy of *Rayne Independent.*)

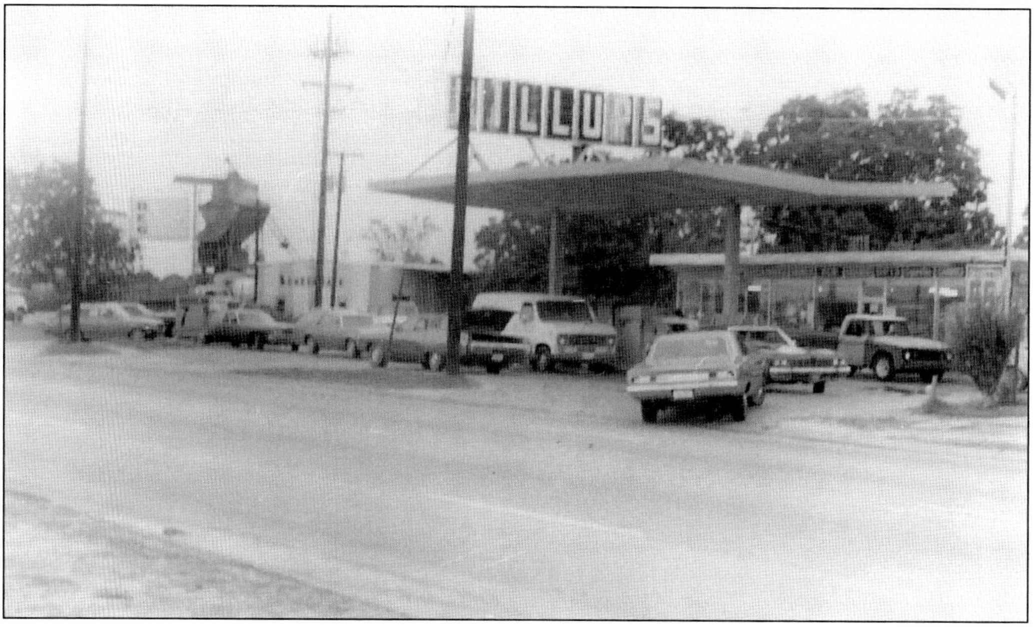

Cars are lined up at the Billups North, across from the Rayne Municipal Pool on the corner of Oak Street and The Boulevard, to get a very limited amount of gasoline during the gas shortage of 1972. At the time, some stations would put out a white flag if they had gas to sell. If they did, a long wait was expected, and often, tempers were short. Smoke 'n' Go is now located in this building. (Courtesy of *Rayne Independent.*)

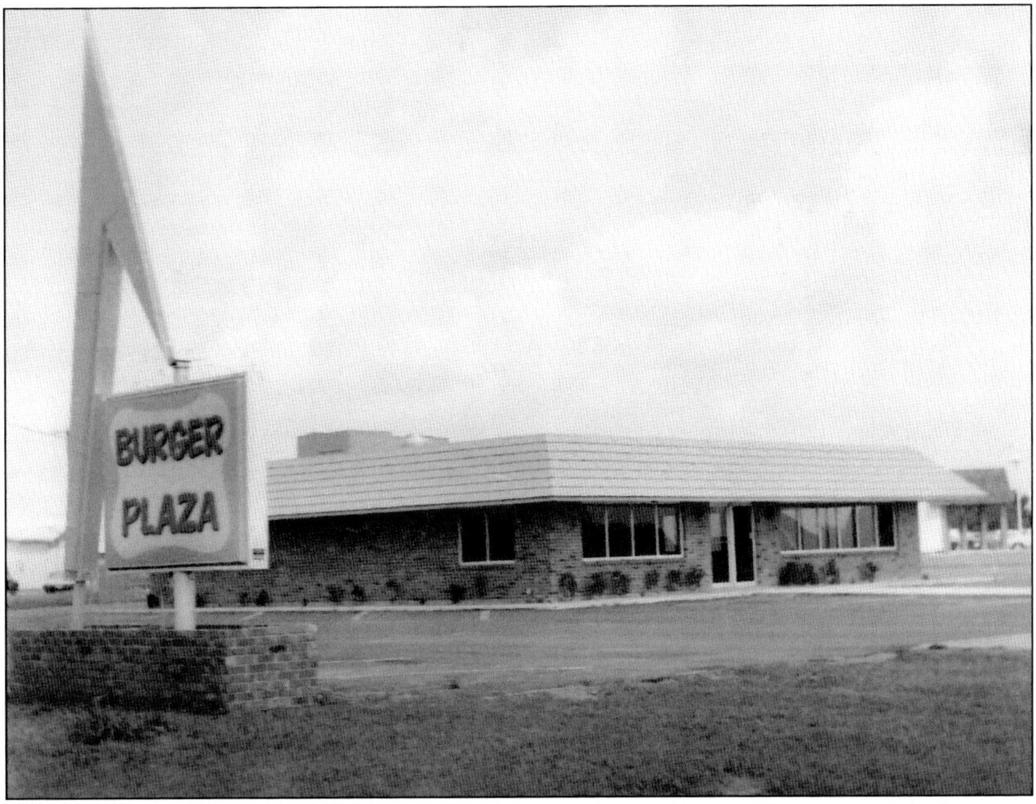

In March 1974, the first fast-food burger restaurant in Rayne, Burger Plaza, opened for business. Owned by Don Whatley, Adam "Latch" Latiolais (who also managed), and Larry Hebert, it opened long before any of the nation's burger chains invaded the area. This building still stands on The Boulevard as Candyland Cottage. (Courtesy of *Rayne Independent*.)

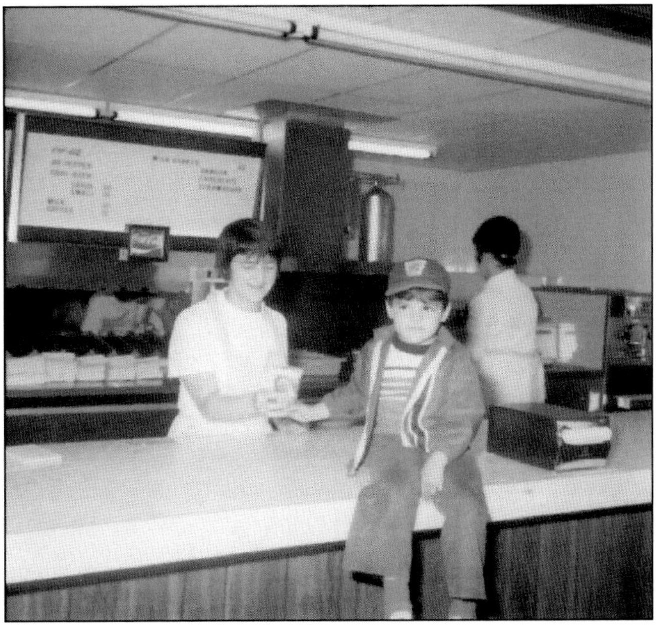

This is a rare inside look at the front counter of Burger Plaza. Diane Broussard serves a drink to the restaurant's first customer, Jason Leger, in March 1974. The restaurant had seating for 76 customers and employed 20 people. It remained open until it was taken over by Burger Chef in 1976. (Courtesy of *Rayne Independent*.)

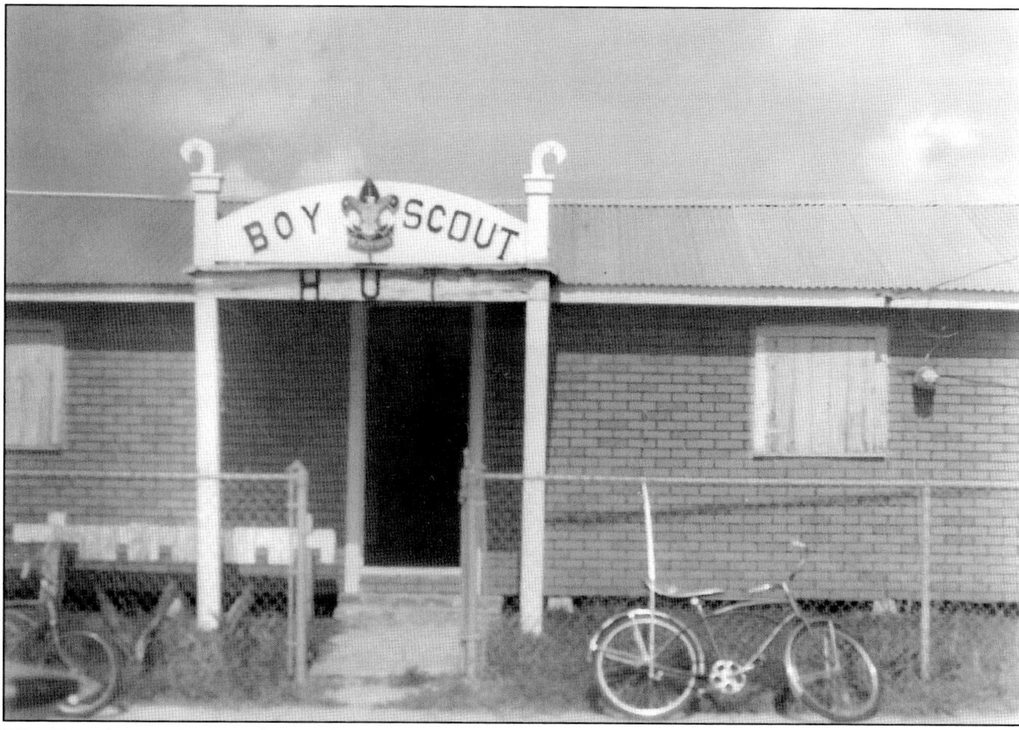

The Boy Scout Hut was located across from the Billups on the west side of The Boulevard. It was used by Boy Scouts, Cub Scouts, Girl Scouts, and Brownies. Milo Duboval and Horace Thibodeaux were Scout leaders for many years. (Courtesy of *Rayne Independent.*)

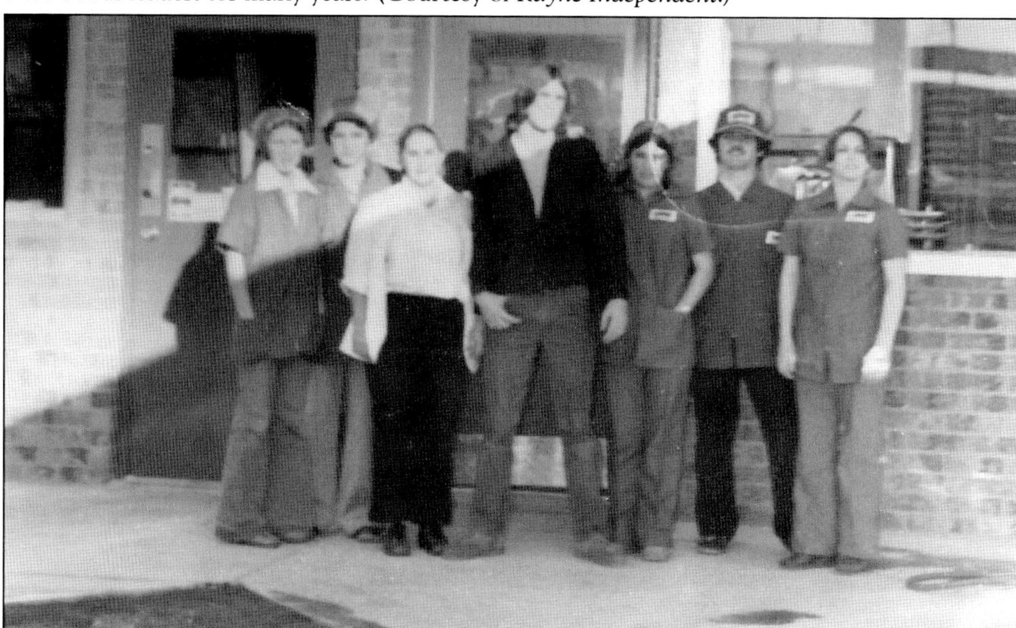

The workers of Sonic pose in 1977, when the restaurant opened in Rayne. Sonic was unique, as carhops usually delivered orders on roller skates. This building still stands; a new Sonic was built in 2013 down The Boulevard. (Courtesy of *Rayne Independent.*)

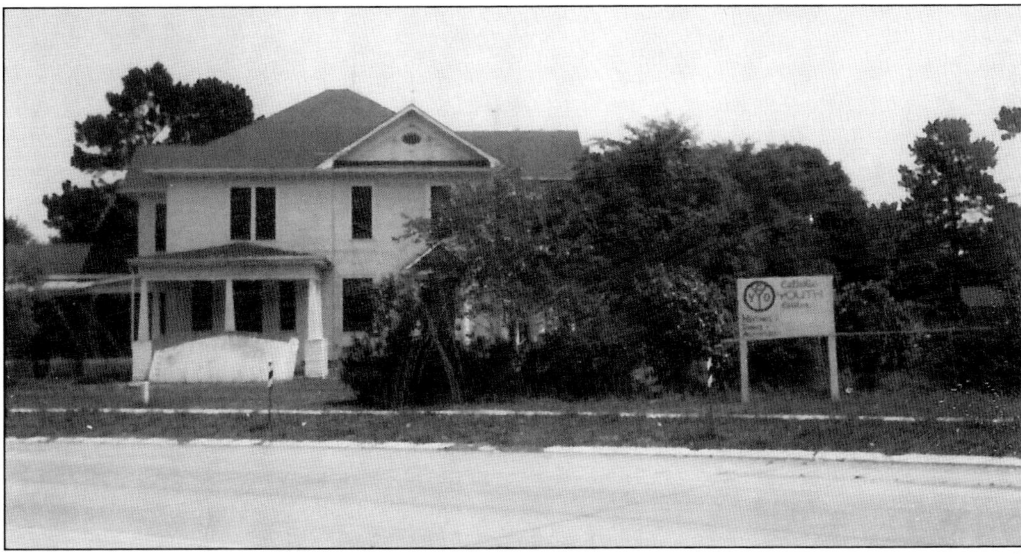

St. Joseph Catholic Church's Catholic Youth Organization was housed in this mansion, formerly the Dermas Petitjean home. Located on The Boulevard's S-curve, it was consumed by fire. (Courtesy of *Rayne Independent*.)

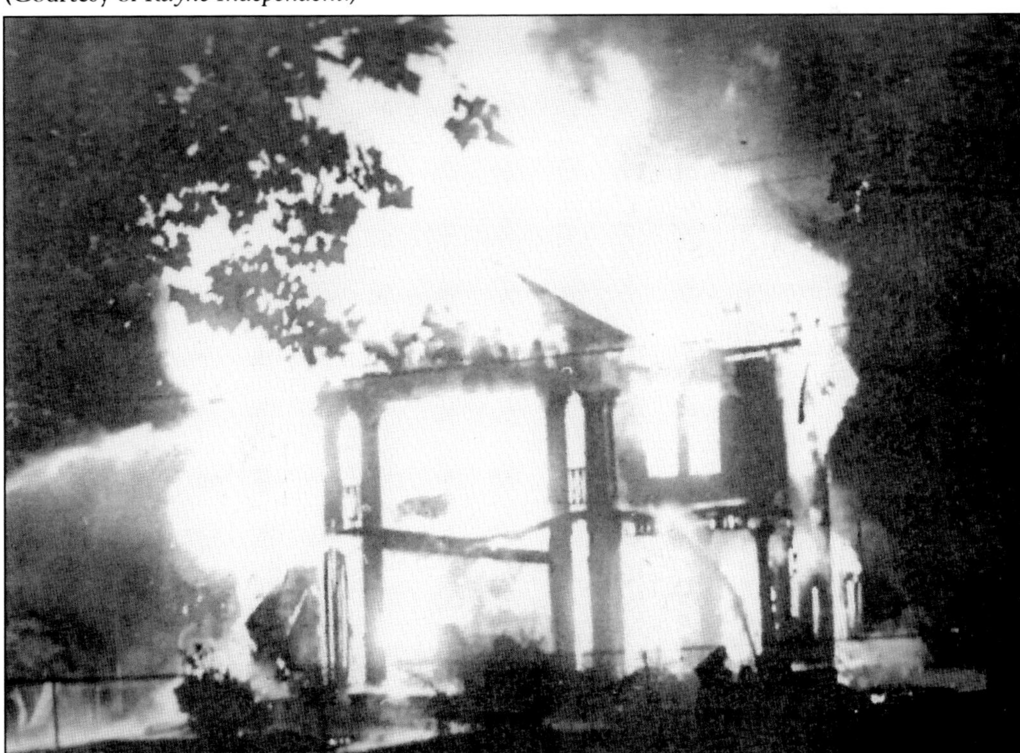

When retired firefighters talk about the big fires in Rayne, this one is usually near the top of the list. In July 1972, the Dermas Petitjean home caught fire and burned to the ground. Not occupied at the time, it was being used by the St. Joseph Catholic Youth Organization. (Courtesy of *Rayne Acadian-Tribune*.)

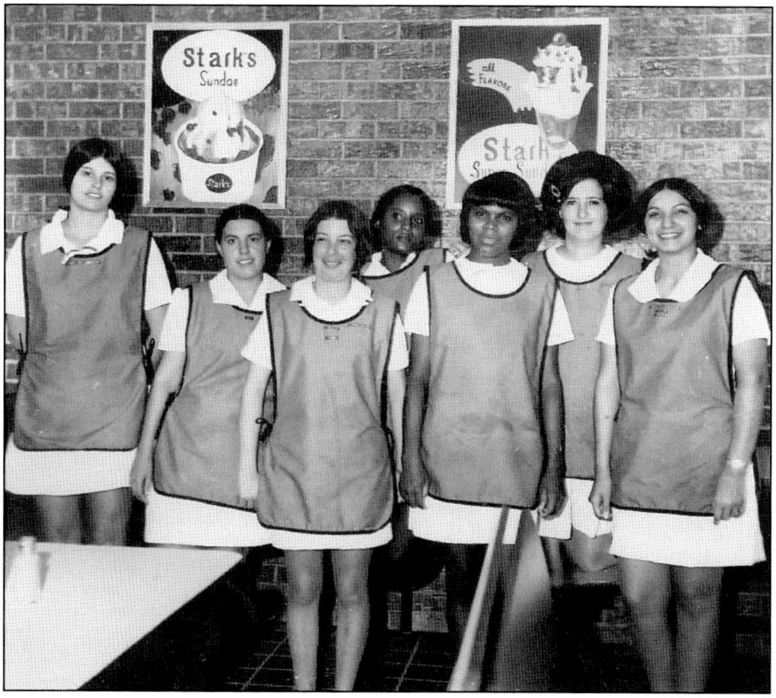

Stark's Family Restaurant was built in the 1980s and featured the Rustler and delicious ice cream. These unidentified workers are posing in the dining room. The restaurant ran daily specials; the author remembers buying a large root beer for only 25¢. Starks was bought out by Dairy Queen, which is operating in the same location today. (Courtesy of *Rayne Independent*.)

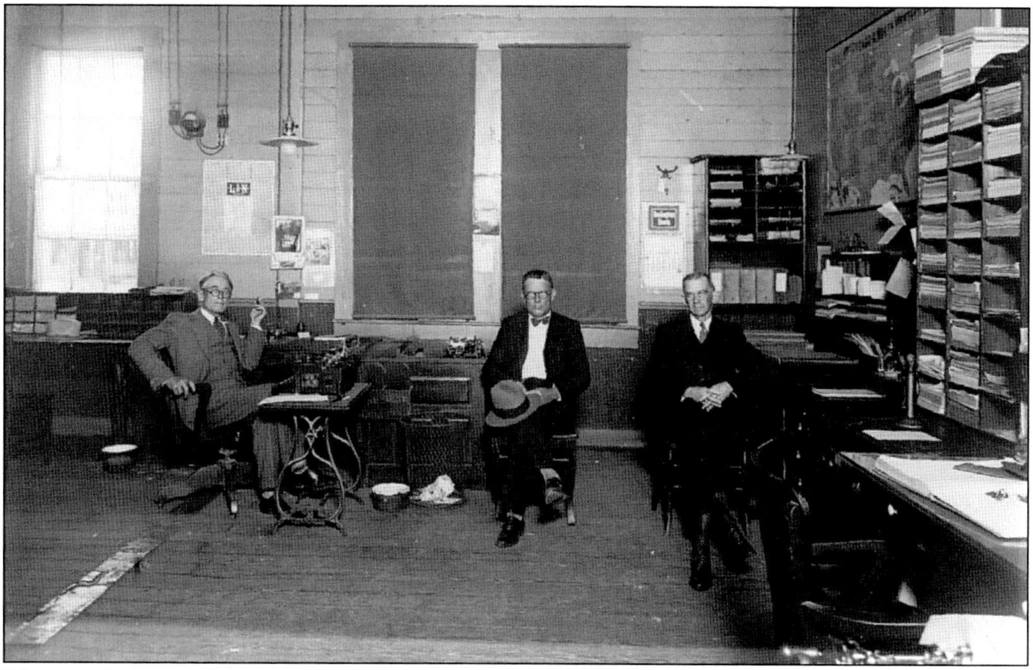

This inside view of the freight depot from 1934 shows employees of Southern Pacific Railroad (from left to right) S.L Ross, agent for the freight office; Charles W. Jennings, telegraph clerk and passenger ticket sales; and F.L. Campbell, cashier and bookkeeper. The depot handled telegraphs, freight, and U.S. mail, and had passenger service until the passenger depot was built on the north side of the tracks in the 1930s. The station operated from 1880 to 1975. (Courtesy of Carl Jennings.)

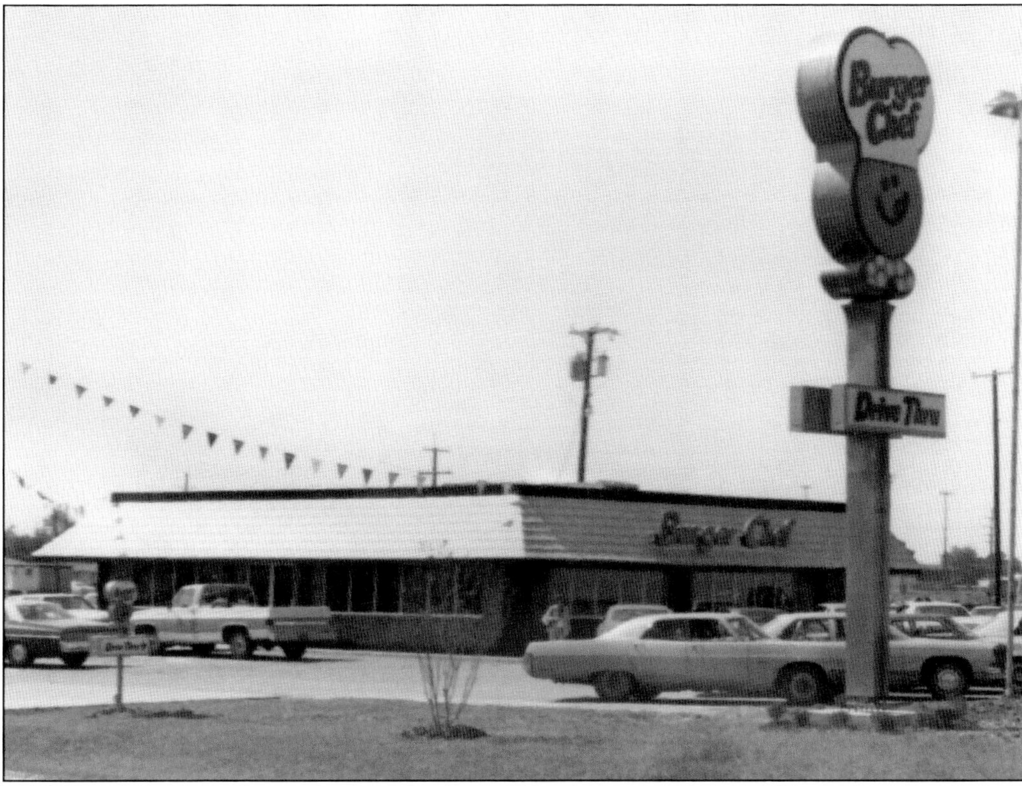

Burger Chef came to Rayne in 1976, when it remodeled the Burger Plaza. Seating was expanded to 84, and a drive-through window and a salad bar were added. Owned by William H. Michot of Lafayette, it was one of 900 Burger Chef restaurants in the United States. (Courtesy of *Rayne Independent.*)

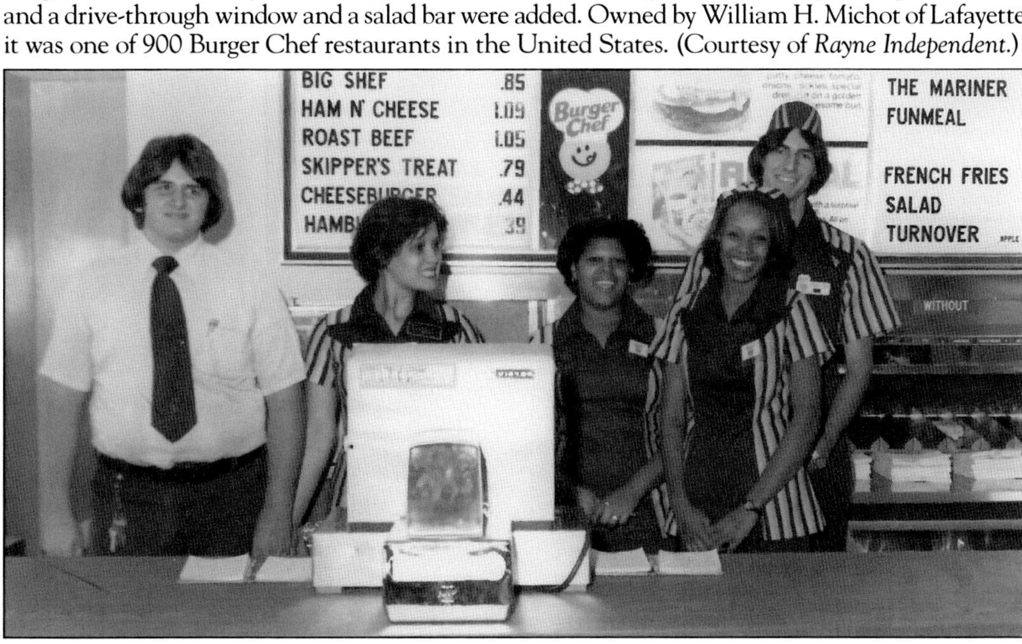

The staff of Burger Chef at its grand opening are, from left to right, Cordell Theriot (manager), Bridget Rochon, Patsy Chachere, Alice Charles, and Jody Constantin. Note the affordable prices on the menu board, including the "Big Shef" for only 85¢. (Courtesy of *Rayne Independent.*)

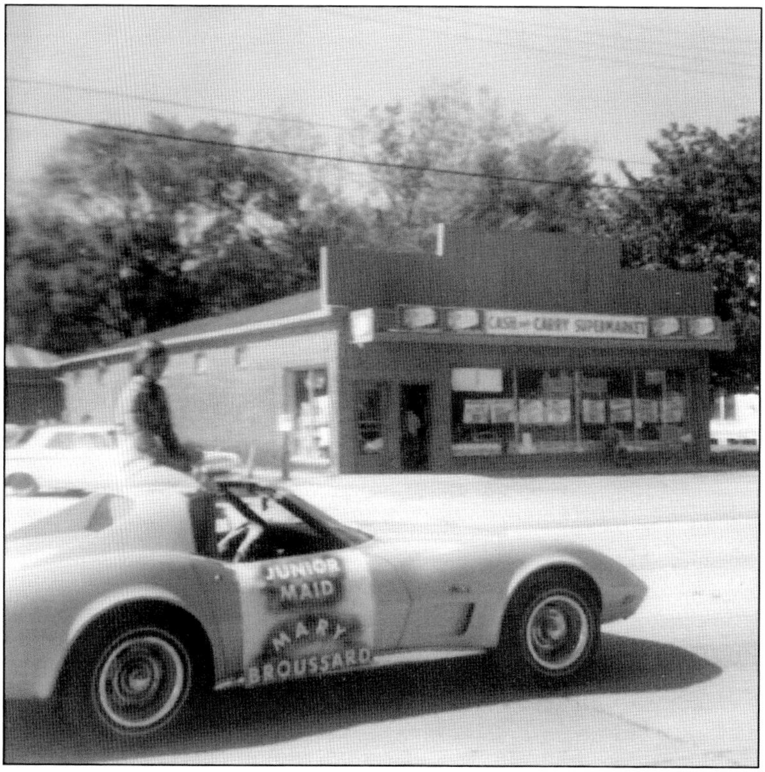

Homecoming junior maid Mary Helen Broussard rides on a Corvette in the 1977 Rayne High School homecoming parade. In the background is Cash and Carry Supermarket, a chain store with locations in Welsh, Oakdale, Dequincy, and Kinder. Joe Alleman was the manager, and Tom LeBlanc was a longtime employee who stocked and bagged. (Courtesy of Mary Helen Broussard Reed.)

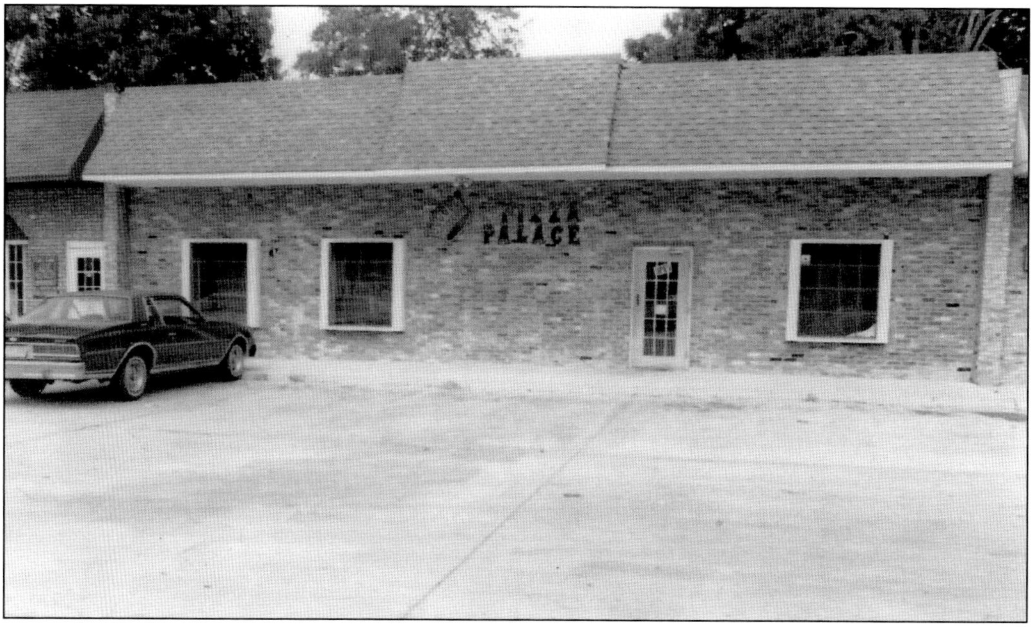

Pizza Palace, located at 804 The Boulevard, was known for its cold beer, salads, and small jukeboxes at the tables. Opened in 1982, it was owned by Mr. and Mrs. Sidney Benton. Raywood Broussard was the manager. Pizza Hut and a Washateria occupy this building today. (Courtesy of *Rayne Independent*.)

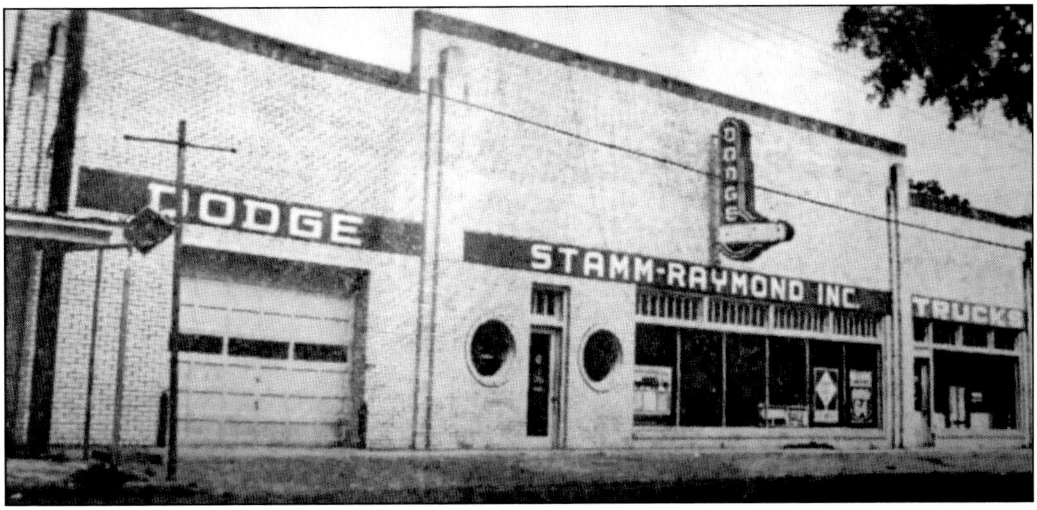

The largest car dealership in Rayne was Stamm-Raymond Motors, owned by John Stamm and Anthony Raymond. Located on the southwest corner of Harrop Street and North Adams Avenue, this landmark took up a large portion of the block. The company sold Fords at its first location on Clegg Street, at Stamm-Scheele in 1918. It later sold Dodge and Chrysler cars and trucks. (Courtesy of *Rayne Acadian-Tribune*.)

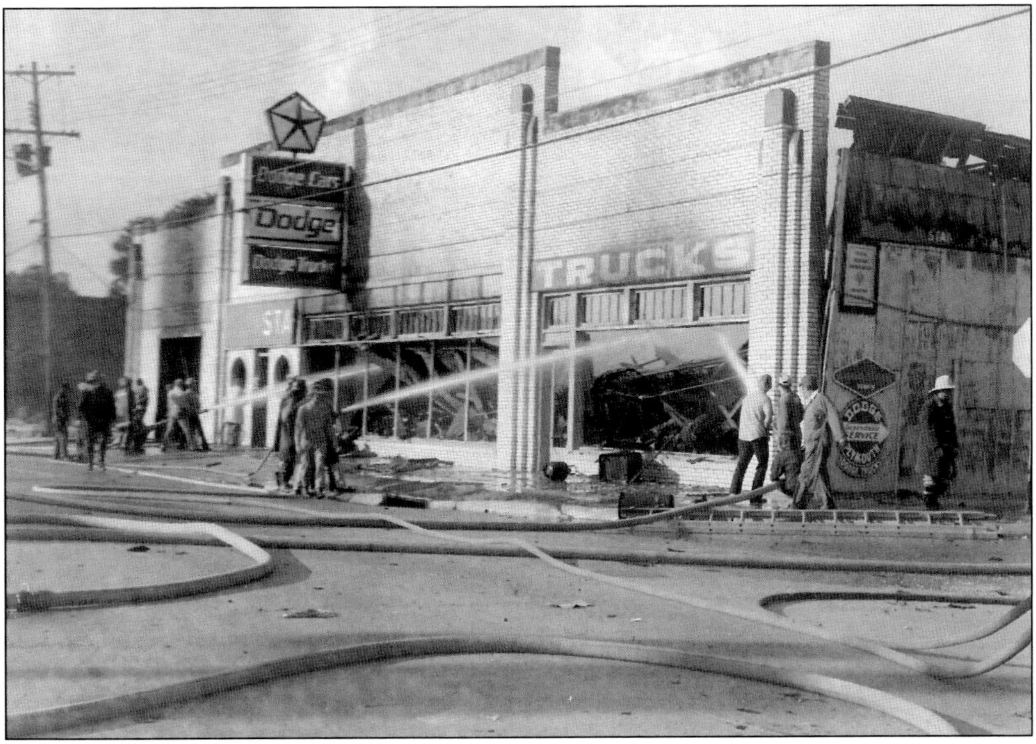

Another large blaze still remembered by firefighters occurred in October 1975 at the Stamm-Raymond dealership. After the fire, all that remained were the exterior brick walls. The intense heat was exacerbated by the new vehicles and the numerous petroleum products in the shop area. Stamm-Raymond was located on North Adams Avenue and West Harrop Street. (Courtesy of *Rayne Independent*.)

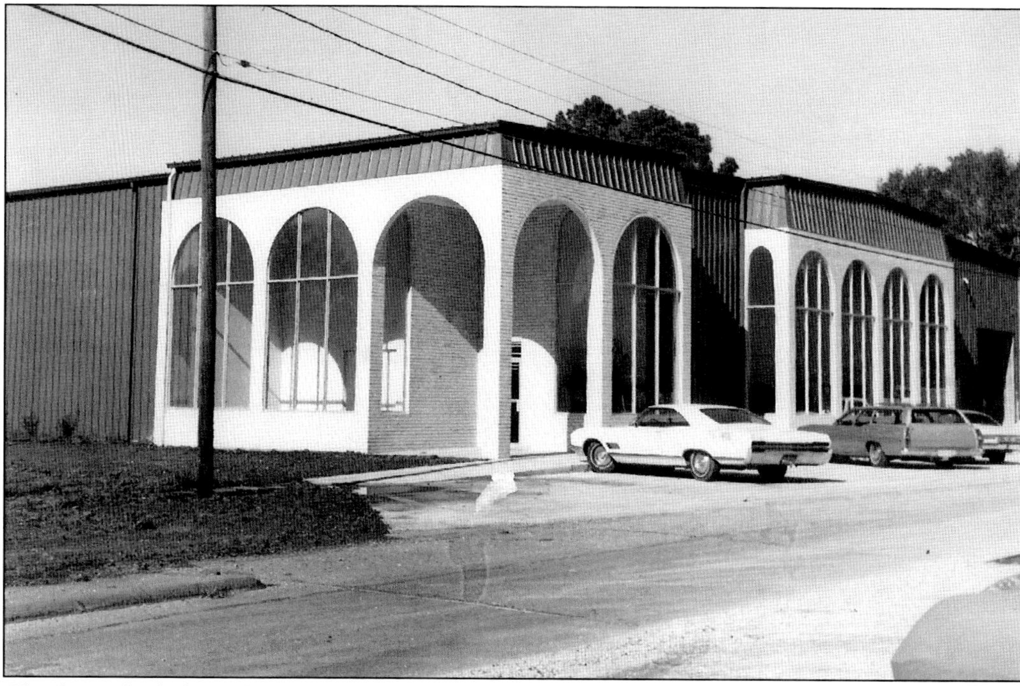

Charles and Gladys Robichaux built the Robichaux Furniture Store on the location of the former Dermas Petitjean home in 1973. They moved to this site from their previous location in the old Besse Furniture store near Stamm-Raymond. This large building featured two stories of shopping. It is still standing today, with other businesses occupying it. (Courtesy of *Rayne Acadian-Tribune*.)

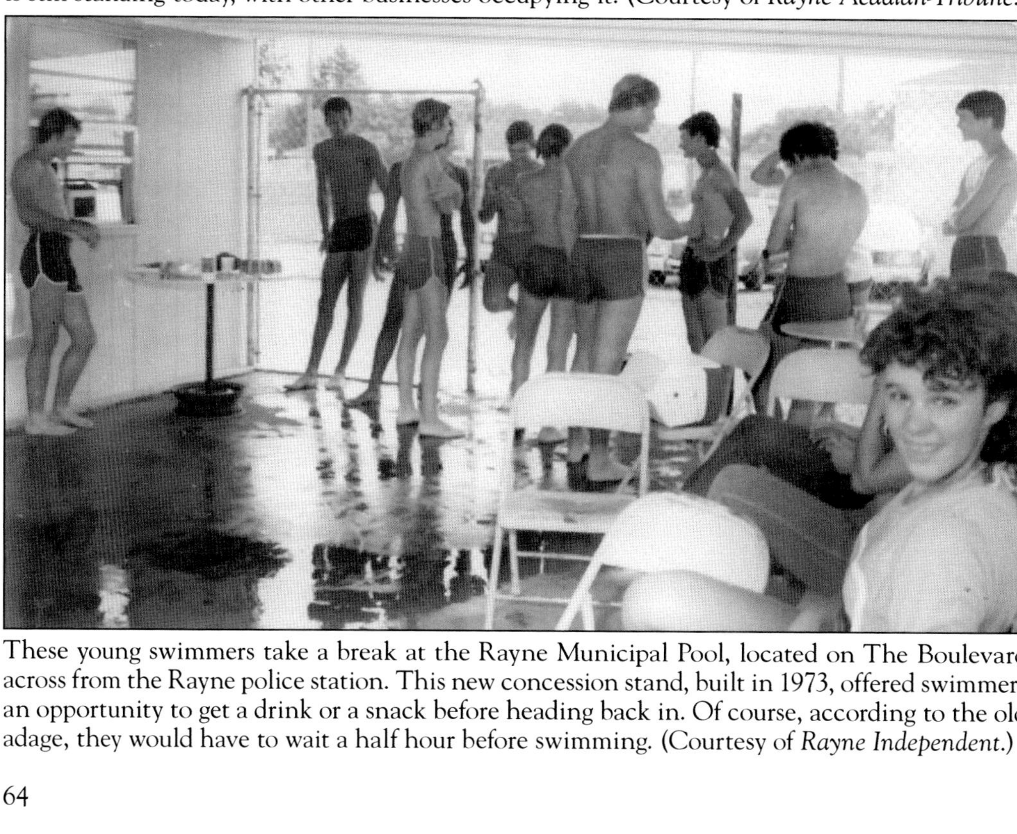

These young swimmers take a break at the Rayne Municipal Pool, located on The Boulevard across from the Rayne police station. This new concession stand, built in 1973, offered swimmers an opportunity to get a drink or a snack before heading back in. Of course, according to the old adage, they would have to wait a half hour before swimming. (Courtesy of *Rayne Independent*.)

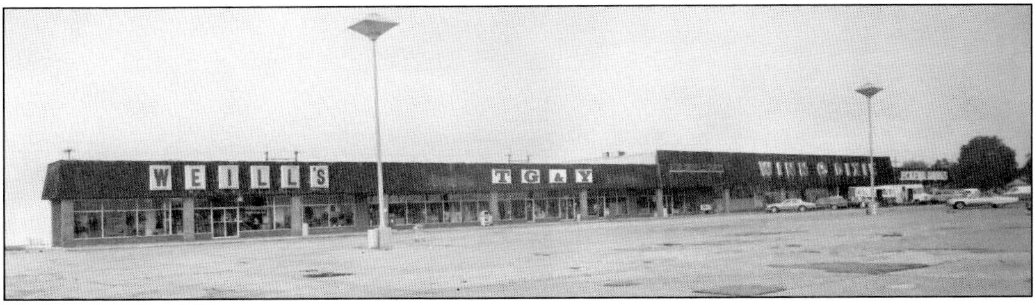

The Rayne Plaza Shopping Center is shown after its grand opening in 1971. It featured, from left to right, Weill's, TG&Y, Top Value Stamp Store, Winn-Dixie, and Eckerd Drug Store. It is still in operation today, with an addition to the north. Winn-Dixie is now located in the new addition. (Courtesy of *Rayne Independent*.)

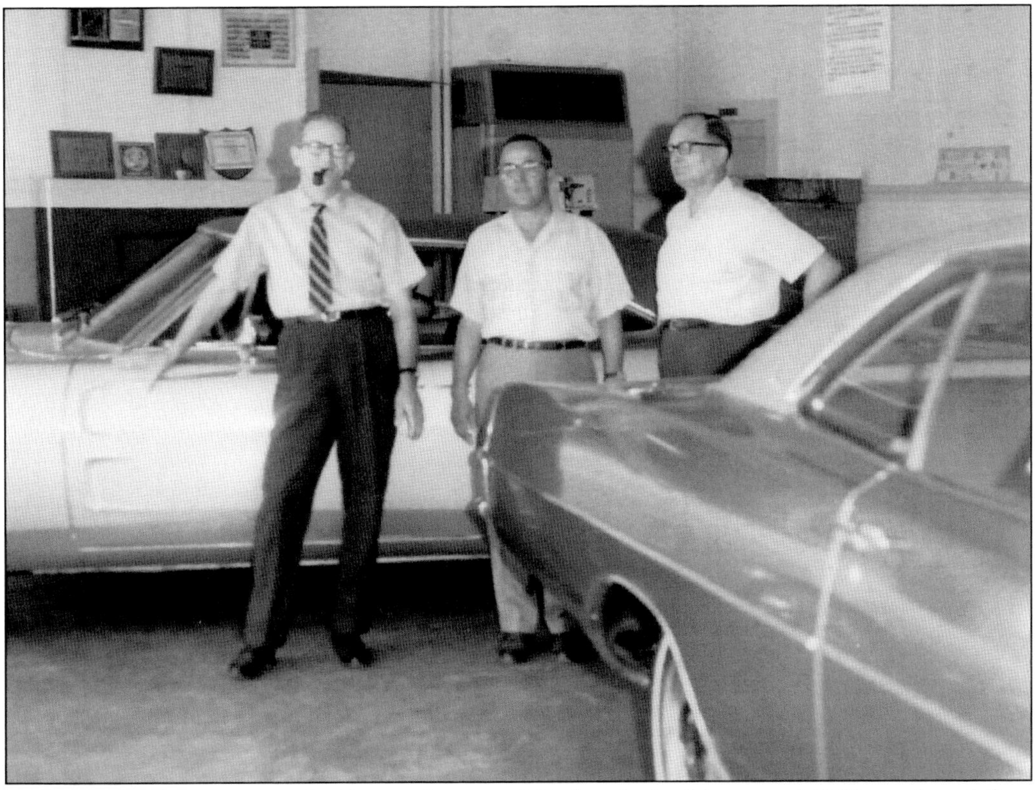

Posing in the showroom at the Stamm-Raymond Dodge dealership around 1970 are, from left to right, Carl "Koochie" Hoffpauir, A.E. "Shorty" Raymond, and Lester Trahan. Unlike today, the introduction of the new-year models was a major event. (Courtesy of *Rayne Independent*.)

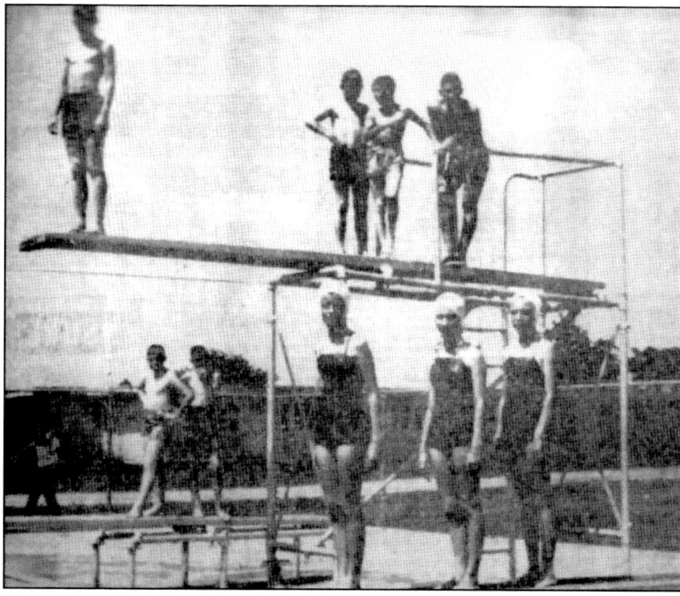

Today, triple diving boards such as these are not common at public pools. Shown here are, from left to right, (low board, foreground) Peggy Hoffpauir, Patsy Ducote, and "Peachie" Pharr; (middle board, background) Norris Cormier and Carol Mouton; (high board) Percy Lapoint, Raymond Primeaux, Wallace Duhon, and Ernest Cormier. This photograph was taken in 1953. The Rayne Municipal Pool was dedicated on July 3, 1949, just in time for the heat of summer. (Courtesy of *Rayne Acadian-Tribune*.)

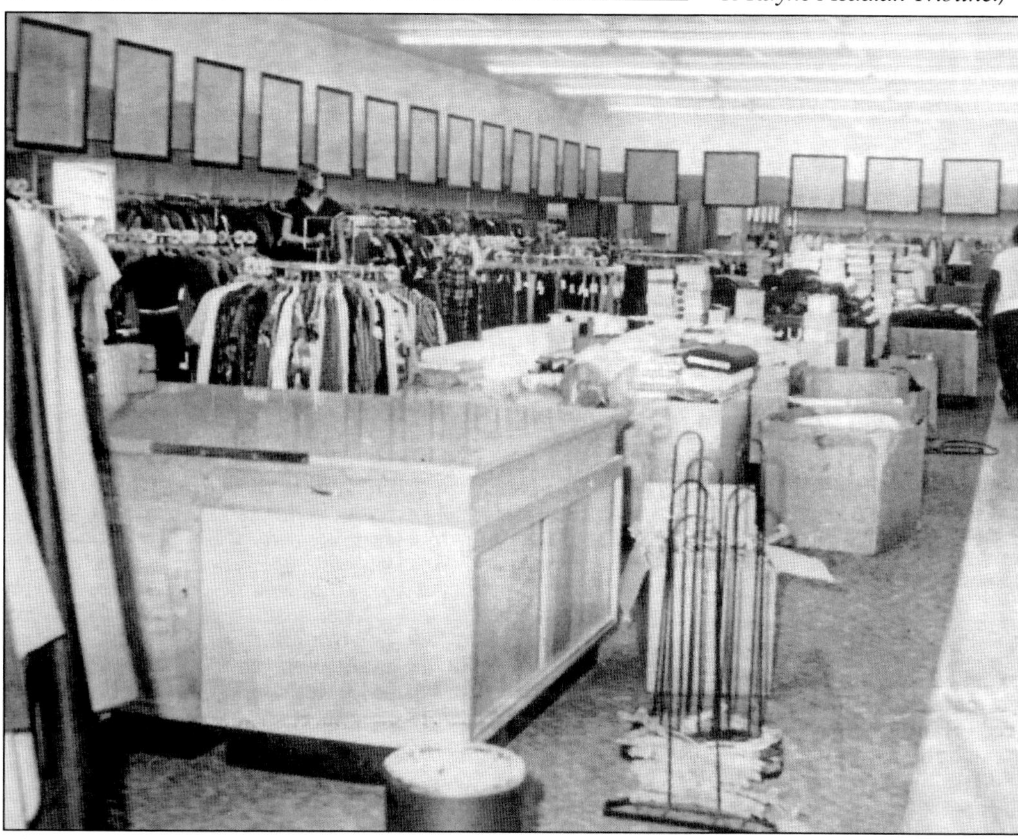

The newly opened Weill's Store is shown here after it relocated to the Rayne Plaza Shopping Center in 1974. It was originally located on East Louisiana and North Adams Avenues, where Dollar General is today. The manager, Jimmy Orillion, was ready for shoppers with the new line of fall clothing arriving in the store. (Courtesy of *Rayne Independent*.)

Four

Streets of Rayne

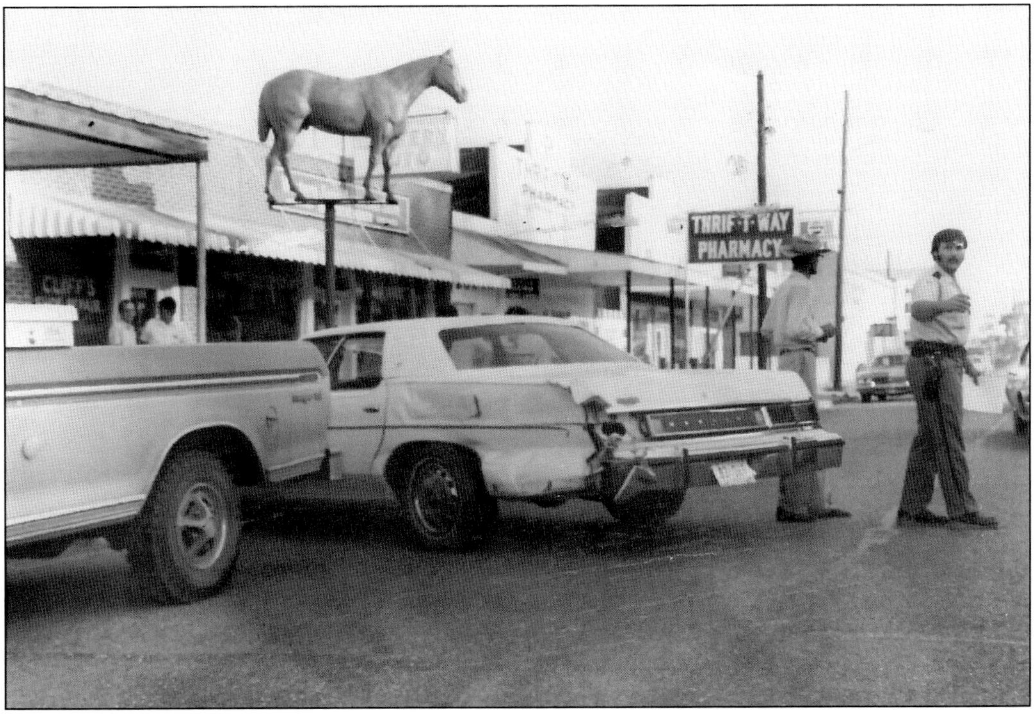

This wreck happened under the watchful eye of the horse perched above Cliff's Shoe Repair. Other businesses along South Adams Avenue were, beginning at center, Western Auto, Thrifty Way Pharmacy, People's Café (Paco's), and Rayne State Bank. The story goes that, one day, someone put a pile of horse manure under the horse. Paco was not too happy with flies around his café. (Courtesy of *Rayne Independent*.)

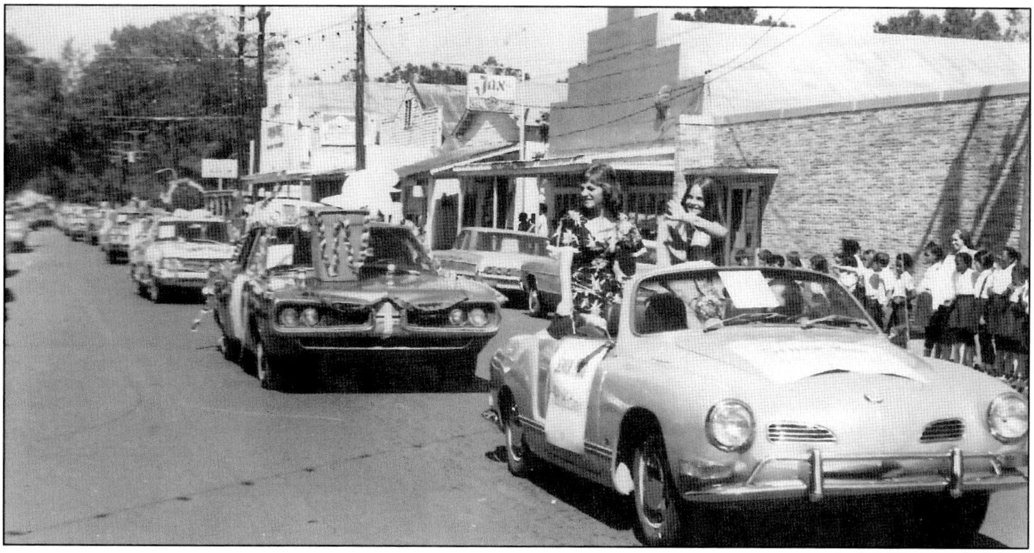

North Polk Street was the scene for the Rayne High School Homecoming Parade in the early 1970s. Rayne Catholic children, supervised by a nun, are lined up next to People's Drug Store. Fortunately, the parade was during the day, and the bars that lined Polk Street were closed. On the right side is the former two-story W.A. Kennedy store, which was Lloyd's Furniture, owned by Lloyd Meche at the time of this photograph. (Courtesy of *Rayne Independent*.)

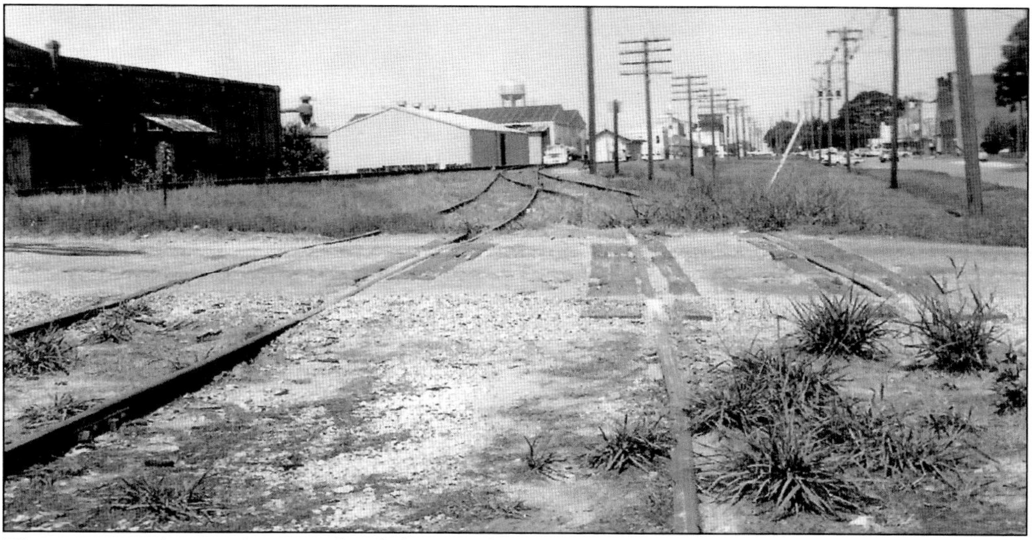

This is a west-facing photograph of the Southern Pacific Railroad tracks at the North Arenas Street crossing, showing the two sidelines that served the Louisiana Rice and the Edmundson-Duhe Rice Mills. The tracks were removed long ago, but the rough crossing is remembered by the older generation. (Courtesy of *Rayne Independent*.)

This aerial photograph, taken by Leonard J. Laperous of The Photo Shop, shows the ever-growing section of southeast Rayne. The main street going left to right is South Arenas Street. At upper center, East Perrodin Street turns left into South Bradford Street. The large area at the top left is where the Rayne Branch Hospital was built in 1958. (Courtesy of Leonard J. Laperous, The Photo Shop.)

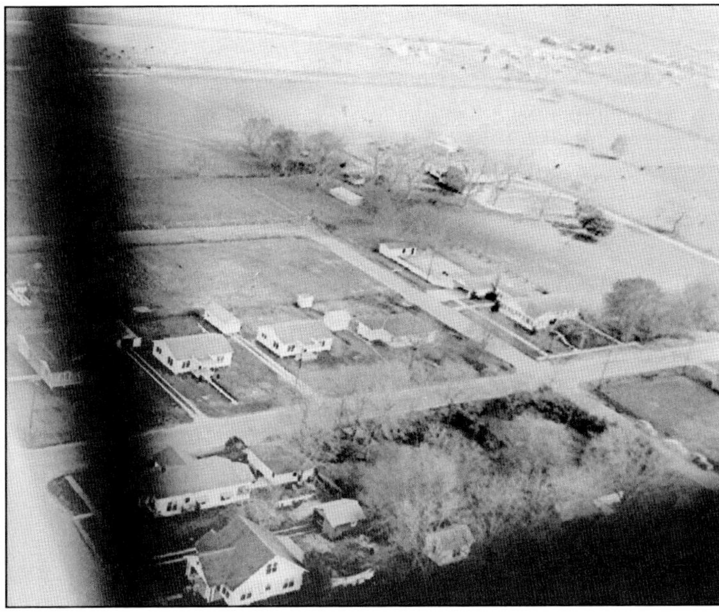

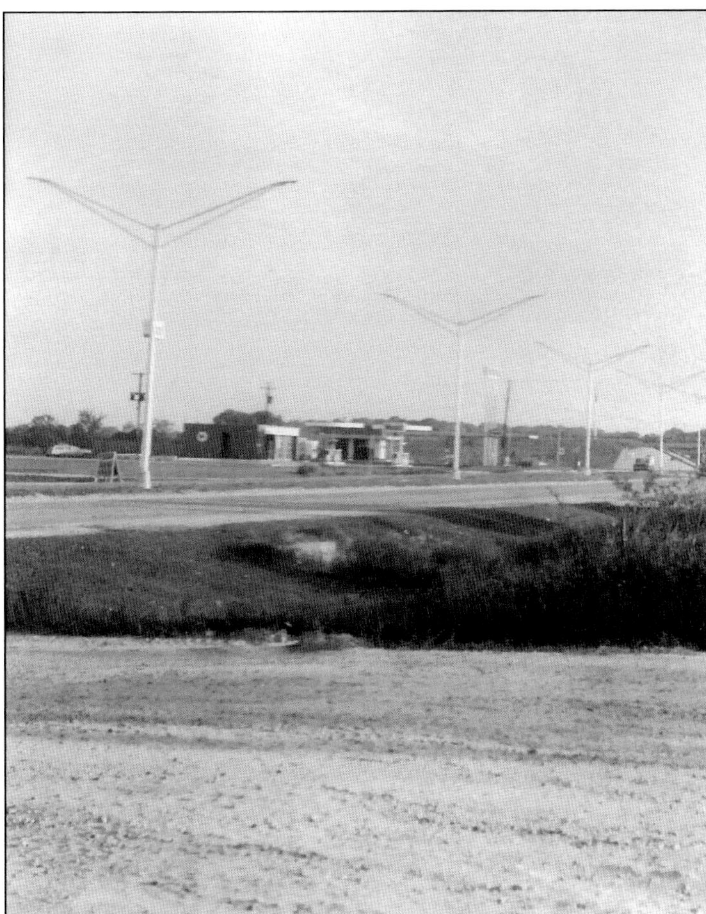

The Boulevard received a boost when these lights were installed to help develop business near Interstate 10. Seen in the background are the Mobil and Texaco service stations. Several cut-throughs have been added, but the lights are still in operation today. (Courtesy of Sidney Stutes.)

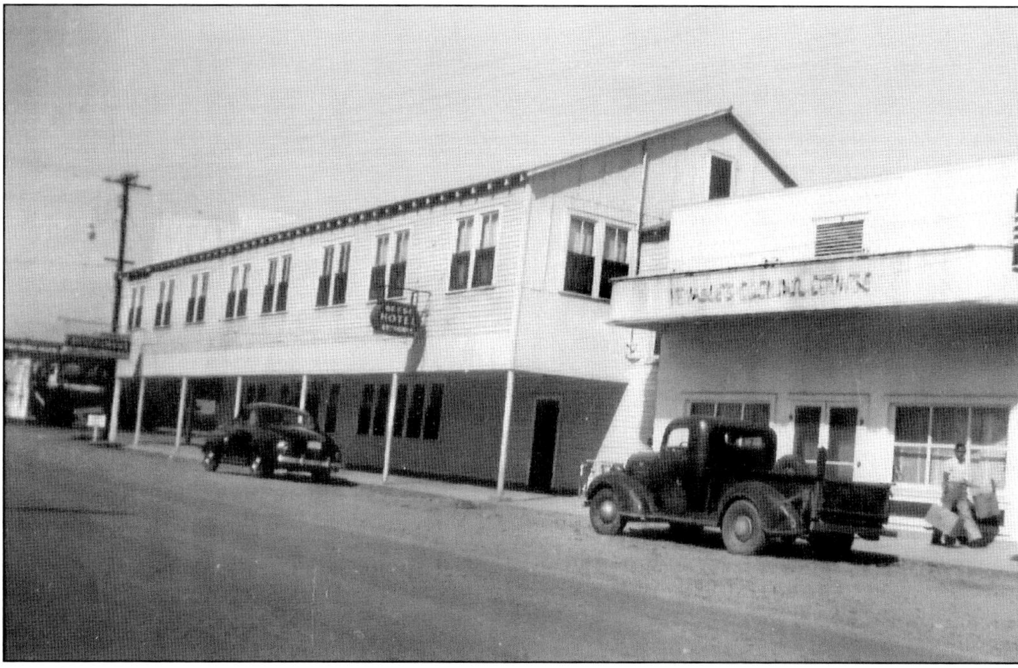

Venable's Cocktail Lounge (right) was owned and operated by Johnny Venable. The Besse Hotel (center) had eight rooms to rent upstairs and a restaurant on the first floor. East Texas Avenue was gravel at the time of this photograph. (Courtesy of Gene Guidry.)

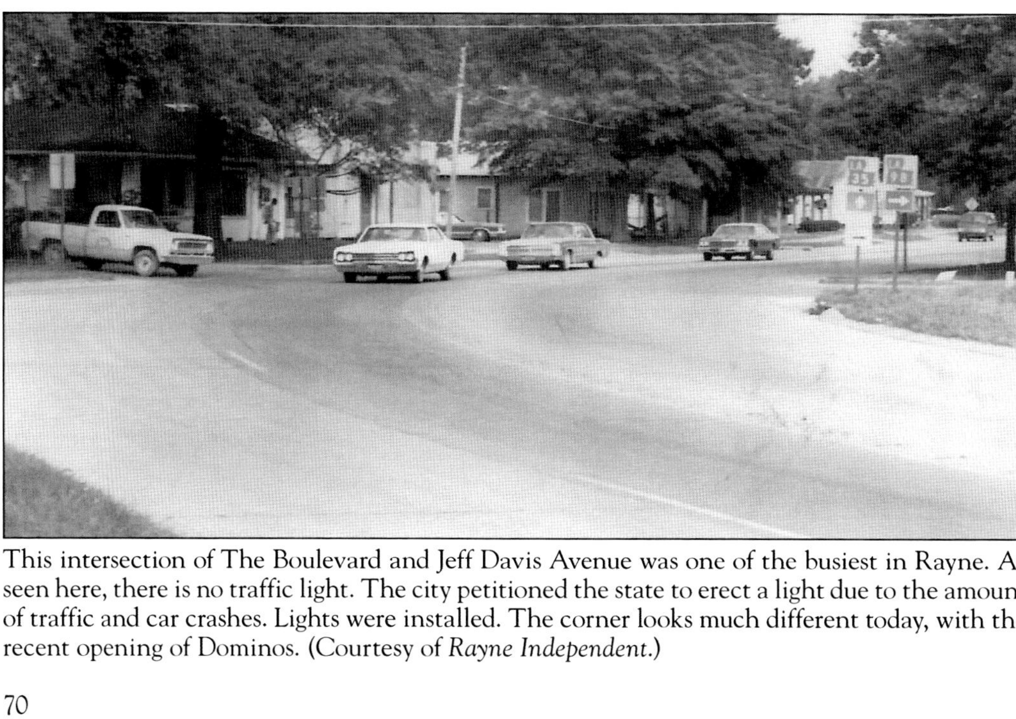

This intersection of The Boulevard and Jeff Davis Avenue was one of the busiest in Rayne. As seen here, there is no traffic light. The city petitioned the state to erect a light due to the amount of traffic and car crashes. Lights were installed. The corner looks much different today, with the recent opening of Dominos. (Courtesy of *Rayne Independent*.)

This south-facing photograph of South Adams Avenue shows the palm trees (right) that were planted in front of the W. Petitjean & Co. Building. As seen here, gas was selling for 29¢ for regular and 32¢ for premium at the Canal Gas Station. Note that the second car from the back is a taxicab. (Courtesy of Sidney Stutes.)

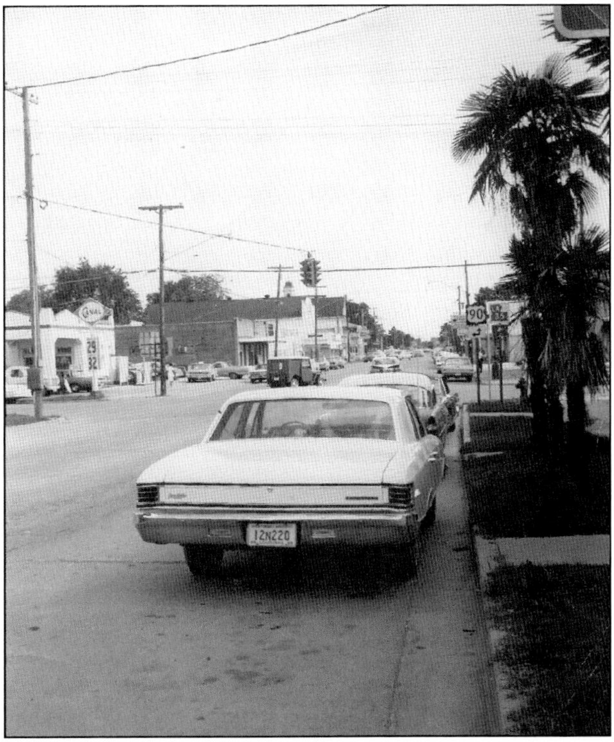

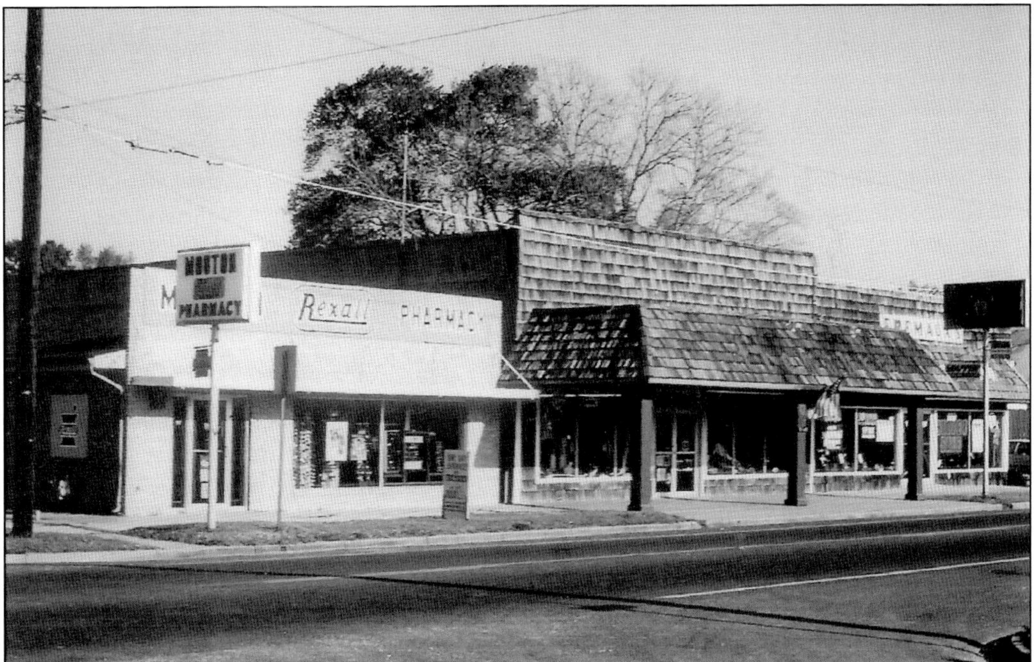

This view of the 300 block of South Adams Avenue in 1983 shows Mouton Pharmacy and E.C. Fremaux's Hardware Store, which took up the majority of the block. The rear of the buildings contained a large repair shop and warehouse. Mouton Pharmacy is still operating at this location; Fremaux's was torn down and is a vacant lot today. (Courtesy of *Rayne Independent*.)

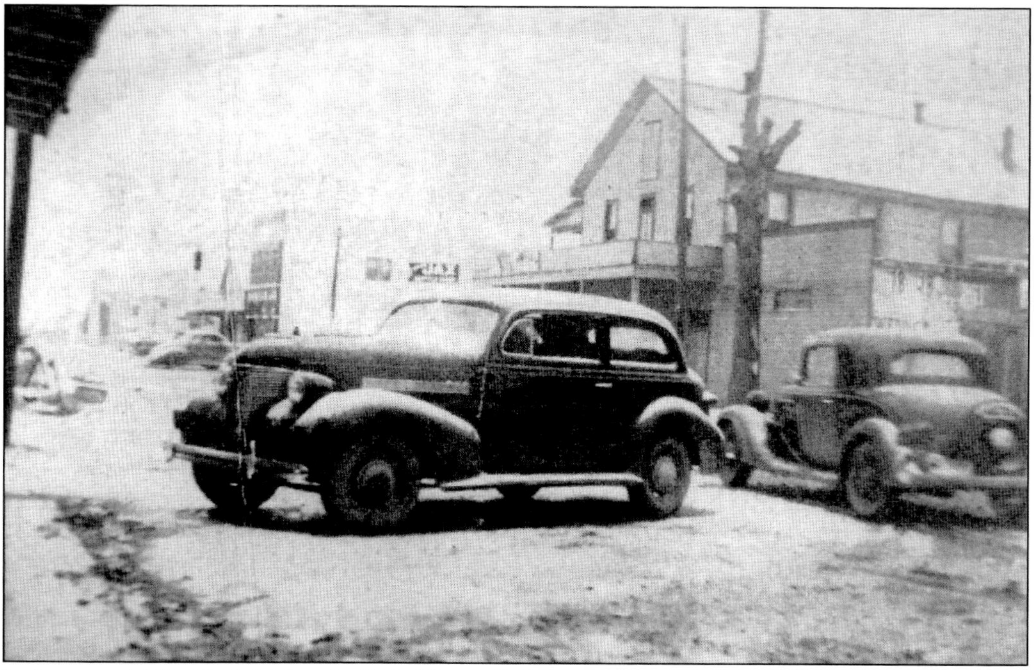

In January 1940, Herb Hebert's 1939 Chevy Sedan is parked in front of his place of business on West Texas Avenue, Pop & Herb's Bar. On the right are Hanks's Bar and Robichaux's Meat Market, where Rayne State Bank stands today. The most unusual thing about this photograph is the heavy snowfall on the ground. (Courtesy of *Rayne Acadian-Tribune.*)

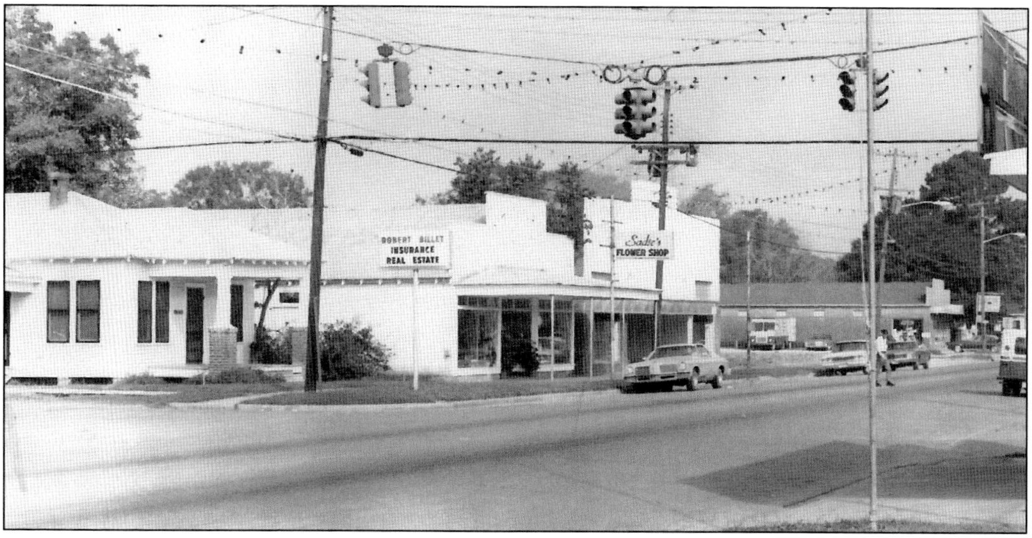

A stoplight controls the traffic at this once-busy intersection at Edwards and North Polk Streets. On the left is the office of Robert Billet Insurance, which was previously the office of Dr. Joseph C. Bruner. Next door is Sadie's Flower Shop, which was originally Bordelon & Lemoine Appliance Store. Next is the Besse Furniture Store. Farther down, on the next block, is the Cash and Carry Supermarket. (Courtesy of *Rayne Independent.*)

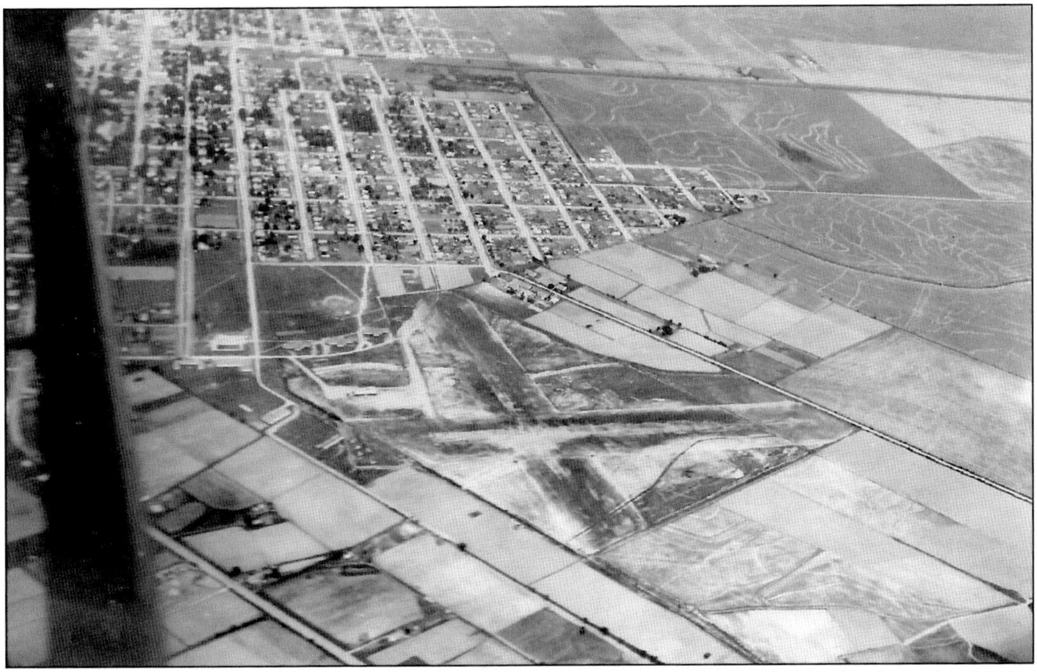

This aerial photograph of north Rayne shows the area where Interstate 10 was built in the 1960s. Here, it is farmland. At center, the runways of Rayne Municipal Airport can be clearly seen, where the baseball parks and the festival grounds are now located. Just above the airport is the rectangle that was the Rayne Pool. (Courtesy of Fair Craig Hash.)

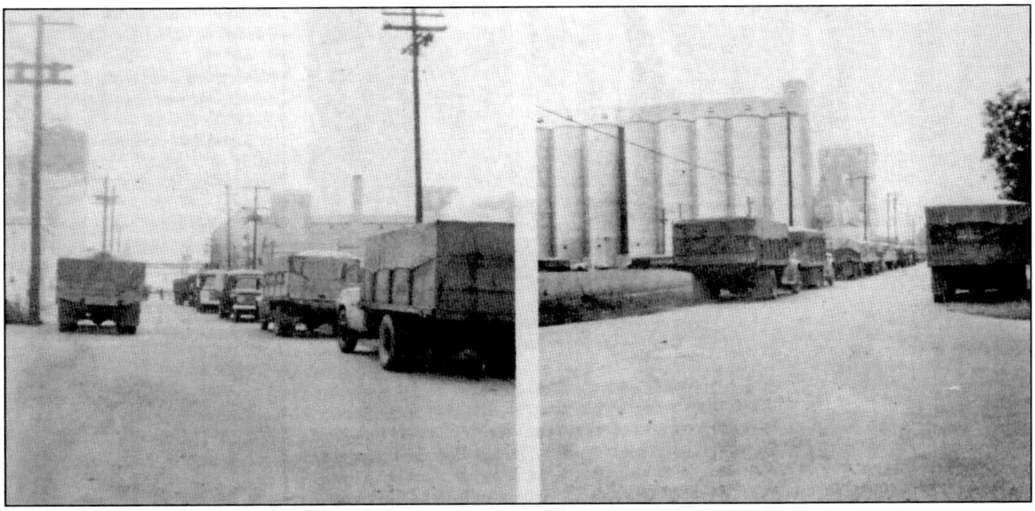

This was a very common sight in the fall, when the rice crops were brought to the rice mill. Today, most farmers have their own bins and dryers, but at the time of this photograph, farmers had to wait their turn to unload their harvest for storage. The picture on the left shows East Edwards Street; the one on the right was taken on North Arenas Street. (Courtesy of *Rayne Acadian-Tribune*.)

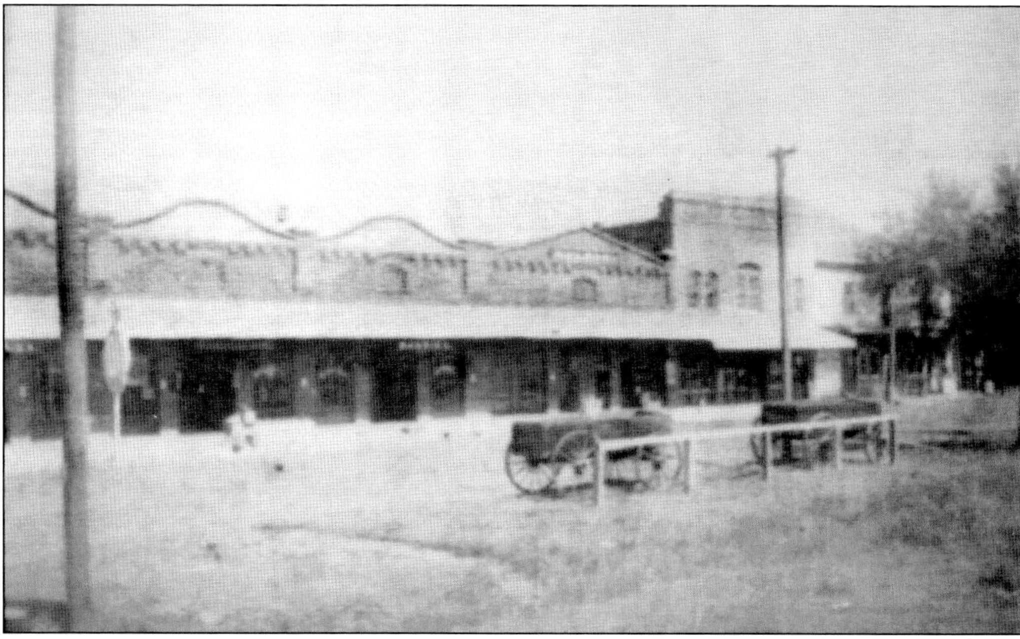

This is Louisiana Avenue as it appeared in 1904. The photograph was taken long before the passenger depot existed. Note the hitching post near the railroad track, as well as the dirt road. Businesses operating at the time were Sol Kahn general merchandise (far left) T-Mier's Bar, a furniture store, and Mervine Kahn Company (far right). (Courtesy of Sidney Stutes.)

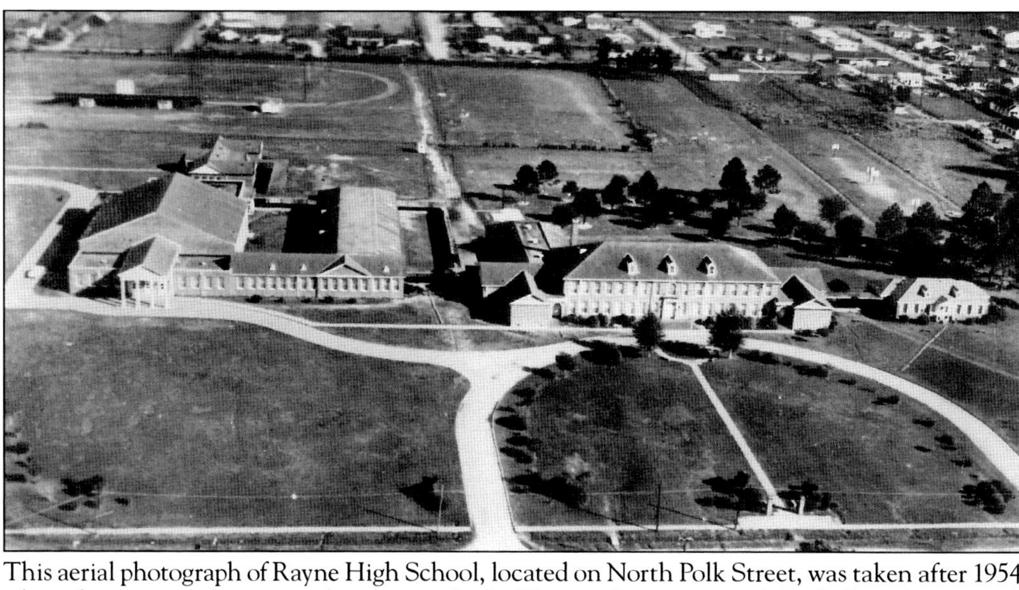

This aerial photograph of Rayne High School, located on North Polk Street, was taken after 1954, when the new north wing and gym were built. The newly constructed football stadium stands were recently finished. The two oak trees in front of the school are small, compared to their size today. (Courtesy of Fair Craig Hash.)

This 1930s view of South Adams Avenue shows the businesses of the time. At far right is Baily Radio Company, and to its immediate left is Royal Tailor Shop, owned by L.J. "Let Me Pitch" Maloz. A big fan of the Rayne Ricebirds, Maloz would holler "Let me pitch!" during the games to the opponents' pitching staff to disrupt their pitches. Reflecting the early days of Rayne, note the large trees along South Adams Avenue. (Courtesy of *Rayne Independent*.)

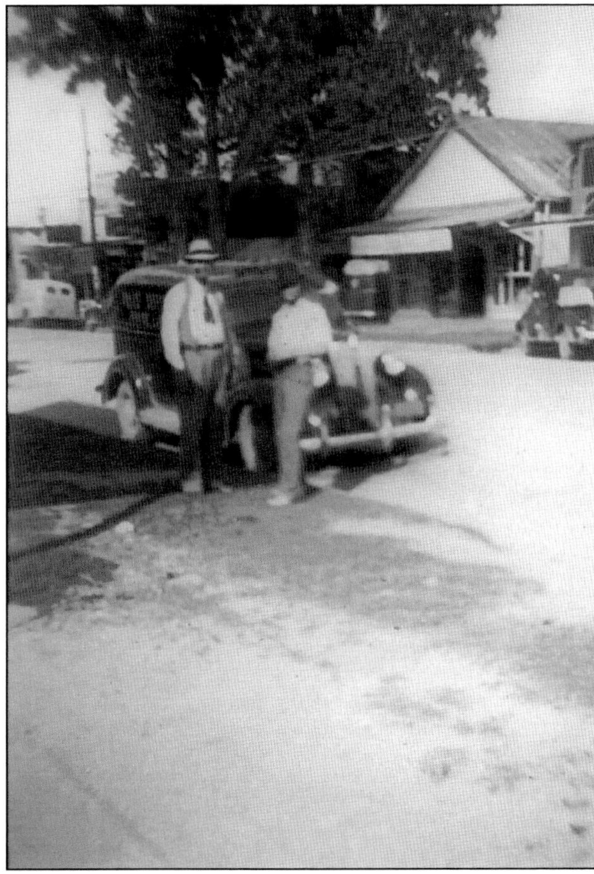

The Centenary Methodist Church, on the corner of East Harrop and North Parkerson Streets, is seen in this early photograph of Rayne. The church was founded in Rayne during the 100th birthday of the Methodist church on property donated by Mary Cunningham, wife of Rayne founder Dr. William Cunningham. Although the new church faces west, the original church faced south. (Courtesy of Sidney Stutes.)

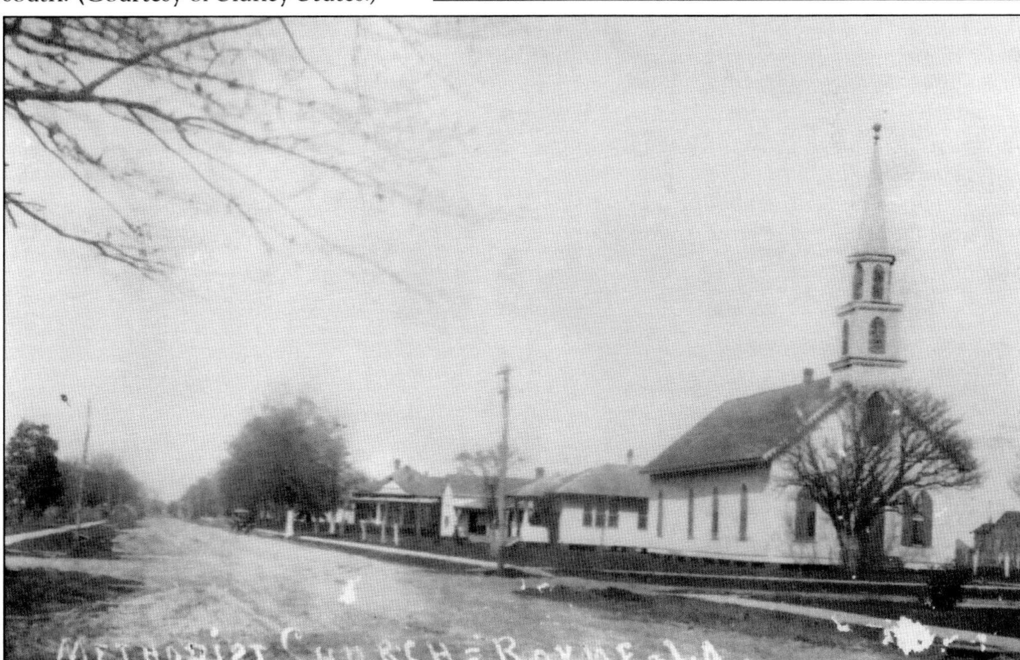

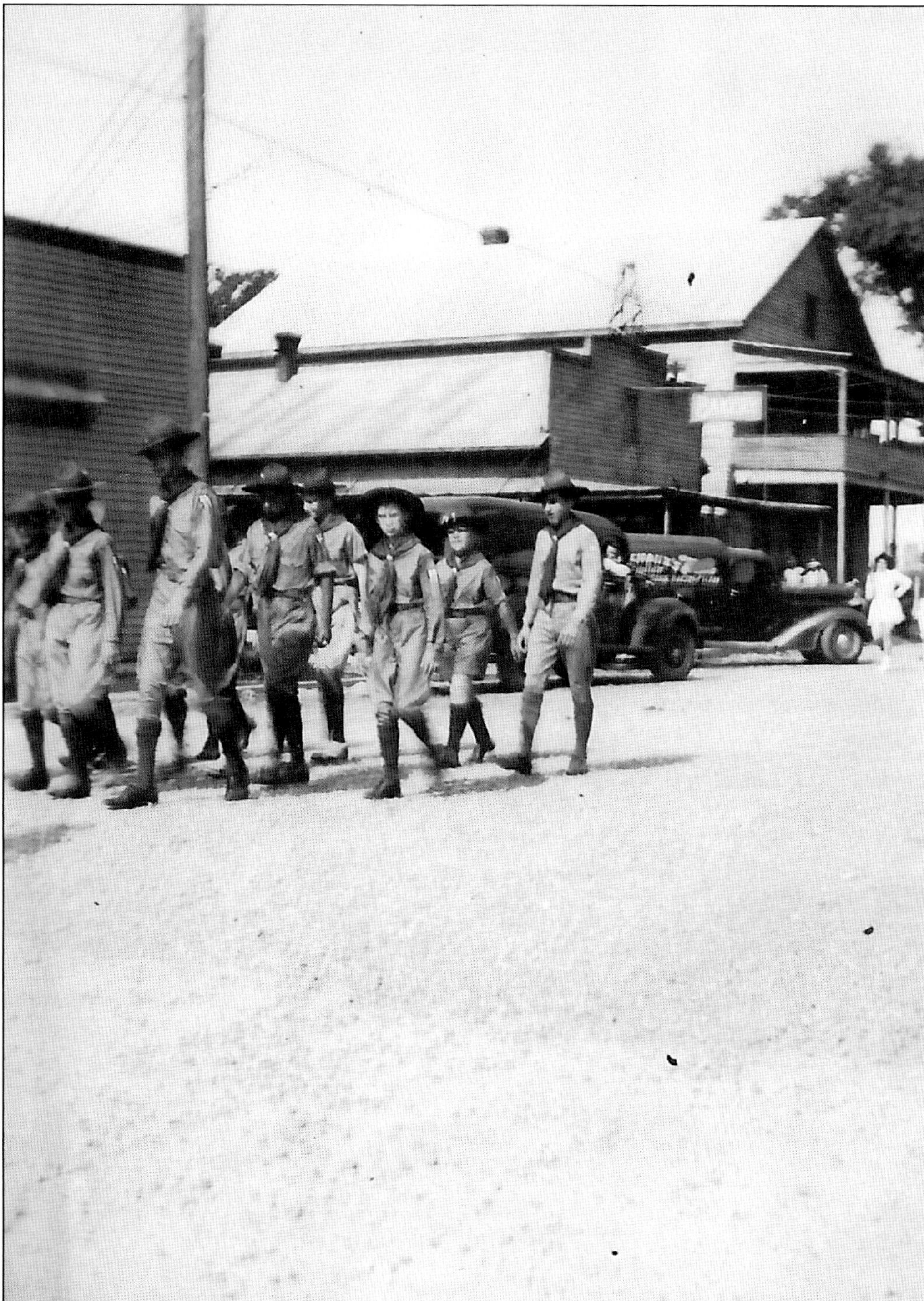

Boy Scouts are marching in a parade on Texas Avenue. Visible at left is the corner of Robichaux's Meat Market. On the right is Privat's Bakery and Joe and Julia Privat's two-story home in the background. The two panel trucks are ready for the next delivery. (Courtesy of Sidney Stutes.)

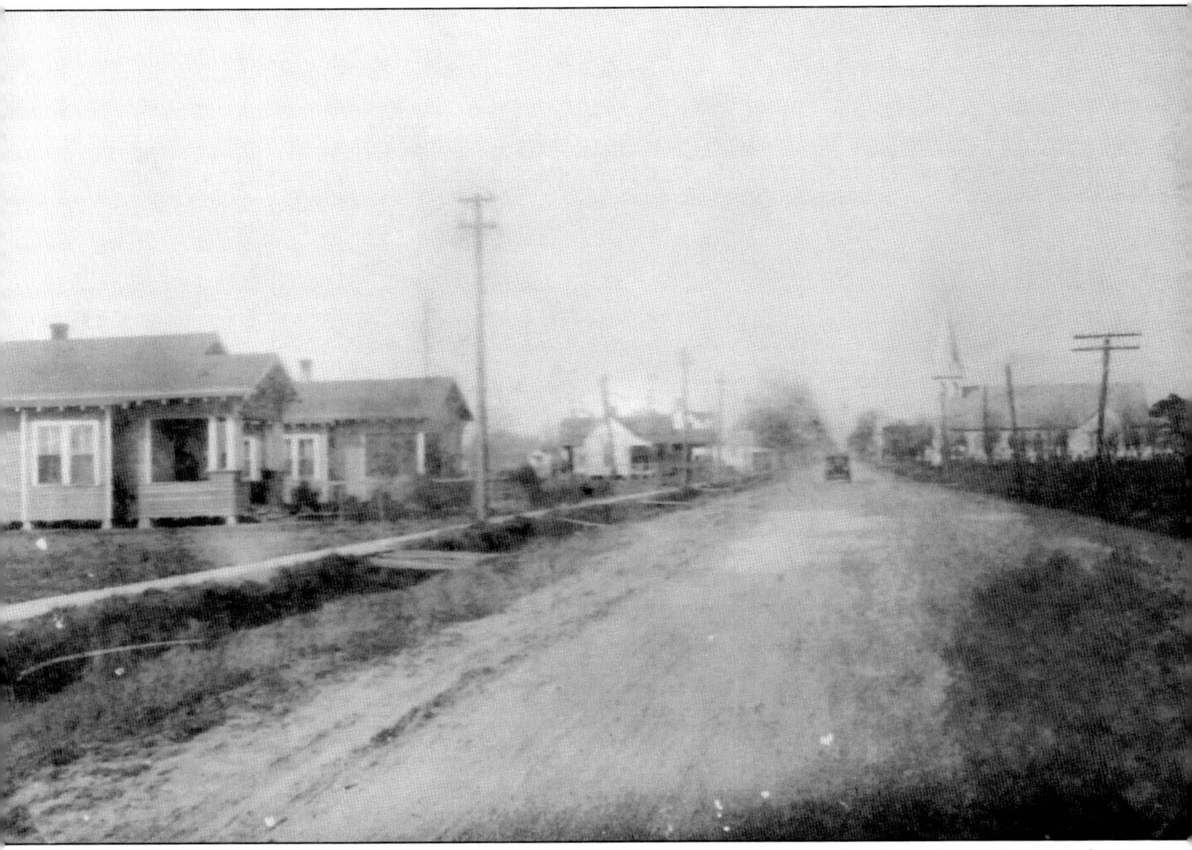

This is South Adams Avenue, looking north in the early 1900s. On the far right is St. Joseph Catholic Church and its graveyard. This section of Rayne was sparsely populated and grew as the town expanded outward. (Courtesy of Steve Raymond.)

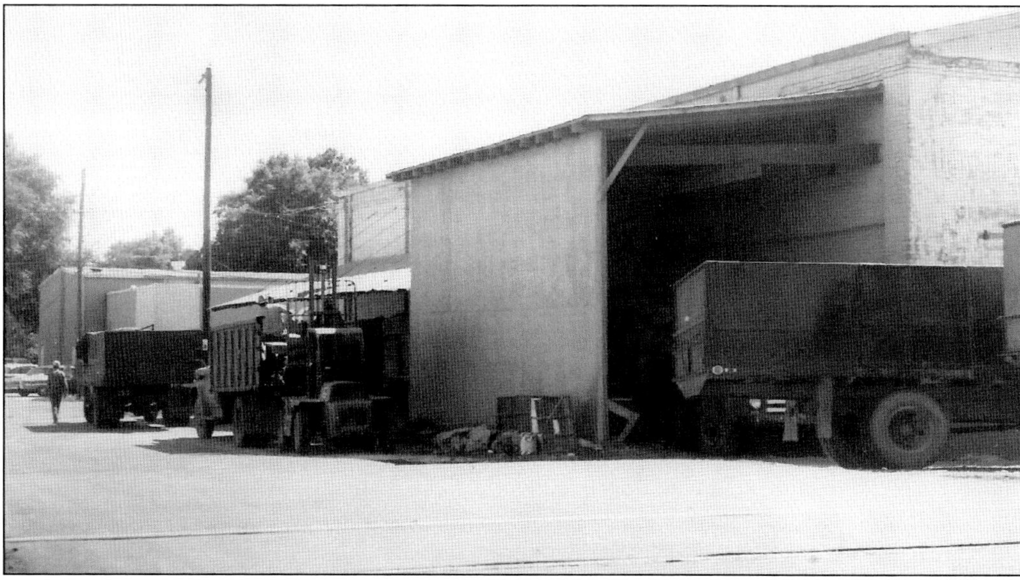

Drivers crossing the railroad tracks on South Parkerson Street could hardly miss seeing Hanks Warehouse. Opened by Dave Petitjean Sr., it was later owned by Delma Hanks, Wallace Hanks, then Ronald and Larry Hanks. The facility bought, milled, and bagged its own rice, as well as sold garden supplies. If it were not for Hurricane Lily, which shifted the roof six feet, the building would still be standing today. The structure was purchased by Doug Ashy Building Materials, which torn it down and used the area for parking. (Courtesy of *Rayne Independent*.)

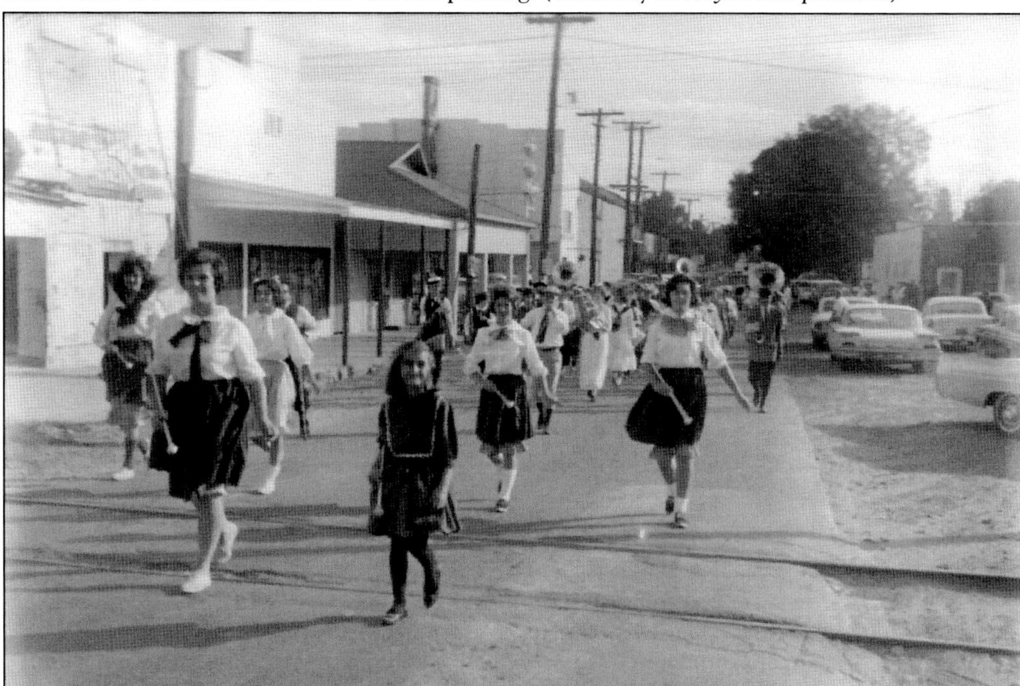

The St. Joseph High School band leads a parade on South Polk Street in the early 1960s. Businesses shown here are, from left to right, the remnants of the Valverde Hotel, Orton Besse's Western Auto, Town House Restaurant, and, across the street, the Joy Theater. (Courtesy of Sidney Stutes.)

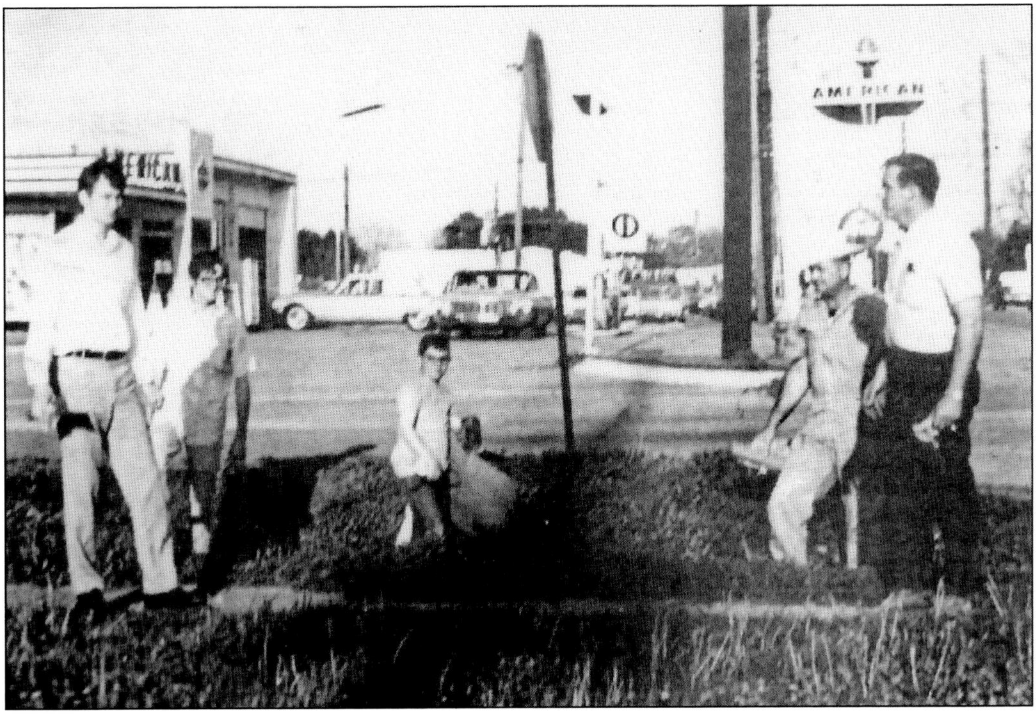

Members of the Young Men's Business Club clean the corner of Wiltz Street and Highway 90 West for a cleanest-city contest in 1970. Seen here are, from left to right, Neil Babineaux, Tommy Cart, Merlin Alleman, and two unidentified men. In the background is the American gas station, located where C.J. Prevost insurance agency now stands. (Courtesy of *Rayne Acadian-Tribune*.)

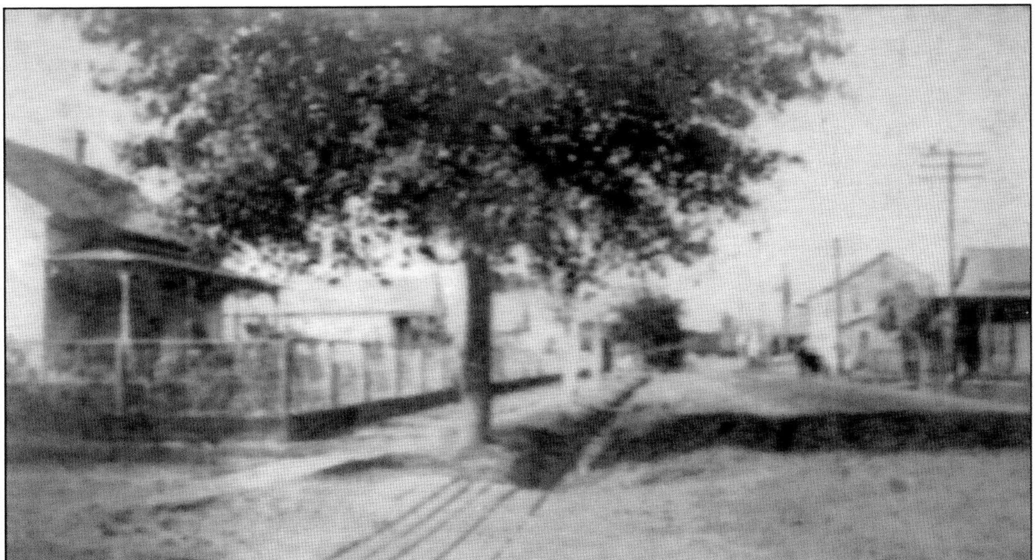

This street scene shows South Polk Street, at the intersection of East South First Street, looking north. At far right is the original Jacques Weil, Leger & Boudreaux building. At the time, there were no concrete culverts, so wood planks were used to cover ditches to allow vehicles to pass. The Auguste Perez house, on the immediate left, is still standing today. (Courtesy of Sidney Stutes.)

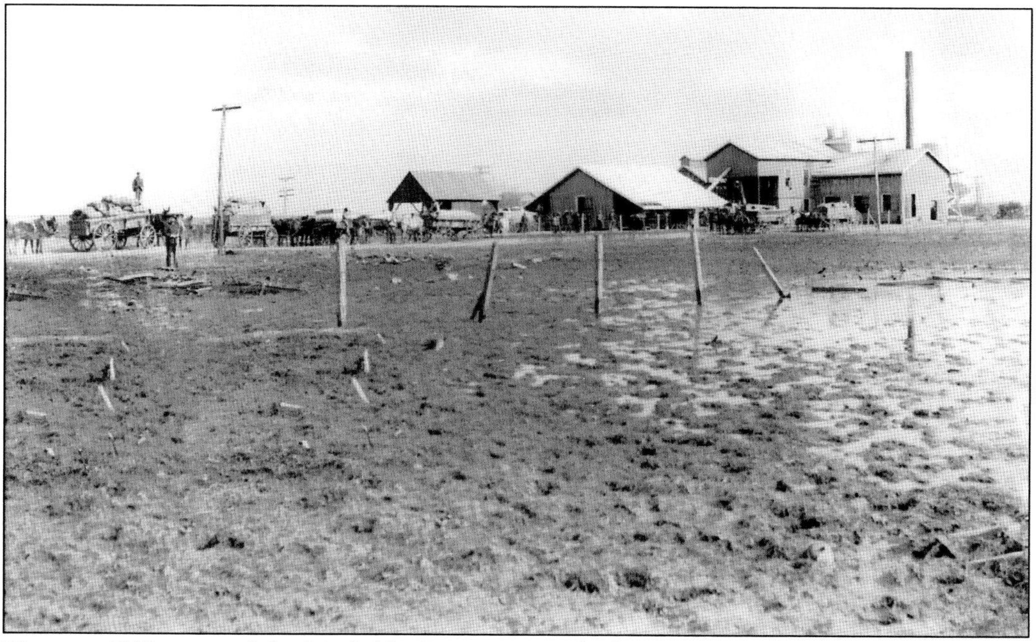

This is a 1900s view of the Mathilde Cotton Gin, which was located on Highway 90 East on the south side of the railroad tracks across from Duhon Funeral Home. It was owned by Jacque Weil and named after his wife, Mathilde. The lack of drainage that was prevalent in the area is apparent, which was ideal for the frog industry, which flourished during that time. This picture was made from a glass negative, which was the finest photography technique available at that time. (Courtesy of Melba Olinger.)

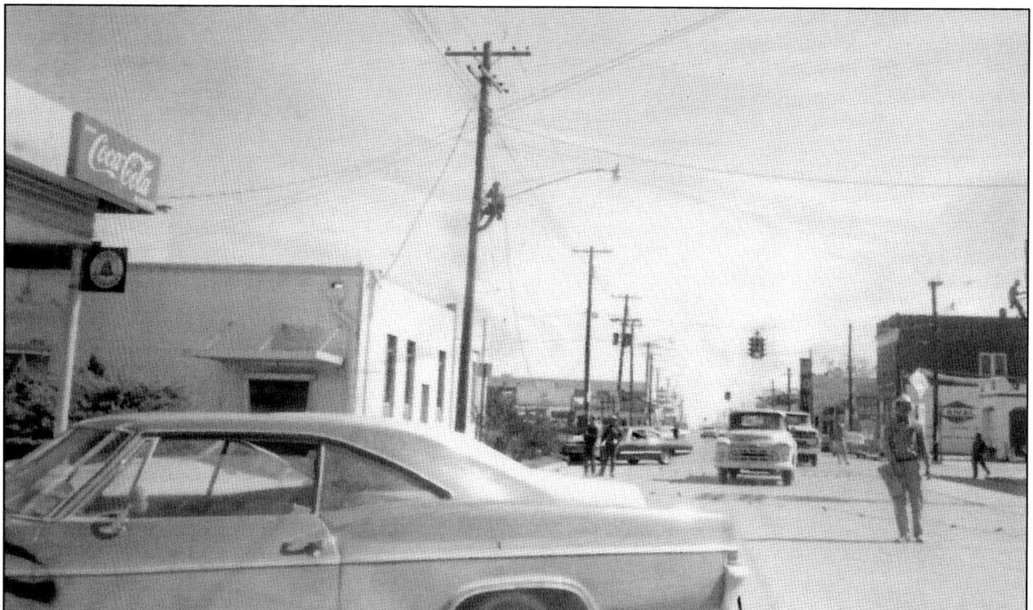

City of Rayne electrical workers hang Christmas lights downtown, to light the way for Santa Claus. The parade used to end at the Southside Community Center, where children could see Santa and bring him letters. (Courtesy of Sidney Stutes.)

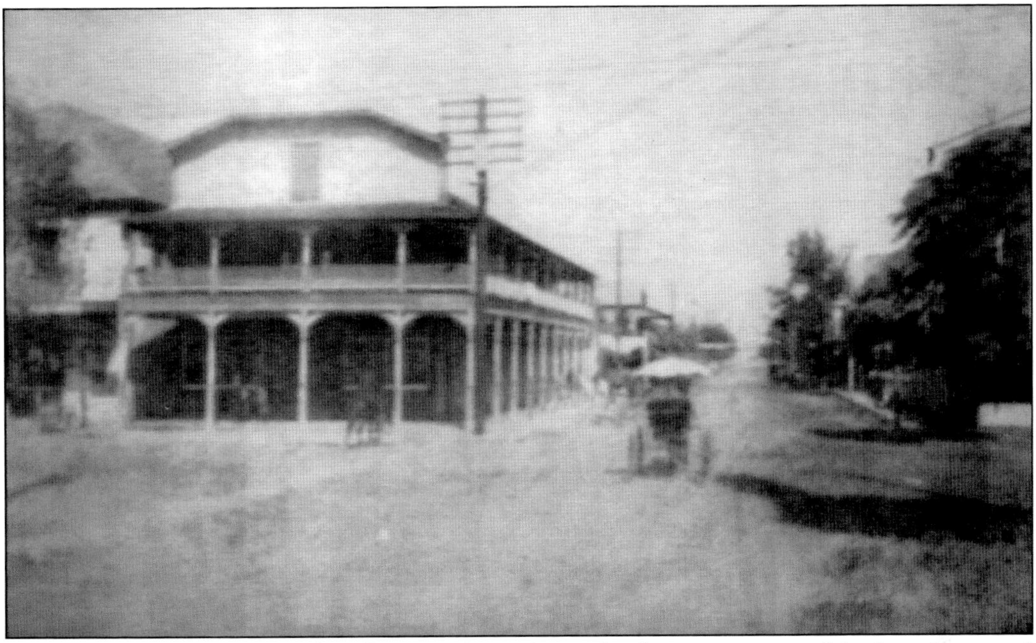

This 1904 photograph of North Polk Street shows the mode of transportation of the day—horse and buggy. The trees along the road provided shade on hot summer days. Rayne's most famous landmark, Mervine Kahn Company, is seen on the left in its early days. (Courtesy of Sidney Stutes.)

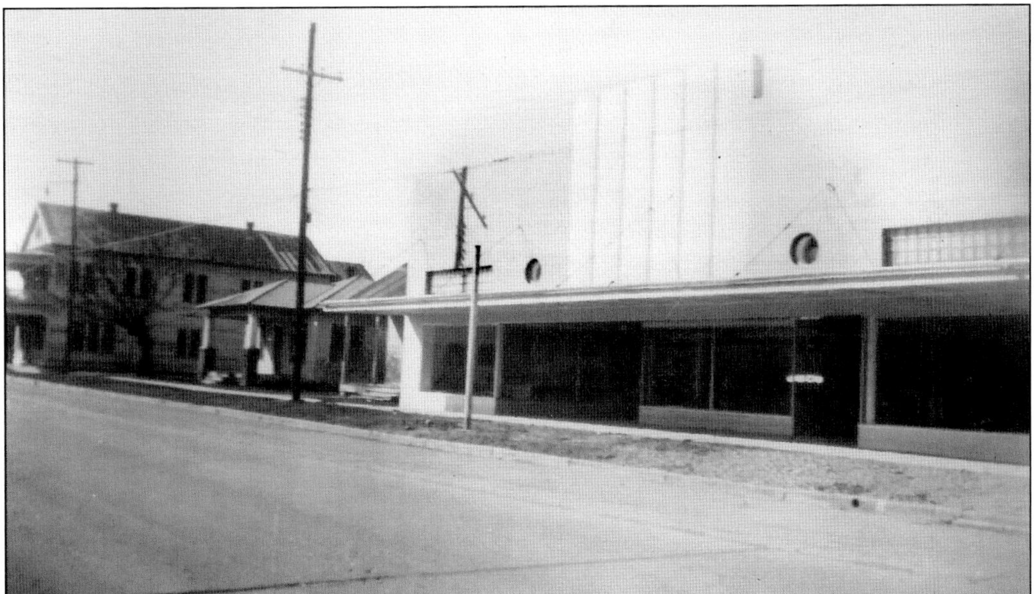

In the 1960s, North Adams Avenue illustrates old and new Rayne. At far left is the Commercial Hotel, and next to it is the office of Dr. Joseph C. Bruner. The occupant of the next building is not known, but it was later the site of a modern building that housed Bordelon & Lemoine Appliances and now is occupied by Sadie's Flower Shop. At right is the new Besse Furniture Store, which featured a walk-around glass showcase along the sidewalk. (Courtesy of *Rayne Acadian-Tribune*.)

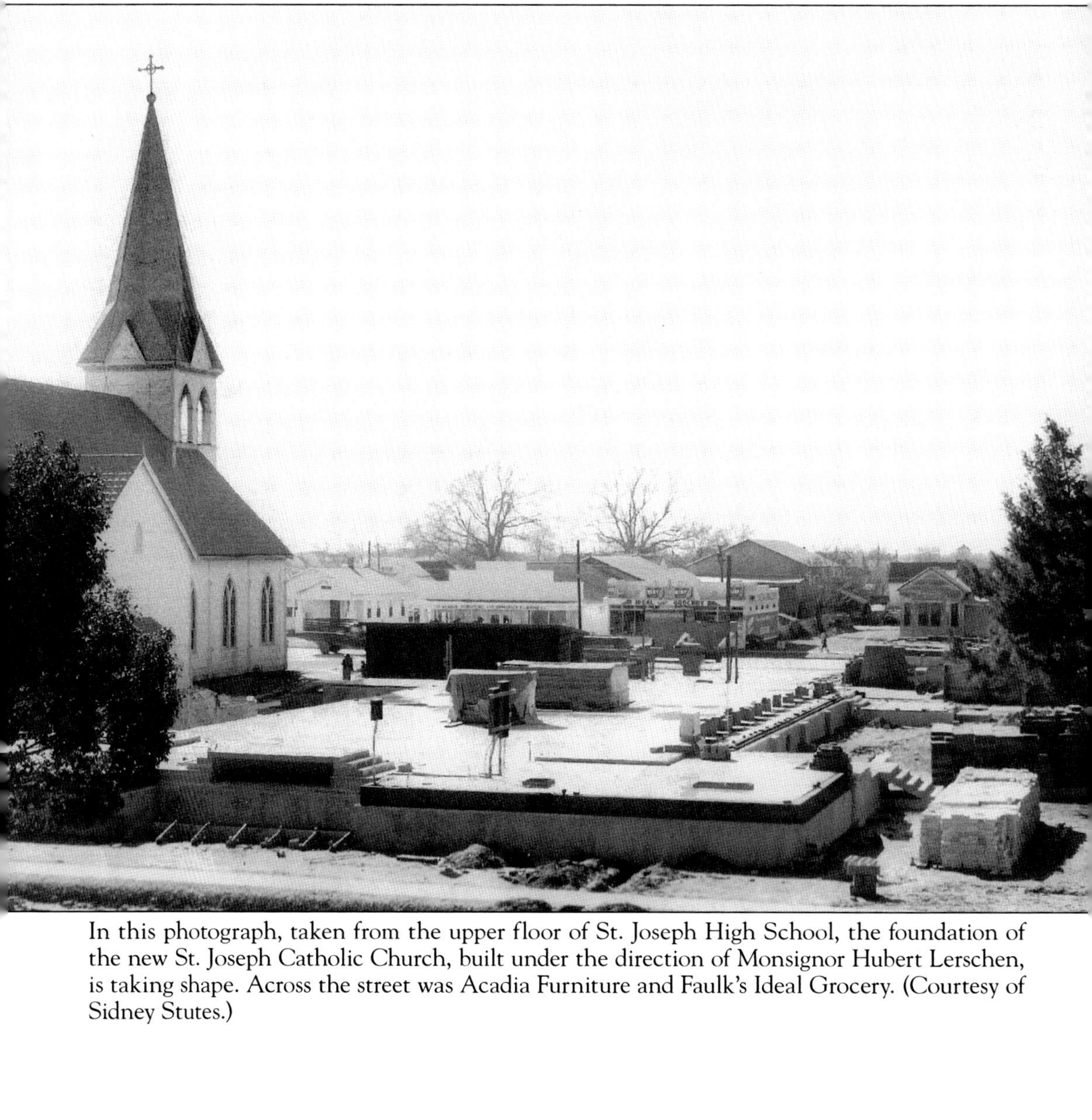

In this photograph, taken from the upper floor of St. Joseph High School, the foundation of the new St. Joseph Catholic Church, built under the direction of Monsignor Hubert Lerschen, is taking shape. Across the street was Acadia Furniture and Faulk's Ideal Grocery. (Courtesy of Sidney Stutes.)

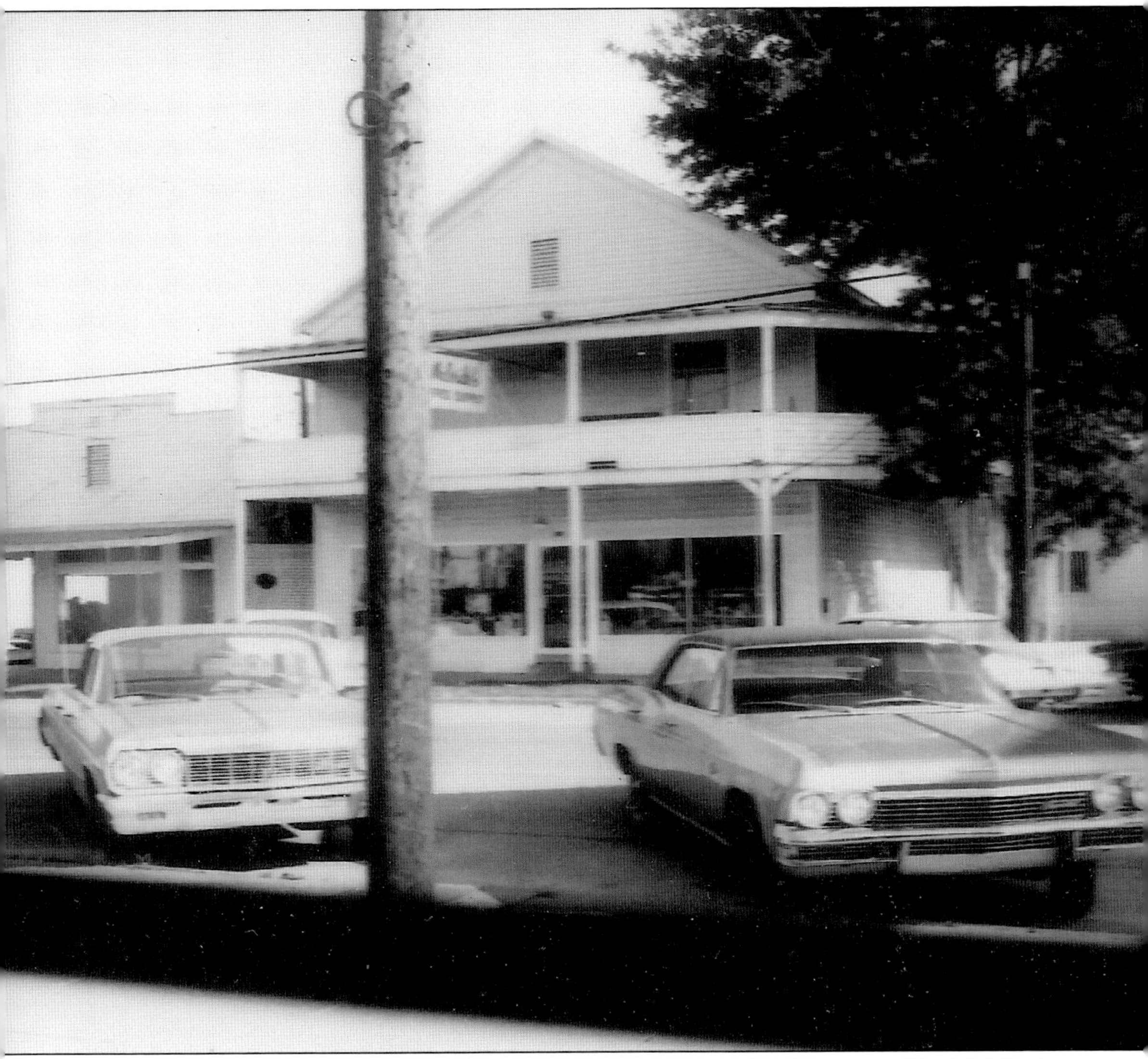

Located on West Texas Avenue, McBride's Office Supply was owned by Warren and Ruth McBride. The business was on the first floor, and the family lived on the second floor. Originally, it served as the family home for the Joe Privat and Ovide U. Landry families. At one time, the home had five mothers-in-law living in it. To the left is Acadia Bakery, later renamed Privat's Bakery, opened by Louis Privat and later operated by his brother Joe. The bakery was first located on the bottom floor of the family home, with the oven behind the home in a separate building. (Courtesy of *Rayne Independent*.)

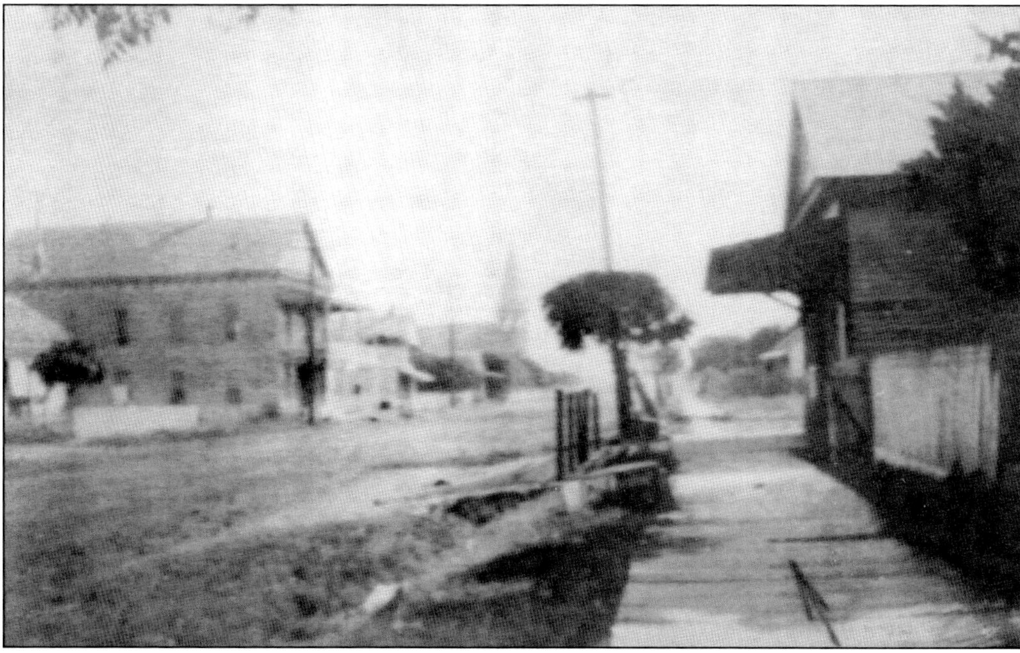

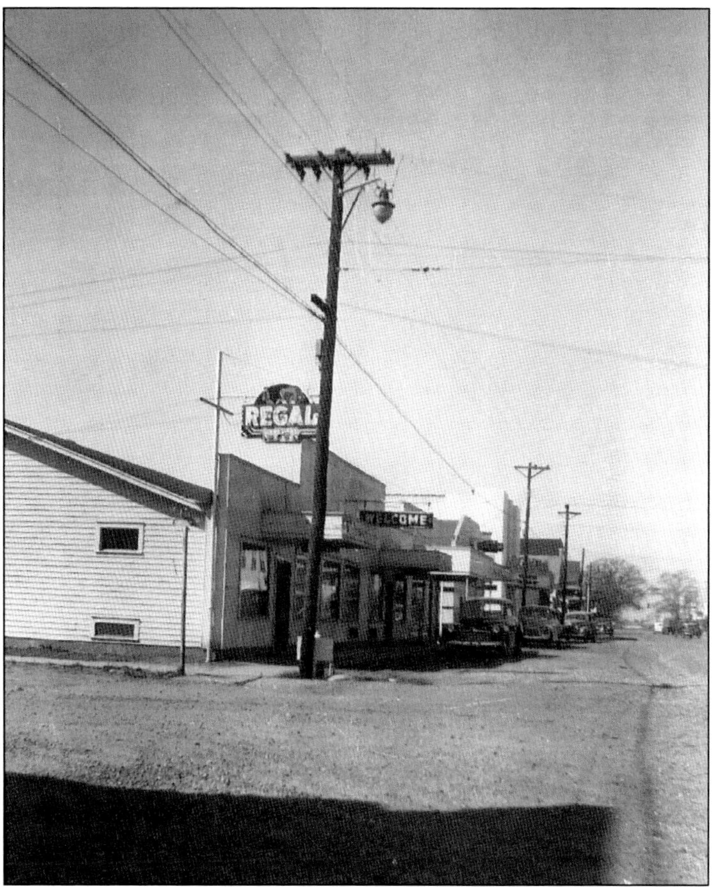

Looking south on Adams Street in 1914, this photograph shows board sidewalks, open ditches, and a muddy road. At left is the two-story Craig Opera House. Farther down the street is St. Joseph Catholic Church. (Courtesy of Sidney Stutes.)

This photograph, taken in front of Privat's Lumber Yard, faces west on East Texas Avenue. The businesses shown here are, from the front, the Welcome Bar & Café, an unknown bar, and the Acadia Theater. Most unusual for the time are the two large trees at the far end of the road. (Courtesy of Gene Guidry.)

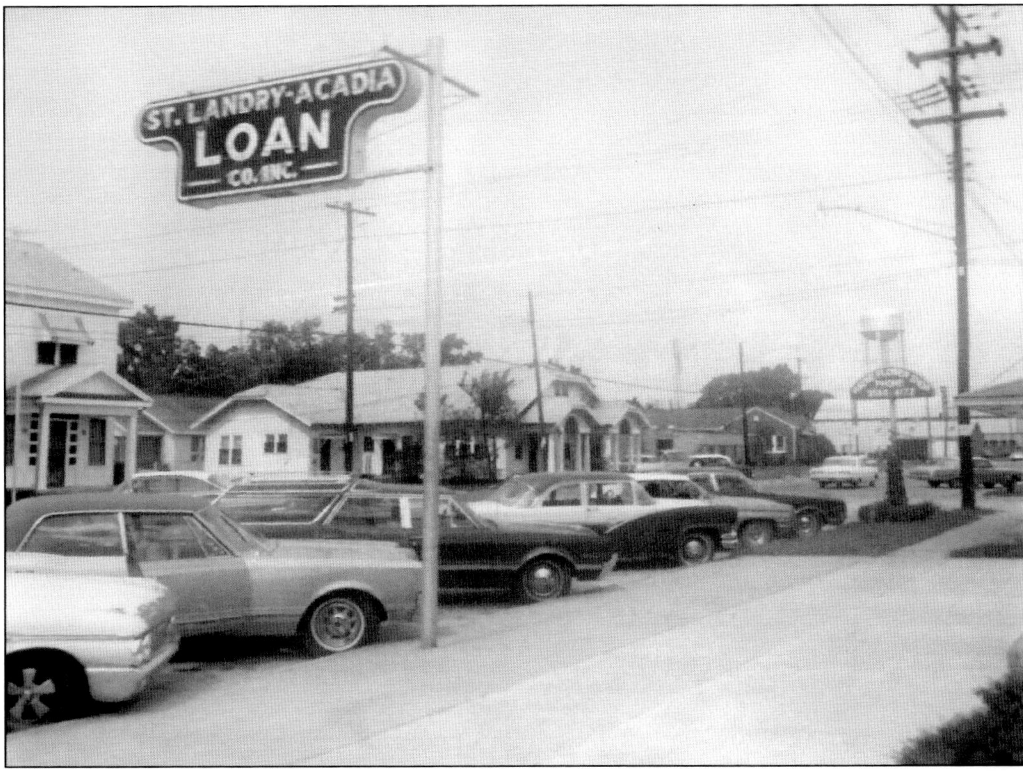

This photograph, taken from in front of the *Rayne Acadian-Tribune* office, shows a busy West Texas Avenue. At left is the old Gossen Funeral Home, and across the street at right is the Ardoin Funeral Home, which later became the Geesey-Ferguson Funeral Home, the American Legion Home, then the South Central Bell switch station. In the foreground is the porcelain sign for St. Landry-Acadia Loan Company, which was managed by Cliff Richard for many years. (Courtesy of *Rayne Acadian-Tribune*.)

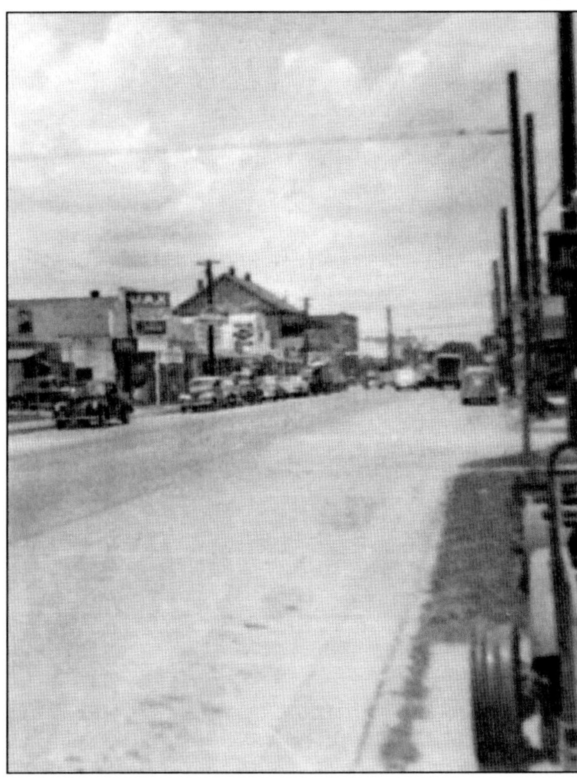

This north-facing photograph of South Adams Avenue was taken from in front of E.C. Fremaux Hardware in early 1945. Visible here are the numerous bars, restaurants, and businesses of downtown Rayne. At far left is the two-story building containing Hanks's Bar, Robichaux's Meat Market, Greasy Spoon, and High Hat Bar. (Courtesy of Julie Anna Ousse and Butch Ousse.)

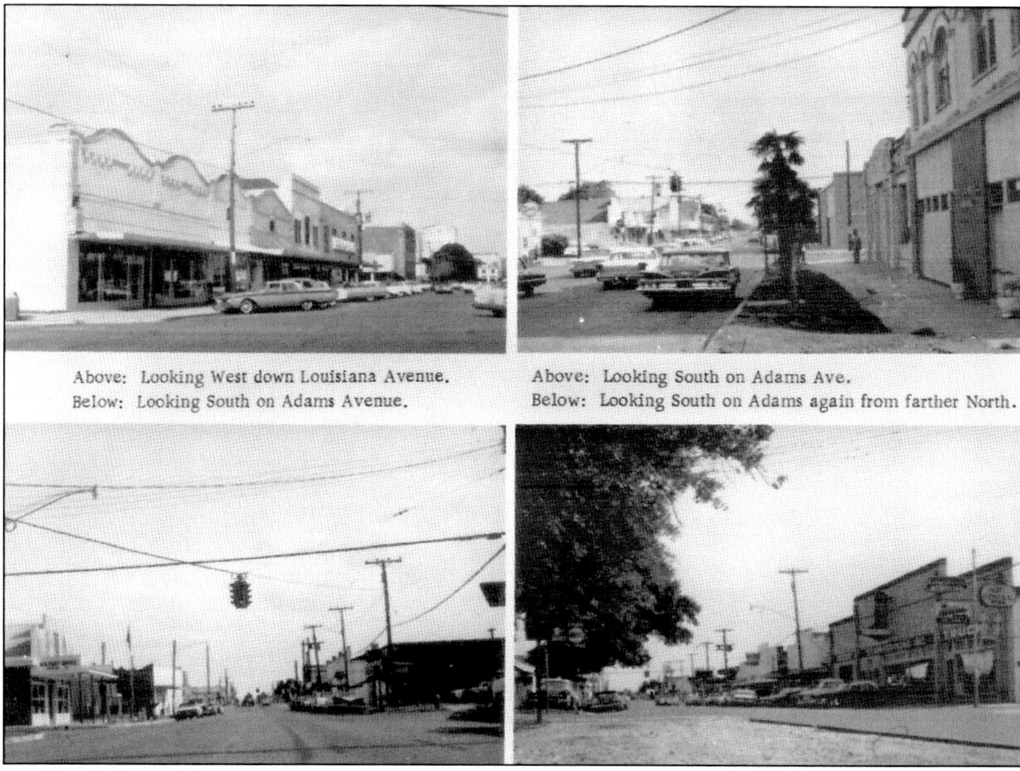

These 1963 photographs show four of the busiest areas of Rayne from different perspectives. Before cameras were as prevalent as they are today, much of Rayne was captured on postcards promoting the city. (Courtesy of Rayne High School.)

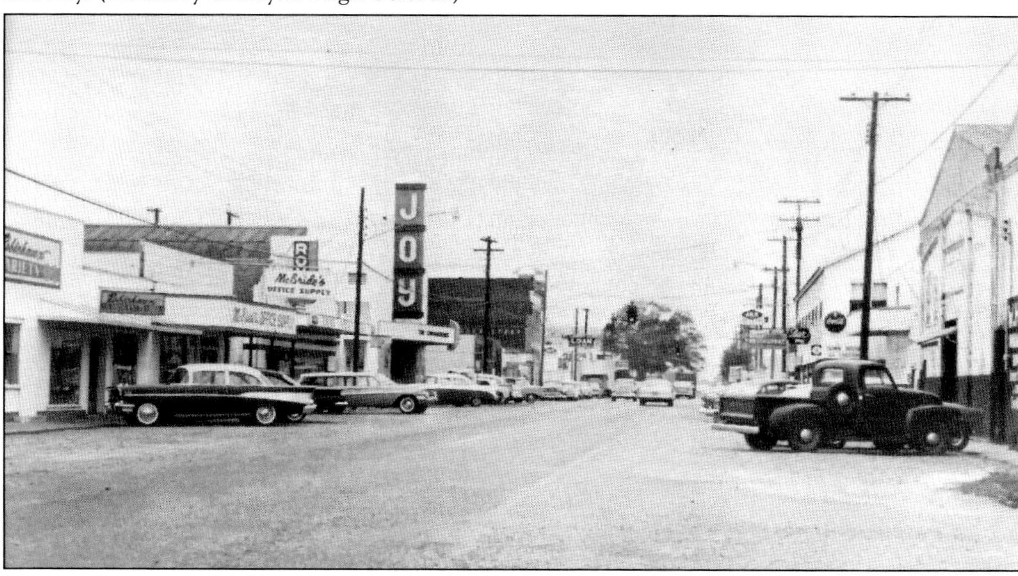

This 1962 photograph offers a westward view of East Texas Avenue, showing the downtown business district. At right is Hanks Warehouse and the Town House Restaurant, which had boarding rooms on the second floor. On the left are Robichaux's 5 & 10 Variety Store, McBride's Office Supply, the Roxy Dress Shop, and the Joy Theater. (Courtesy of Rayne High School.)

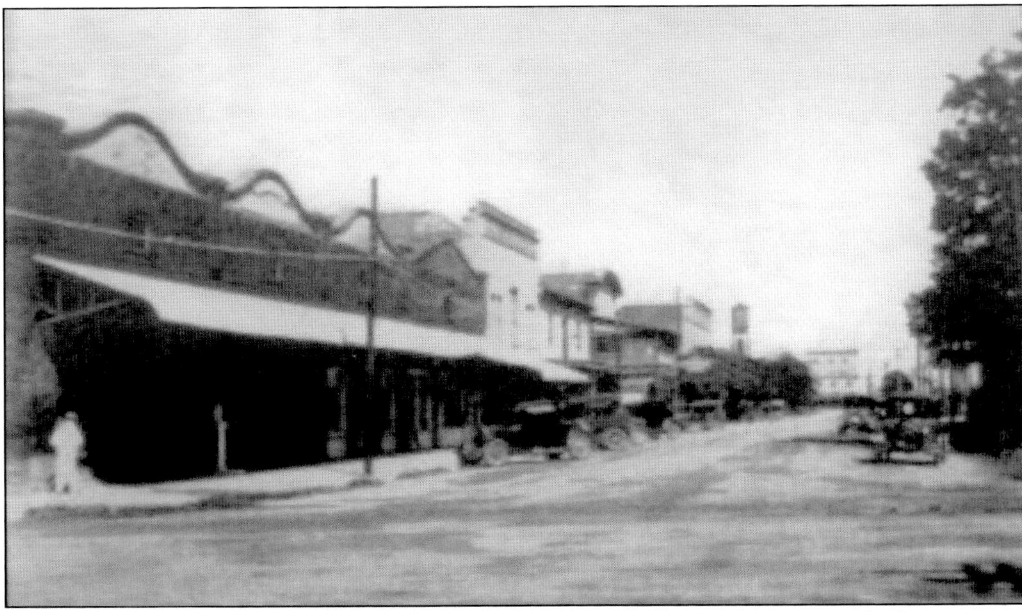

This photograph, taken from a postcard, shows East Louisiana Avenue in 1938. The large awning in front of the Sol Kahn Store kept the sun out and the business cool. Visible in the distance is the rice mill water tower. (Courtesy of Melba Olinger.)

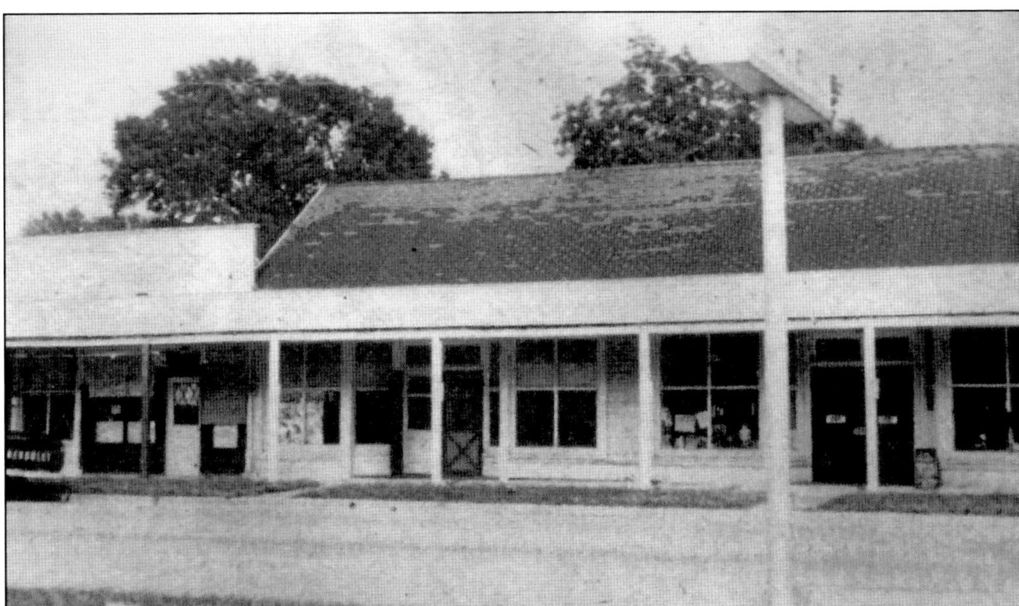

This busy 200 block of North Adams Avenue was the home of many businesses owned by the H.J. Sills estate. In 1967, it included, from left to right, Trahans' Plumbing Store, operated by Austin Trahan; Simoneaux's Meat Market, owned by Lionel Simoneaux Jr.; and Batson's Grocery Store, owned by Batson Richard. (Courtesy of *Rayne Independent*.)

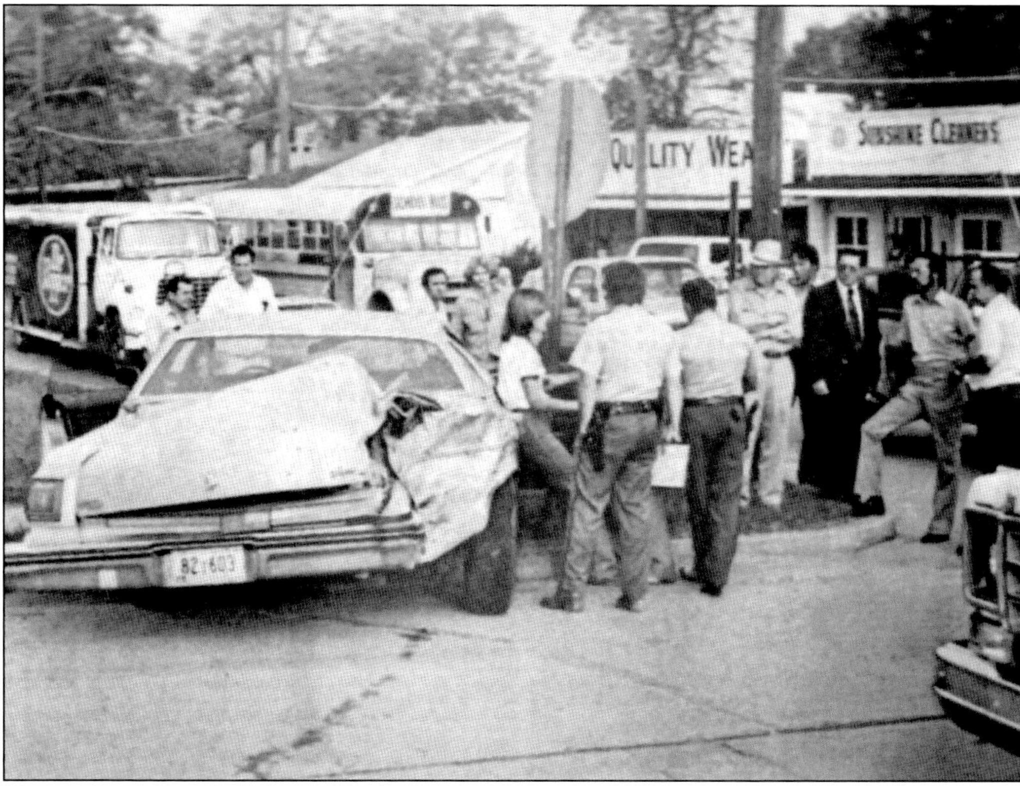

No one was seriously hurt in this crash, which occurred when a northbound Southern Pacific freight train struck a car on Adams Avenue in 1978. Visible in the background are Quality Wear and Sunshine Cleaners, both located to the west of Worthmore's 5 & 10 store. (Courtesy of *Rayne Acadian-Tribune*.)

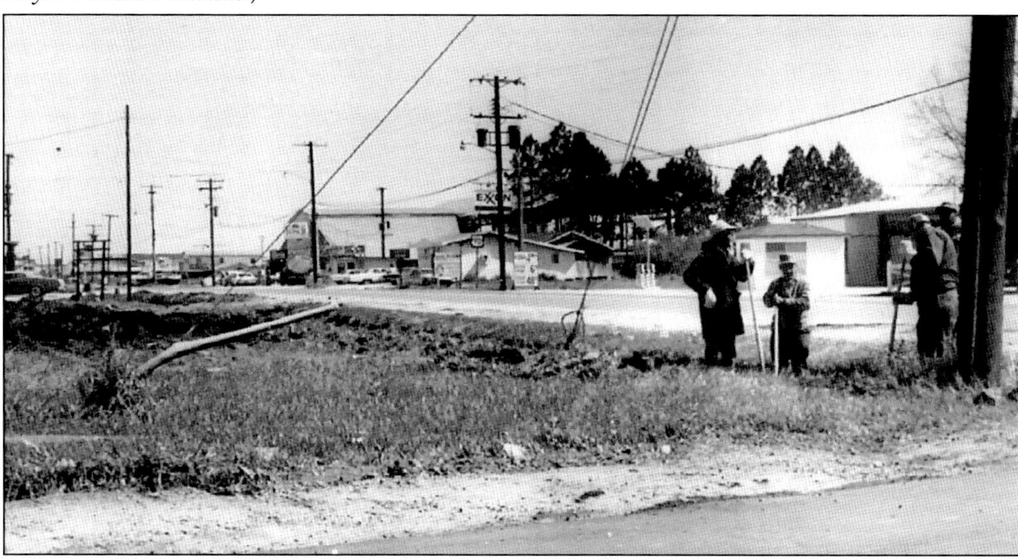

Workers prepare a vacant lot on South Arenas Street and East Highway 90 for the coming of the Glen Oaks Manufacturing Plant parking lot. Looking east on Highway 90, a gas station is seen on the near right. Farther down the street is the Villa Bar. (Courtesy of *Rayne Independent*.)

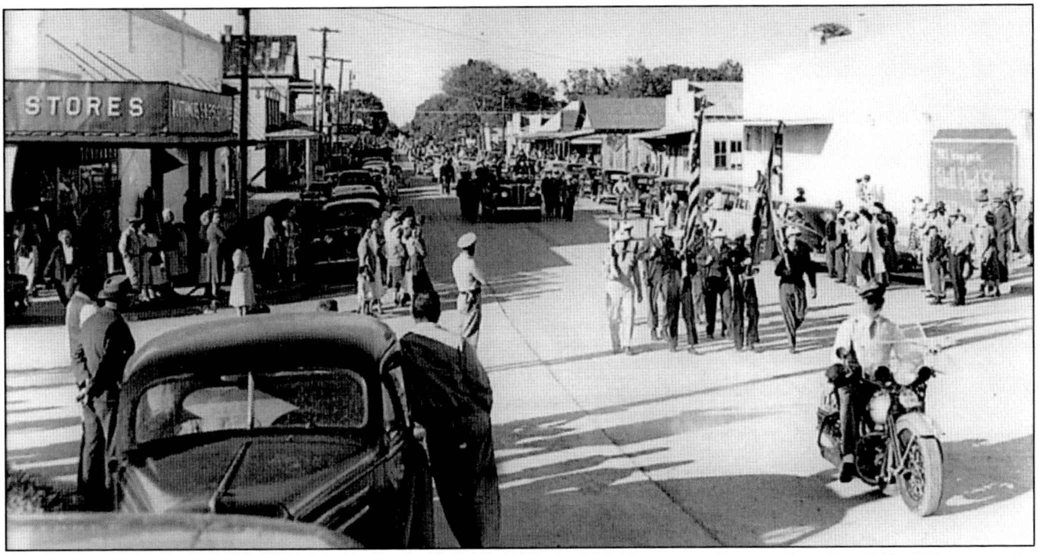

The American Legion Parade heads up North Adams Avenue on November 8, 1948. The parade heralded the annual fund drive in support of American Legion Arceneaux Post 77. A police motorcycle leads the way, followed by a color guard and members of the Rayne Volunteer Fire Department escorting the fire truck. (Courtesy of Andrus Fontenot.)

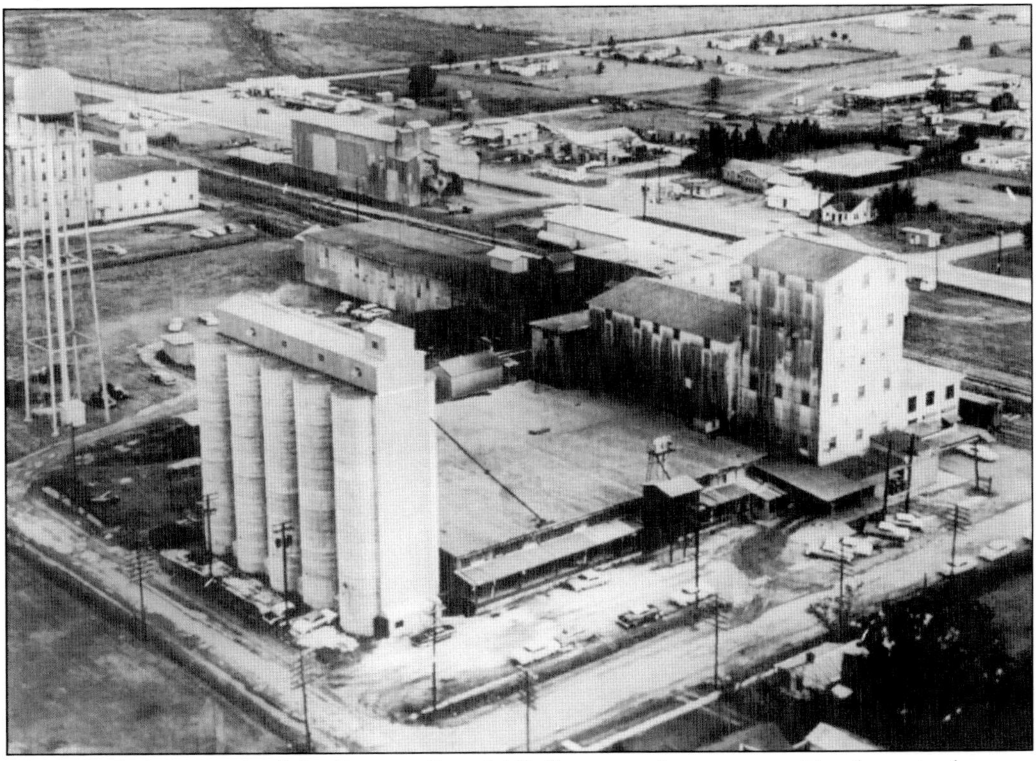

This aerial photograph of the Riviana Rice Mill illustrates the amount of land required to run such a large operation. At the top of the photograph, businesses are seen along Highway 90, including Clovis Kennedy Rice Mill on the south side of the railroad tracks. (Courtesy of *Rayne Acadian-Tribune*.)

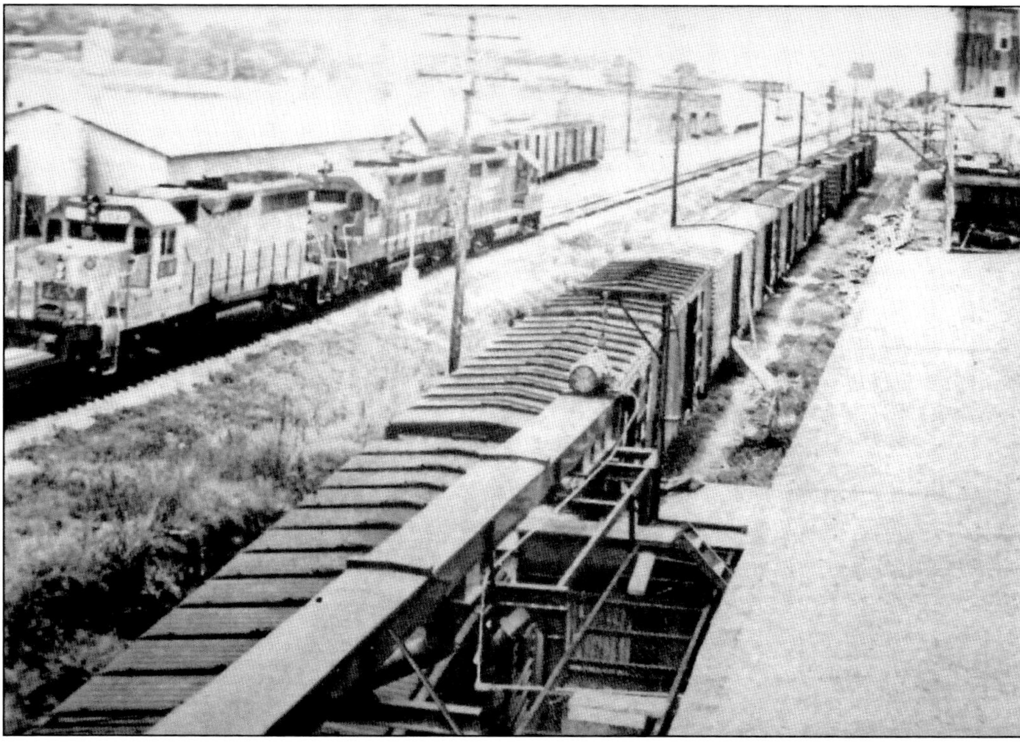

When a business was built next to railroad tracks, the railroad company would put in a side line to supply it with easy access to railcars. This is evident here, where railcars are being loaded at the Edmundson-Duhe Mill. There are two locomotives on the main line (center) and another line at left. This historic 1969 photograph shows rice being loaded, in a move to supply brown rice to the Republic of South Korea. The rice would be milled there, a first for America since the Korean War. (Courtesy of *Rayne Acadian-Tribune.*)

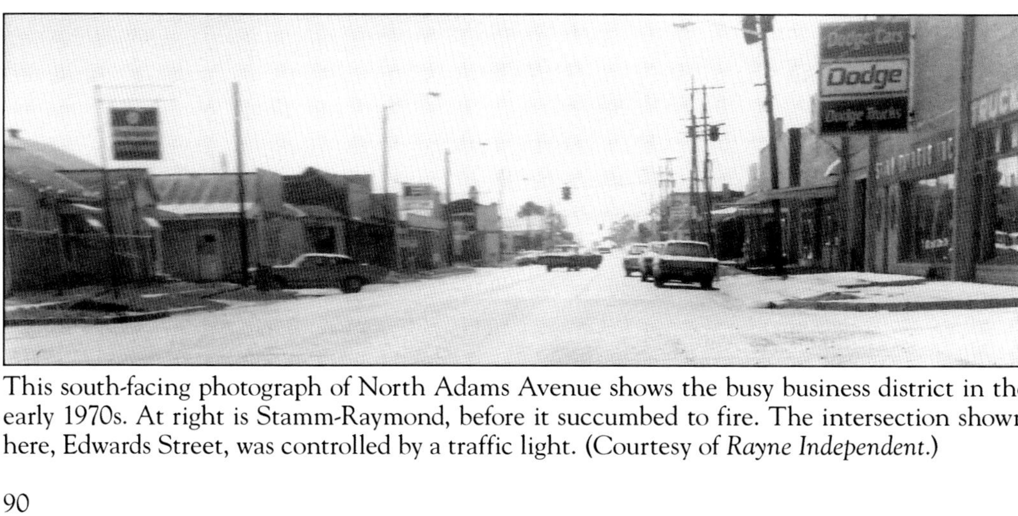

This south-facing photograph of North Adams Avenue shows the busy business district in the early 1970s. At right is Stamm-Raymond, before it succumbed to fire. The intersection shown here, Edwards Street, was controlled by a traffic light. (Courtesy of *Rayne Independent.*)

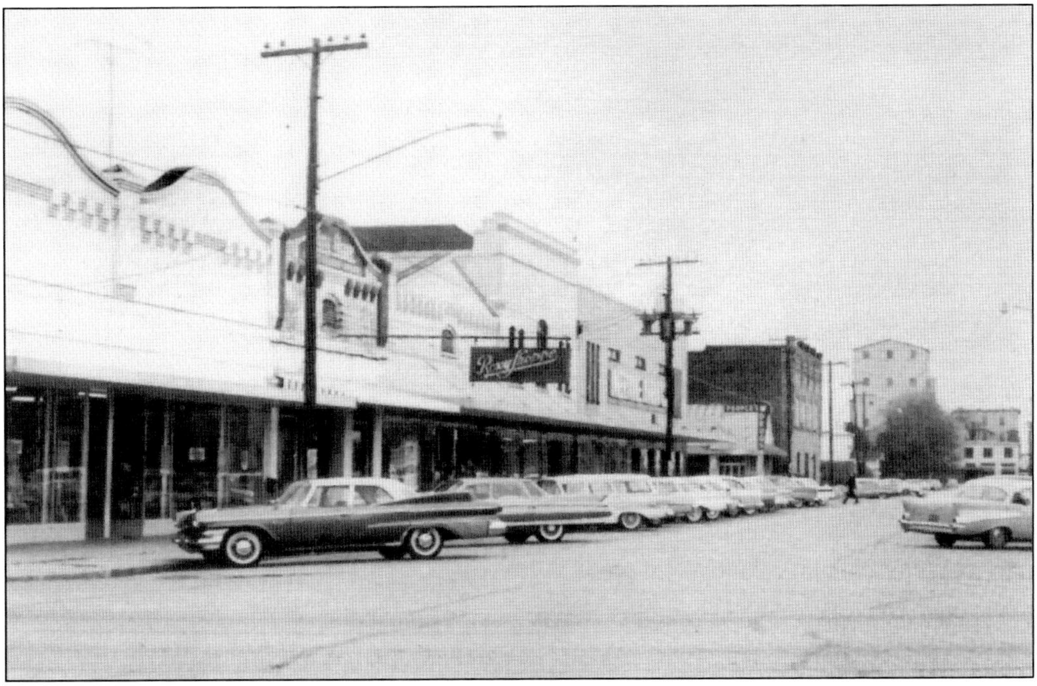

This 1962 photograph of East Louisiana Avenue shows the sign for the Roxy Shoppe. This section of the avenue is wide because, at one time, the passenger depot was on the south side near the tracks. After it was torn down, extra room became available. This area was also used for many years for 18-wheeler trailers that parked for political speeches and events. (Courtesy of *Rayne Acadian-Tribune*.)

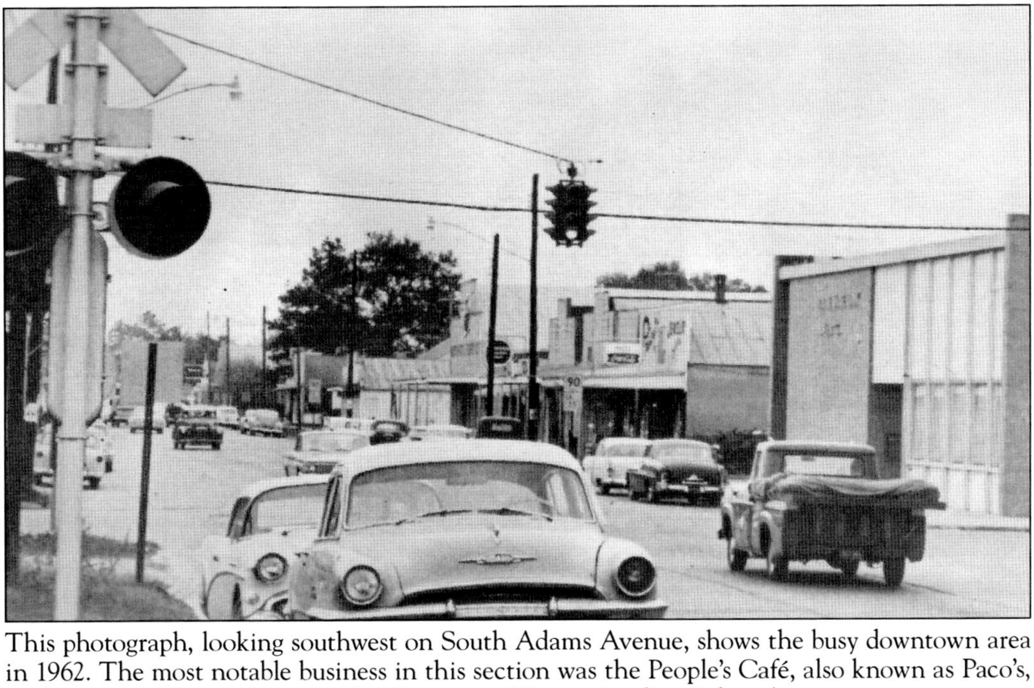

This photograph, looking southwest on South Adams Avenue, shows the busy downtown area in 1962. The most notable business in this section was the People's Café, also known as Paco's, to the south of Rayne State Bank. (Courtesy of *Rayne Acadian-Tribune*.)

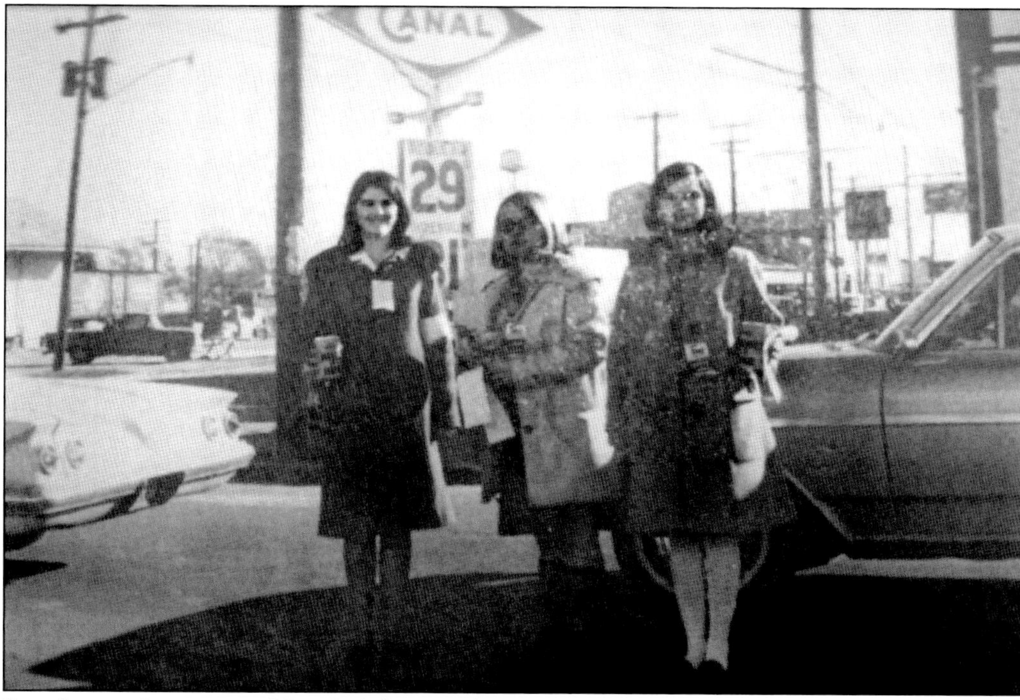

Standing at the corner of South Adams and East Texas Avenues in 1967 are, from left to right, Mary Landry, Louisette Nugent, and Charlotte Petitjean. They were three of the sixteen girls from St. Joseph's High School helping with street collections for March of Dimes on a frigid day. (Courtesy of *Rayne Acadian-Tribune*.)

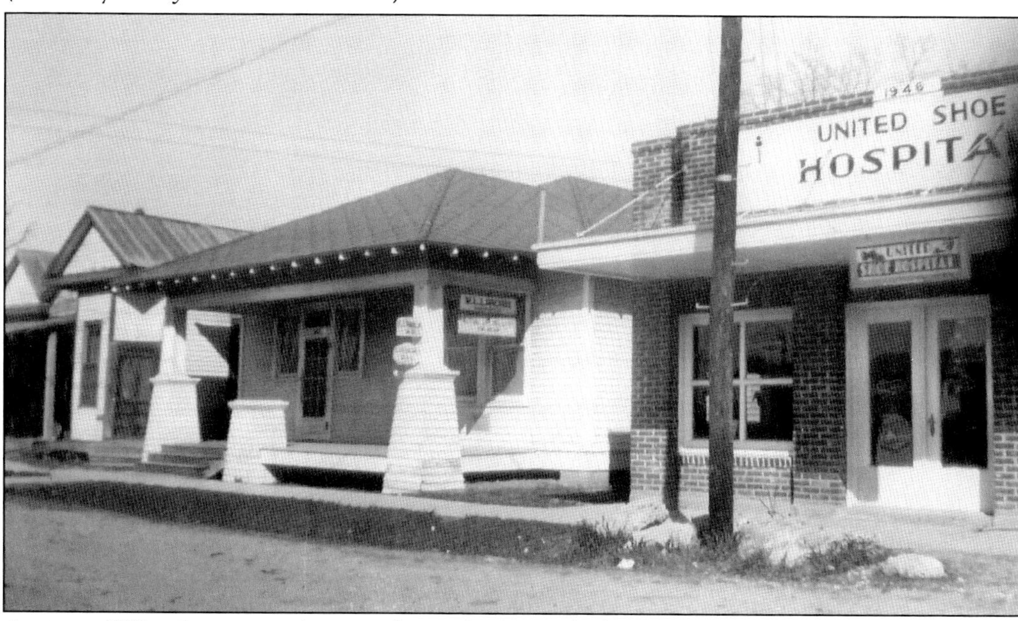

A view of West Louisiana Avenue shows the United Shoe Hospital, established in 1946. The building later housed Benoit's Quality Wear and Morris Touchet's Army Store. To the left are the offices of Dr. E.C. Faulk, Dr. Leon J. Elazar, and W.L.L Larcade Insurance. (Courtesy of Gene Guidry.)

Five

AROUND TOWN

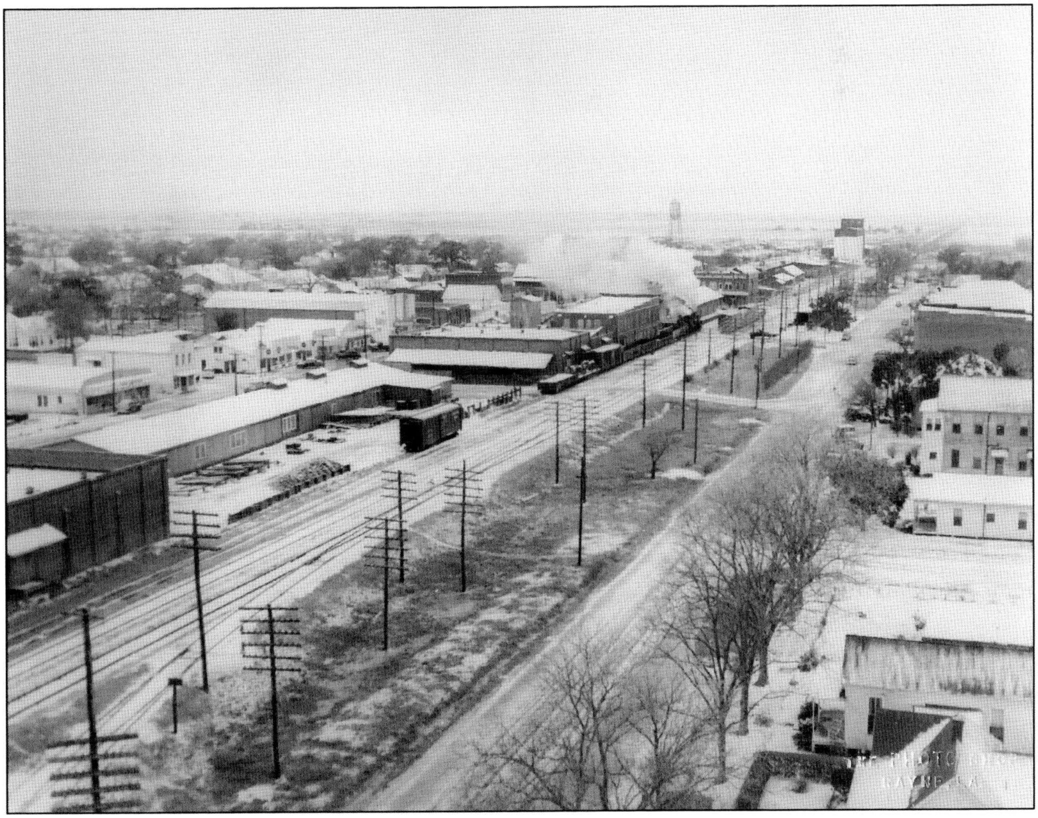

The headline of the *Rayne Tribune* newspaper read, "Yes—This was Rayne Louisiana on January 31, 1949." Leonard Laperous of The Photo Shop climbed to the upper floor of the Louisiana State Rice Mill to get this photograph of downtown. The Mervine Kahn Rice Warehouse (far left) and Privat's Lumber Yard can be seen across the street. Steam comes from the locomotive engine parked at the Depot Square. (Courtesy of Leonard J. Laperous, The Photo Shop.)

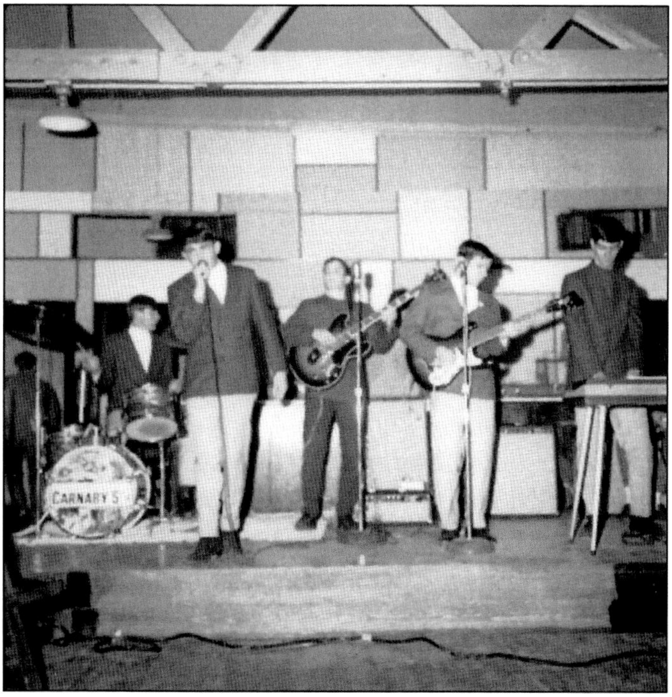

At this Friday-night dance, teenagers enjoy an evening at the Hangout, listening to a local band, 19th Street Uprising. Band members are, from left to right, Ted Cobena (drums), Eddie Blanchard (singer), Bert Broussard (guitar), Tucker Johnston (guitar), and Rusty Guidry (keyboard). Originally used during World War II by the National Youth Administration, this building was moved from the Rayne Municipal Airport grounds to Fourth Street Park. Fair Craig Hash was the first director of the venue, and she booked popular local bands and held pool and foosball tournaments. (Courtesy of *Rayne Independent*.)

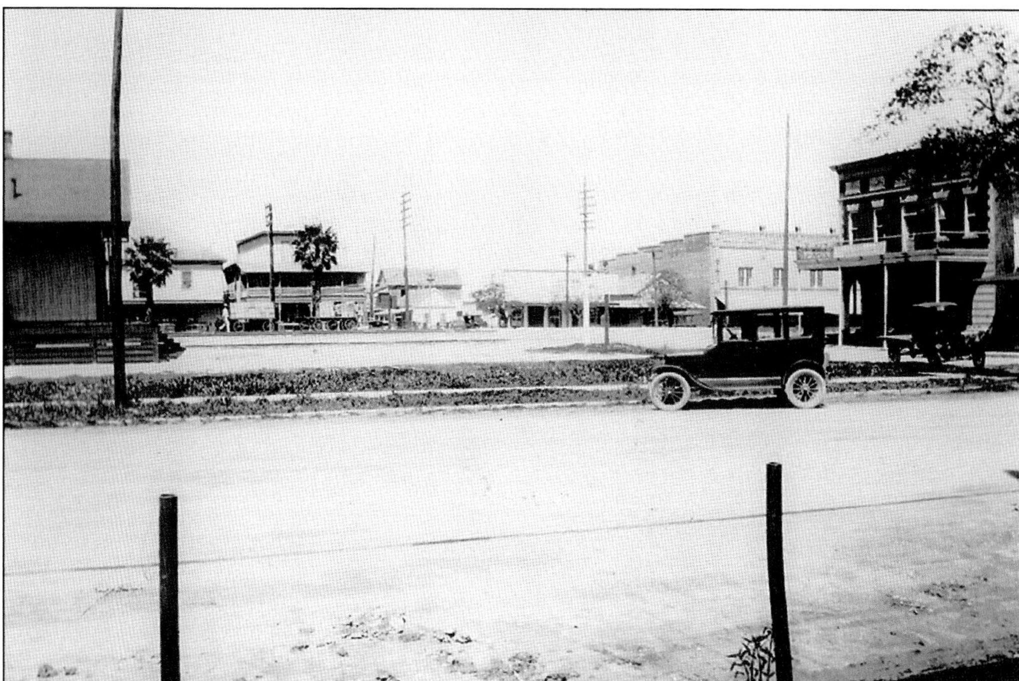

This early 1900s photograph of downtown Rayne shows the depot area. In the right foreground is the Valverde Hotel, before it burned down in 1917. Across the tracks is the Mervine Kahn Company Store behind the palm tree. To the right, with posts in front, is People's Drug Store, then Dr. J.P. Mauboules's medical office, and, at far right, the Mervine Kahn Warehouse. (Courtesy of Ann and Eddie Palmer.)

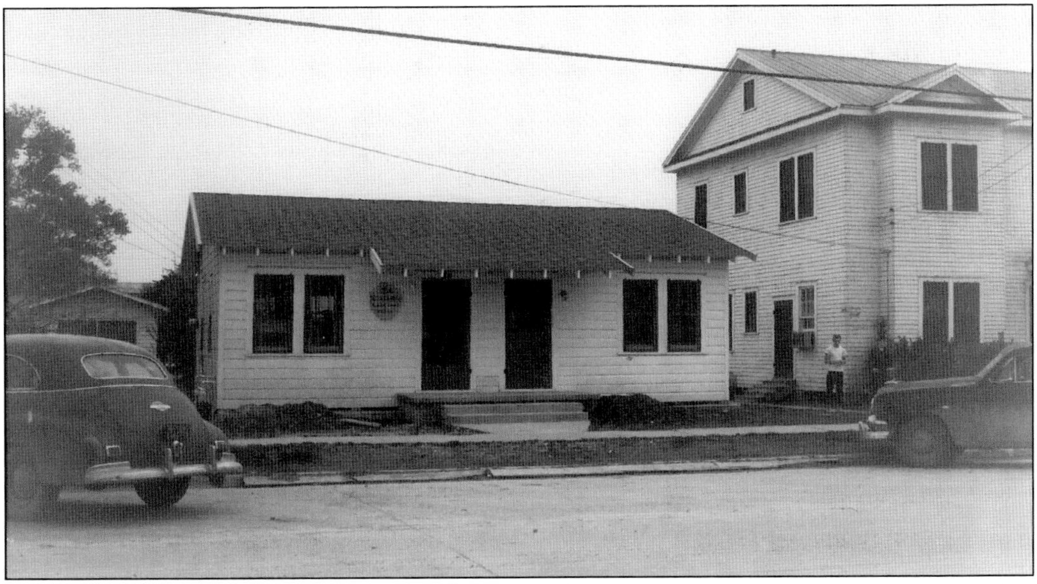

The offices of the *Acadian* newspaper, billed as the "oldest operating paper in Acadia Parish," is pictured in 1952 on West Texas Avenue (American Legion Drive), next to Gossen Funeral Home, which was torn down in 2015. In 1954, it consolidated with the *Rayne Tribune* to make the *Rayne Acadian-Tribune*, which is still published today. (Courtesy of *Rayne Independent.*)

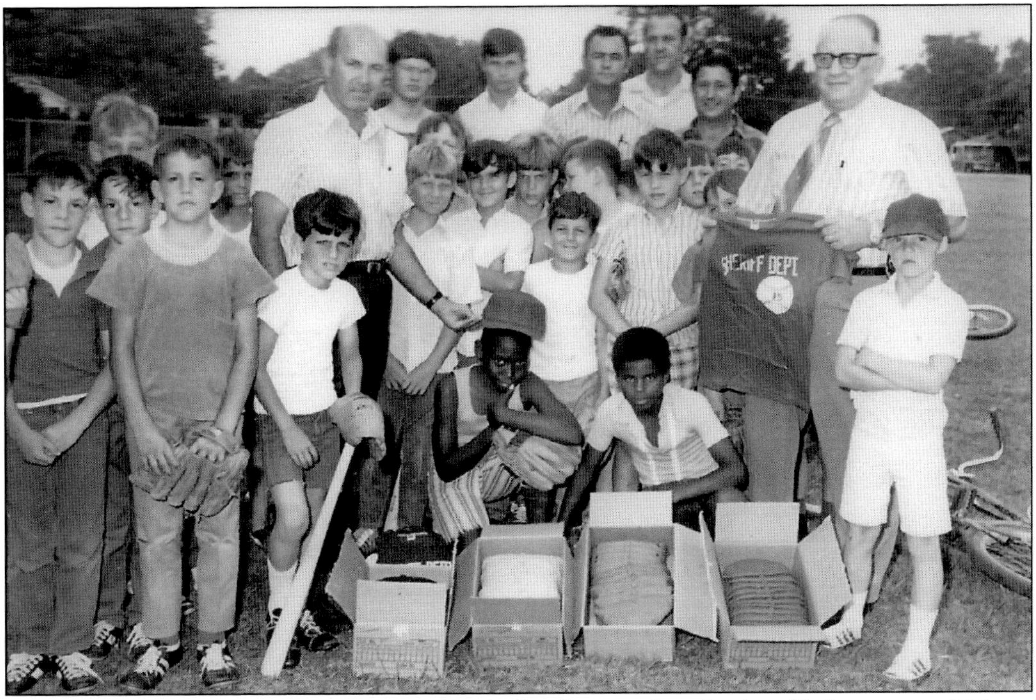

Any youth who played Rayne recreation baseball will remember the sheriff's department T-shirts and caps given to all players. Longtime Acadia Parish sheriff Elton Arceneaux, seen holding a shirt at right, donated the uniforms to the city. Many coaches and players are pictured, along with recreation director Rodney Trahan, shown in the white shirt holding a cap over a player's head. (Courtesy of *Rayne Independent.*).

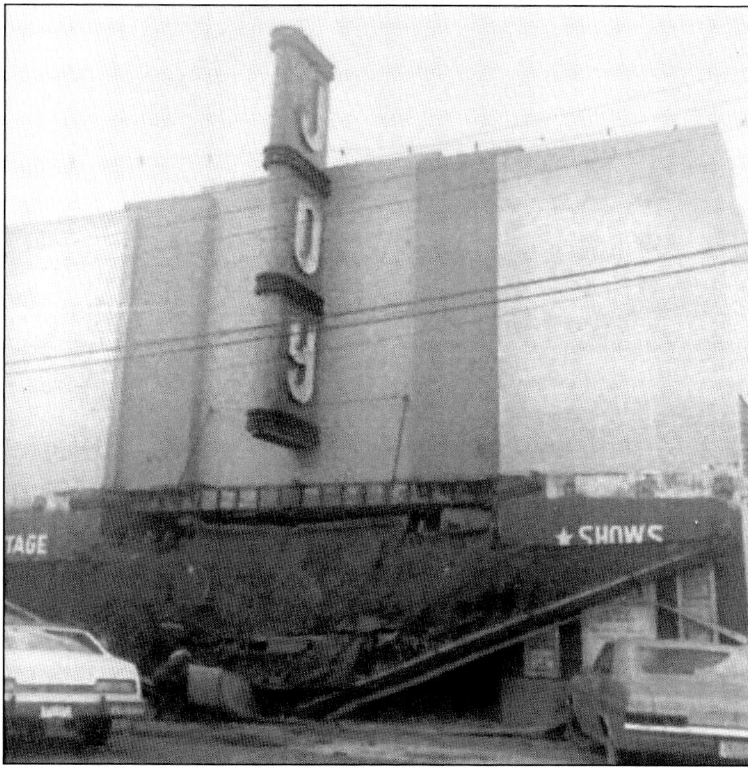

In May 1976, due to old age and the heavy rains that fell on Rayne, the original Joy Theater marquee collapsed onto the sidewalk. Fortunately, no one was injured, and a new overhang was built. The theater, built by the Weil brothers—Jacques, Edmond, and Gontran—was first operated under the name Le Moulin Rouge, reminiscent of their home city, Paris, France. (Courtesy of *Rayne Independent*.)

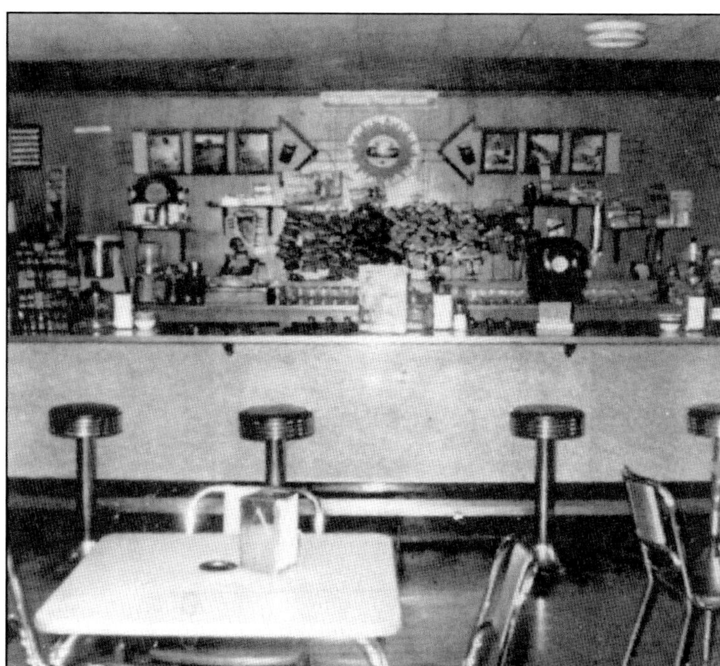

"I'll have a cheeseburger and a cherry Coke" was heard many times at this counter of the original Johnson Drive Inn, located on the east side of South Adams Avenue. Owned by Flemon, Jasper, and J. Glady Johnson, it was the hot spot for Rayne teenagers. (Courtesy of Rayne High School.)

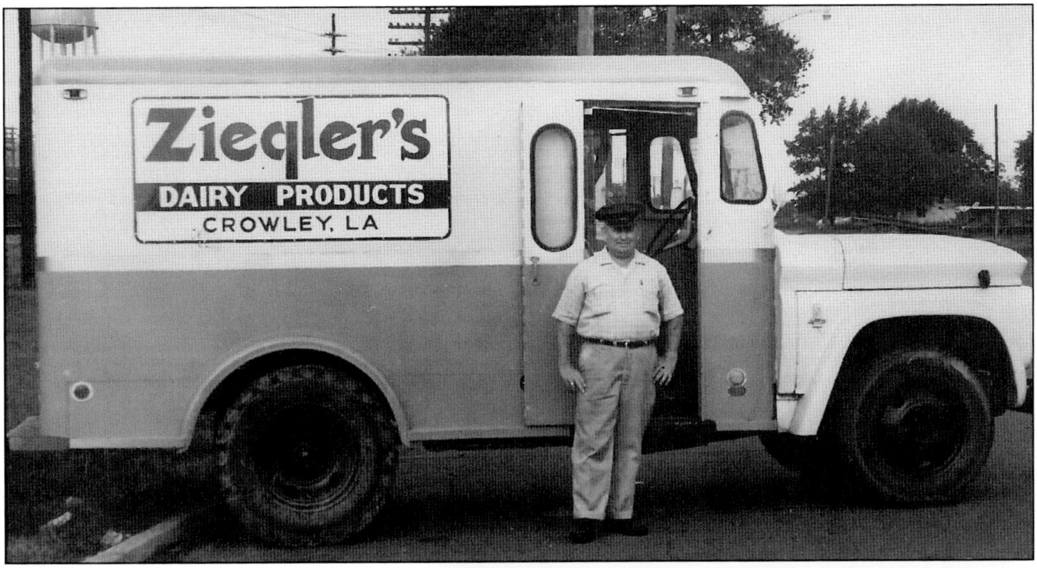

This truck was a popular sight in Rayne for many years. Claude Blanchard, the Rayne agent for Ziegler's Dairy Products of Crowley, is shown next to his new delivery truck. Residents would put empty milk bottles on the front porch before going to bed. In the morning, the empty bottles were replaced with full bottles. The firm operated every day but Sunday. (Courtesy of *Rayne Independent*.)

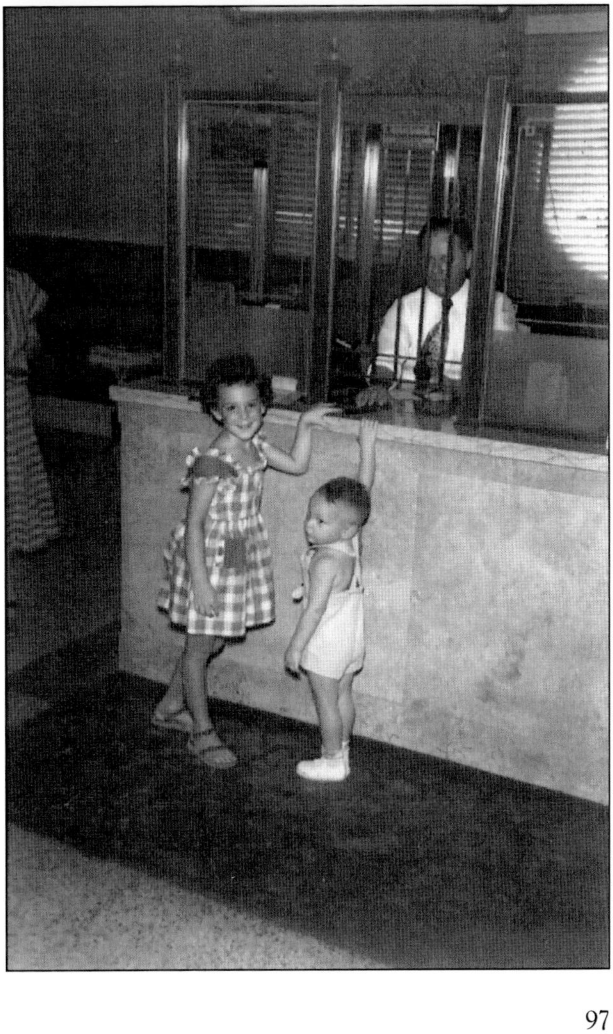

In a publicity photograph for Rayne State Bank, youth are seen making a deposit into their savings account. In this October 1953 photograph from the *Weekly Acadian*, Louise Catherine, five, and Albert Dwight Owers, 19 months, daughter and son of Mr. and Mrs. Fred Owers, are giving their deposit to Aaron Nugent, cashier for Rayne State Bank & Trust Company. (Courtesy of Donald Petitjean.)

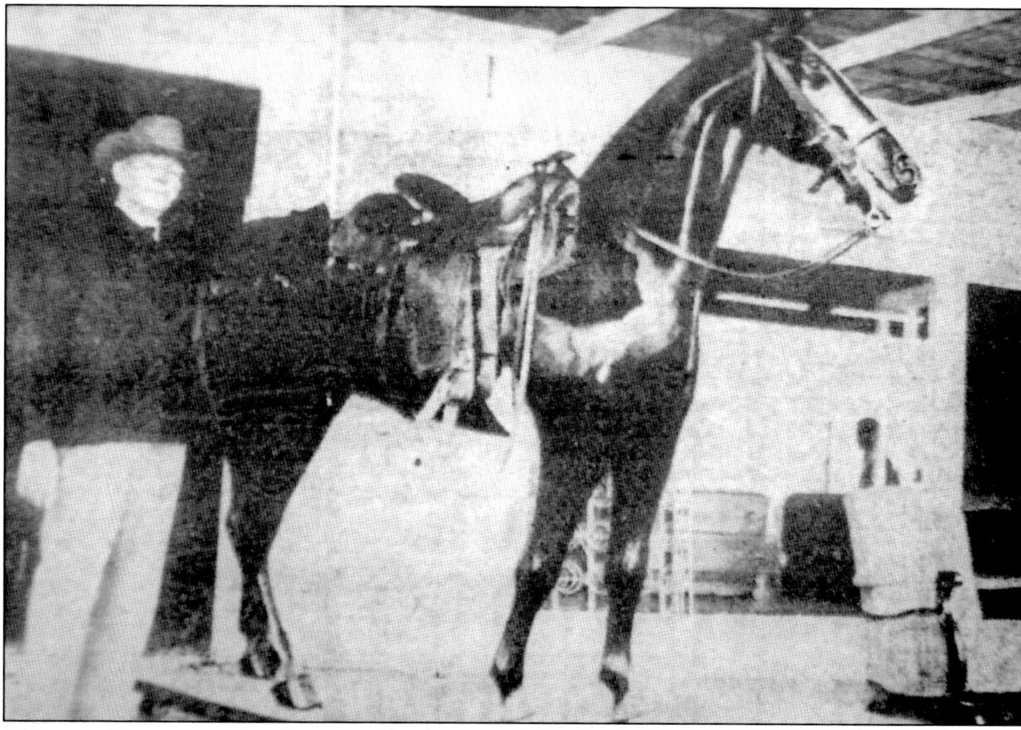

This wood horse stood in Farmers Hardware for many years and was a favorite of Rayne youth. When the business closed in 1954, it was sold to a hardware store in Lafayette. Kids would look into the picture window at the horse, which would sometimes be hitched to a wagon. Originally black, it was later repainted to resemble a palomino. It is not known if the horse is still standing tall or was used for firewood. (Courtesy of *Rayne Acadian-Tribune*.)

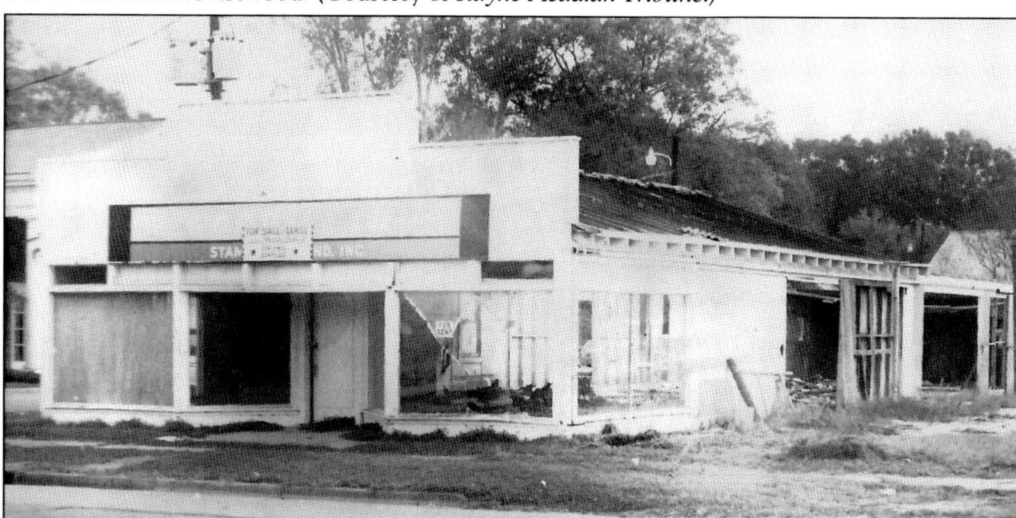

This abandoned building being torn down had been used by numerous businesses over the years. Judging from the sign, it was last used as the office for Stamm-Raymond's Used Cars. It was located across from the Bank of Commerce, on the corner of Harrop Street and North Adams Avenue. (Courtesy of *Rayne Independent*.)

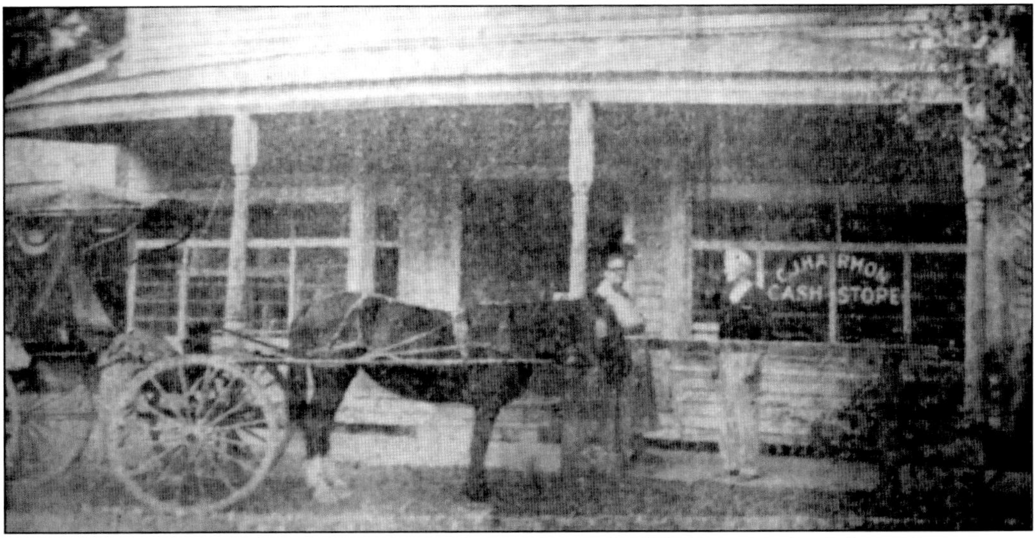

The C.J. Harmon Cash Store is pictured in 1909, with C.J Harmon (right) speaking to an unidentified person. The building was the home for many businesses and is still standing on West Edwards Street, next to Koury's Jewelry Store. (Courtesy of *Rayne Acadian-Tribune.*)

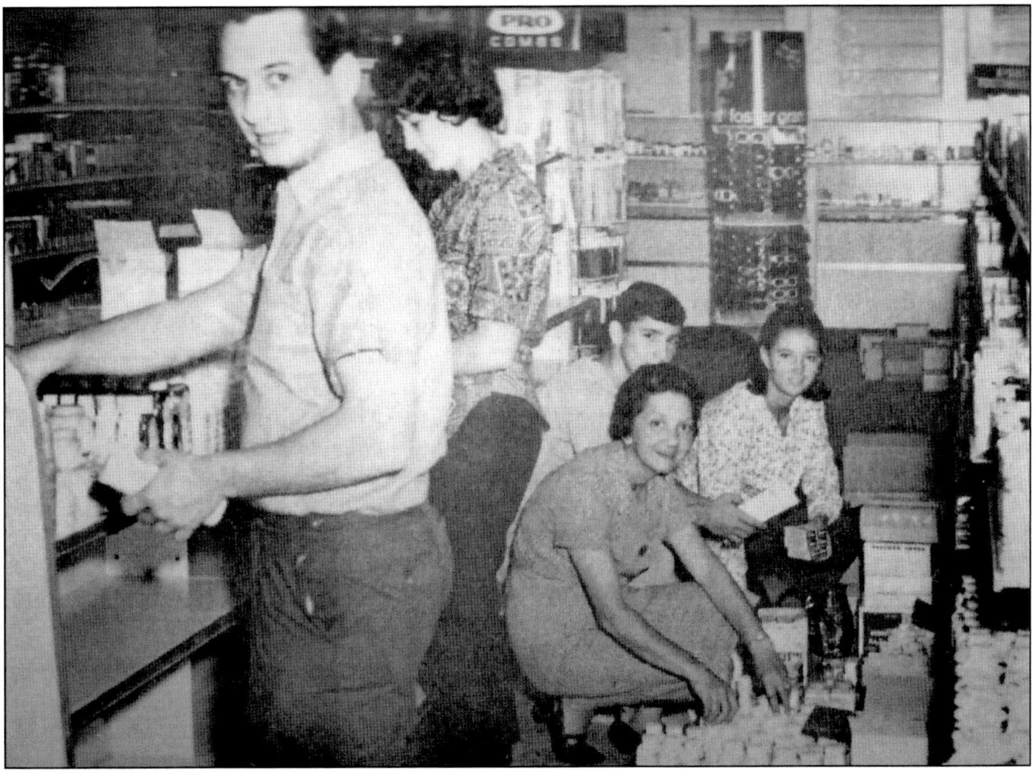

Workers are stocking shelves of the newly opened Brown's Ethical Pharmacy, located near Paco's on South Adams Avenue in 1967. Cyril Dodge would be the supervisor, with help from Barbara Babineaux, Mildred Alleman, Price Hains Jr., and Diana Guidry, all from Rayne. Brown's later became Eckerd Drugs, located in the Rayne Plaza Shopping Center. (Courtesy of *Rayne Acadian-Tribune.*)

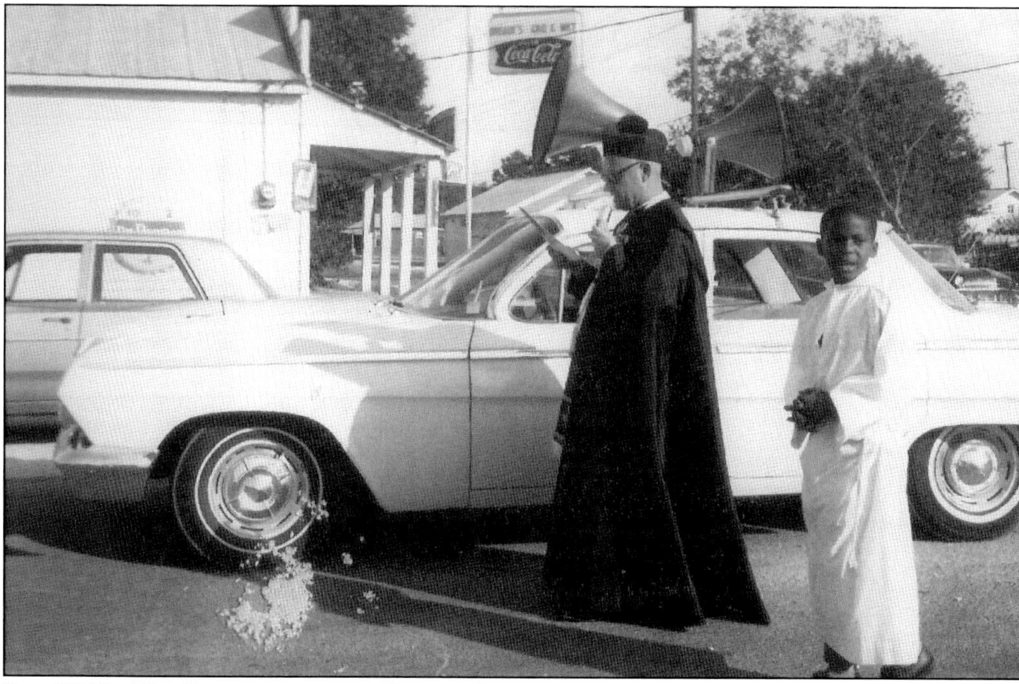

Rev. Wilfred DesRossiers, pastor of Our Mother of Mercy Shrine, bestows a blessing outside the church on West Jeff Davis and Lyman Avenues. Judging by the size of the loudspeakers on the car, a large crowd must have gathered to hear the priest speak. Breaux's Grocery & Market can be seen in the background. (Courtesy of *Rayne Independent*.)

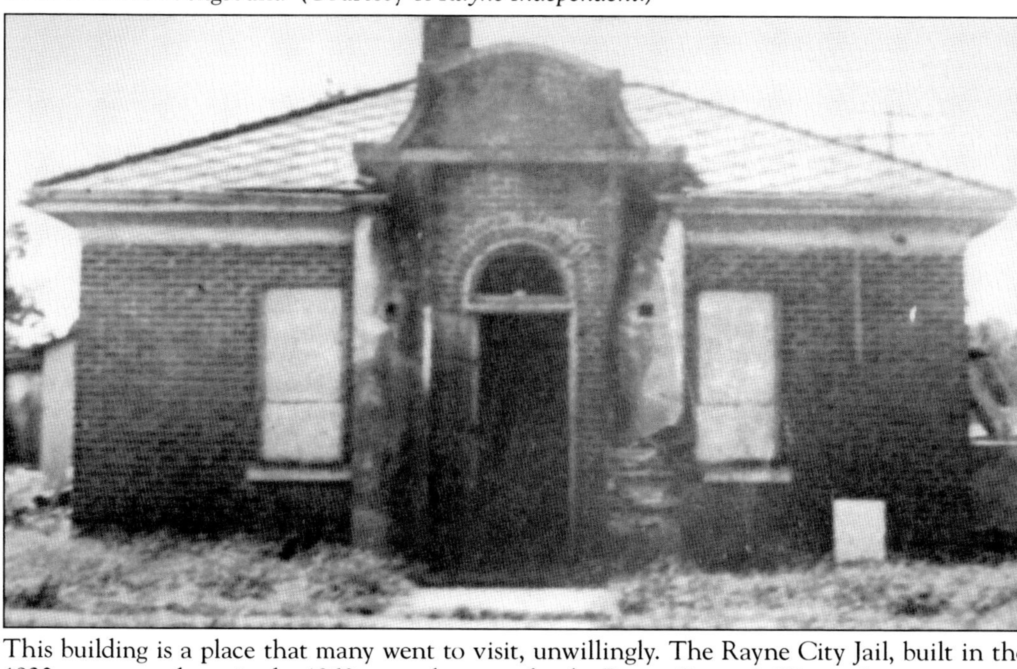

This building is a place that many went to visit, unwillingly. The Rayne City Jail, built in the 1930s, was torn down in the 1960s to make room for the Rayne Power & Water plant expansion. Erected during the tenure of Mayor Joseph Gossen, the jail featured two cells and was located on the corner of West Texas Avenue and Fourth Street. (Courtesy of *Rayne Acadian-Tribune*.)

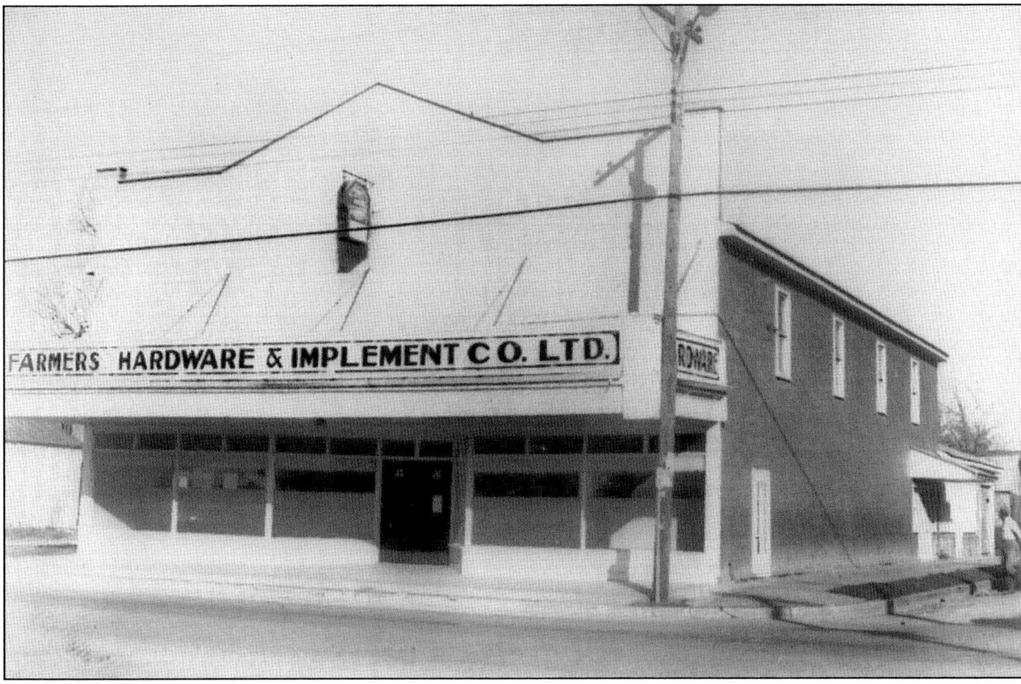

The Farmers Hardware & Implement Company was in operation from 1913 to 1954. After it closed, it later became the home of Rayne Furniture, NAPA Motor Parts, and, today, Farmers True Value Hardware. (Courtesy of *Rayne Independent*.)

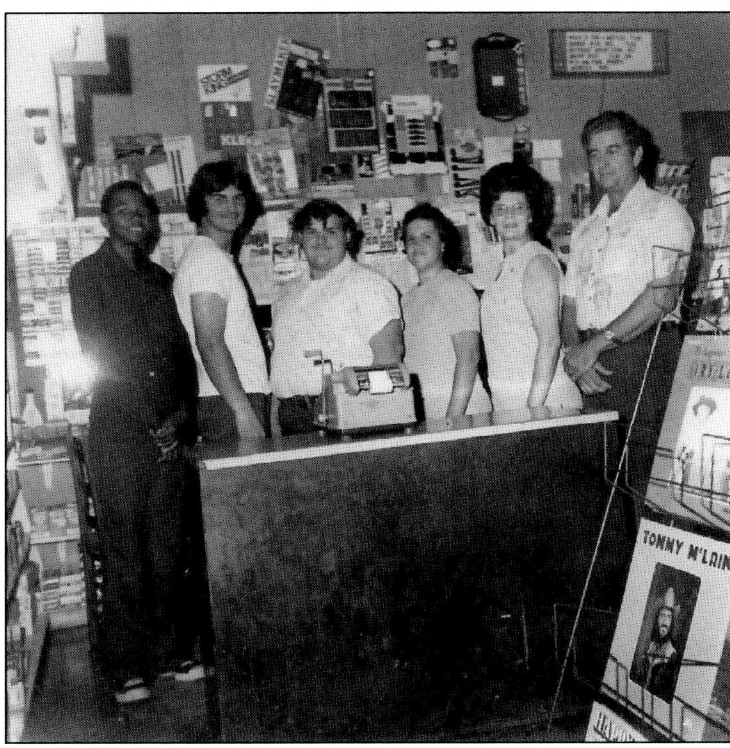

The staff of Venable's Grocery Store, located on Reynolds Street at the corner of West Jeff Davis Avenue, pose for a 1976 photograph. They are, from left to right, Cleve Guillory, Ronnie Venable, John Meaux, Elaine Venable, and owners Laura and Preston Venable. There is no computer; rather, an old adding machine is on the counter. The store in still in operation today under different ownership. (Courtesy of *Rayne Independent*.)

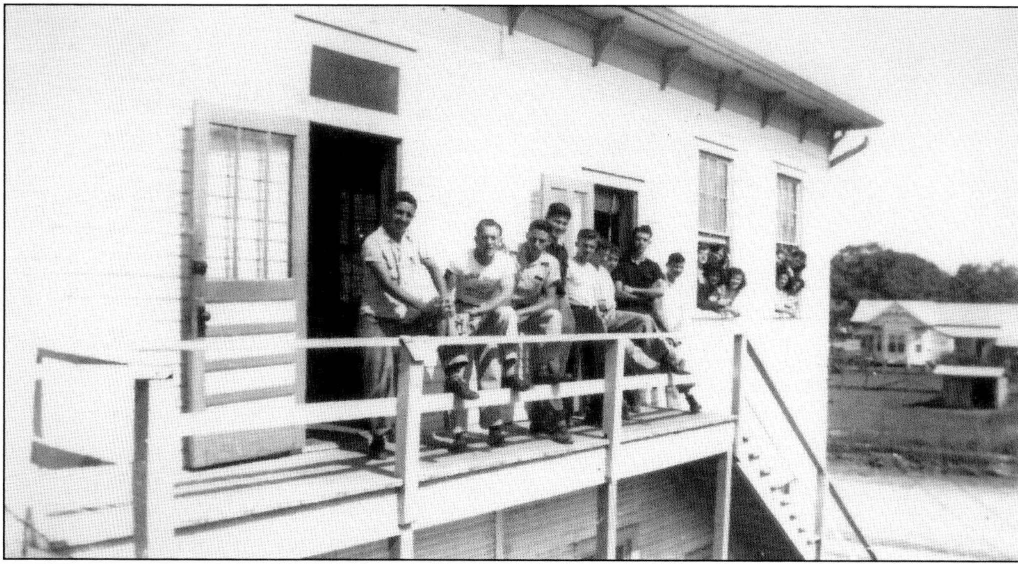

These students of St. Joseph High School pose on the second floor of their school. The building was torn down, and a new structure was erected in its place in 1953. All Catholic high schools in the parish consolidated to make Notre Dame High School of Acadia Parish in 1967. (Courtesy of Donald Petitjean.)

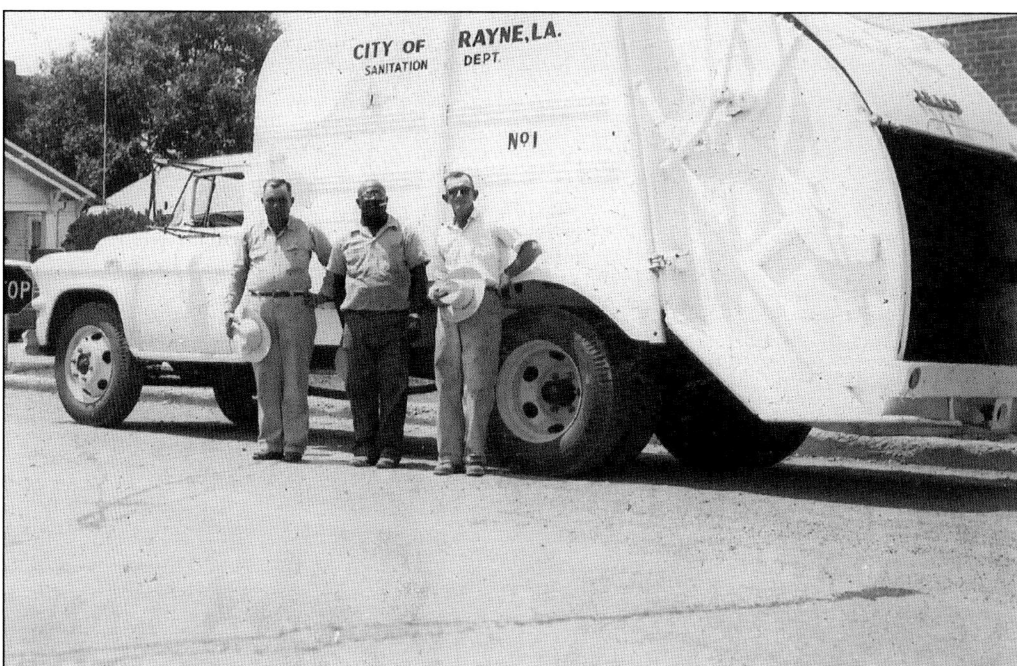

These three city employees pose next to city sanitation department truck No 1. in front of the former Rayne City Hall on East Louisiana Avenue. Trash was collected in different parts of the city each day and brought to the city dump, just north of Rayne on Roberts Cove Road, next to the bayou. This practice was discontinued when a parish-wide tax was passed, and the sanitation service contract was awarded to Browning Ferris Inc. (BFI). (Courtesy of *Rayne Acadian-Tribune*.)

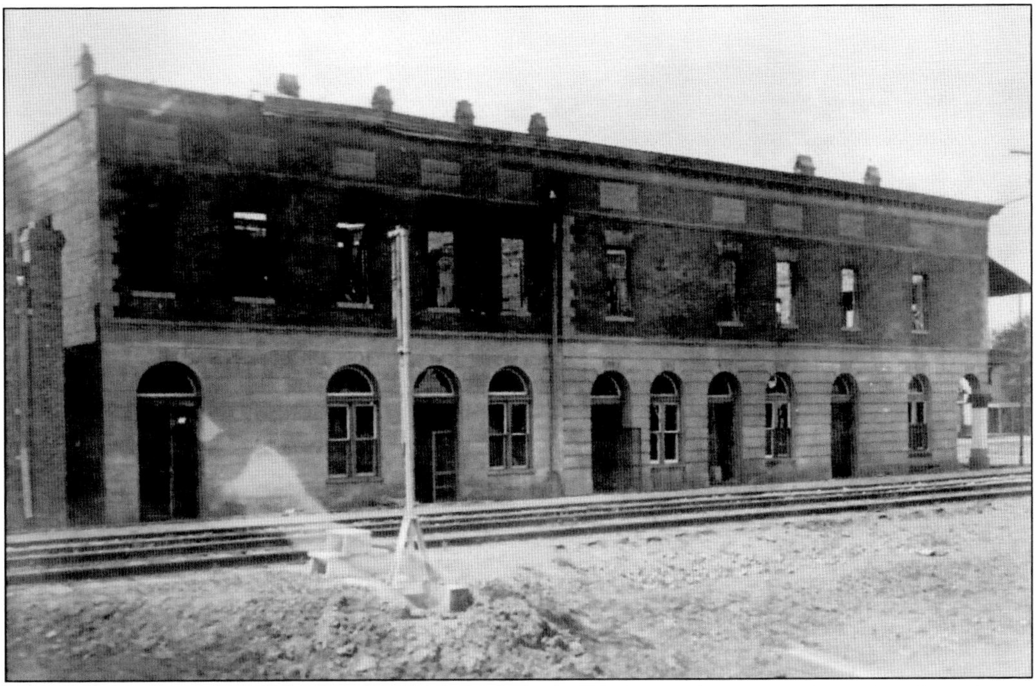

This is the north side of the Valverde Hotel, which was located next to the railroad tracks on South Polk Street. The hotel caught fire in 1917. People trapped on the second floor had to be rescued. This building was remodeled and housed the Bruce Theater and, of all things, a bowling alley on the second floor. (Courtesy of Sidney Stutes.)

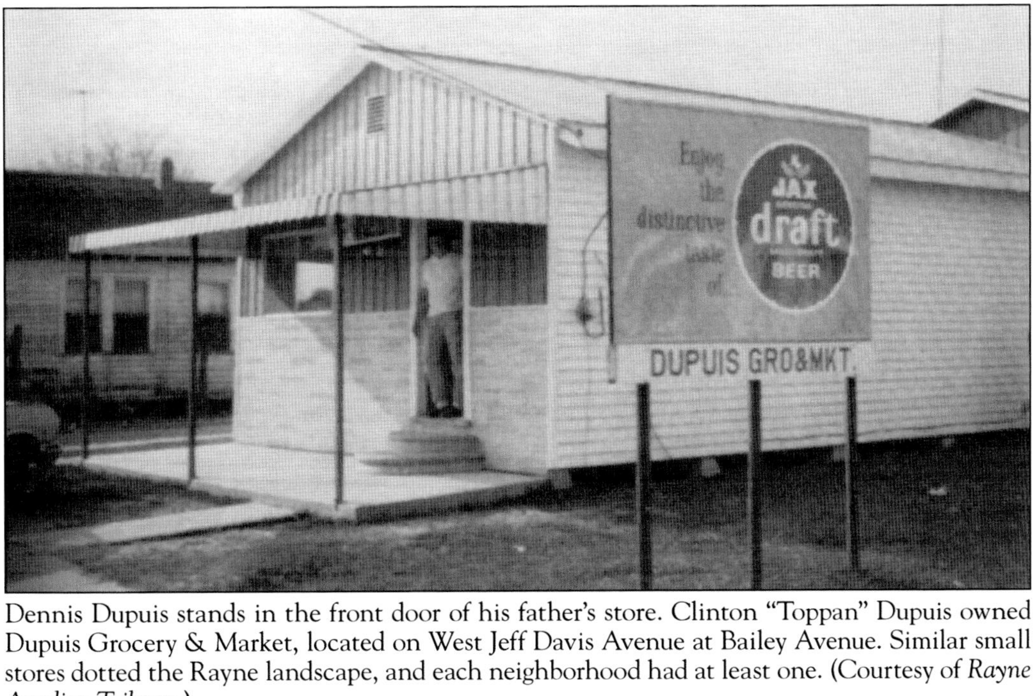

Dennis Dupuis stands in the front door of his father's store. Clinton "Toppan" Dupuis owned Dupuis Grocery & Market, located on West Jeff Davis Avenue at Bailey Avenue. Similar small stores dotted the Rayne landscape, and each neighborhood had at least one. (Courtesy of *Rayne Acadian-Tribune*.)

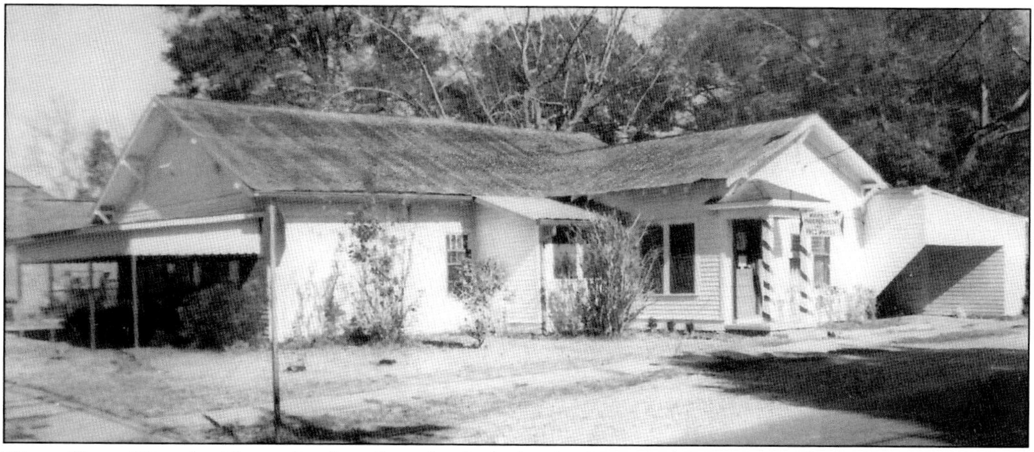

The office of Bertha Doty, the first female clerk for the Town of Rayne, was located at the corner of South Polk and East South First Streets. The front porch was filled with African violets, which she grew as a member of the African Violet Society. The building was later purchased by Jo and Robert Cart and served as the home of the *Rayne Independent* until the last edition was printed in May 2013. (Courtesy of *Rayne Independent*.)

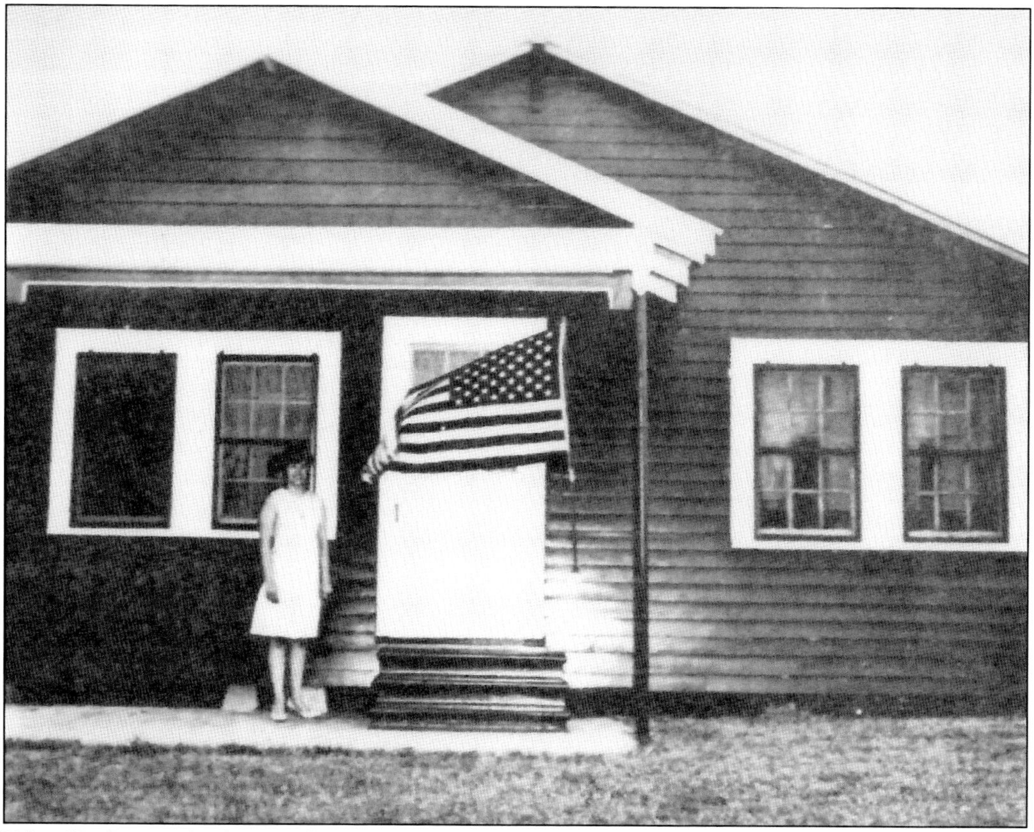

Edna "Pudgie" Whatley stands in front of the Little Red School House on East "F" Street in 1968. It was a preschool where students learned shapes, colors, and the alphabet. A promotion ceremony was usually held at the South Side Community Center, where the school's students recited stories and songs, and received diplomas. (Courtesy of *Rayne Acadian-Tribune*.)

The results of the flood of 1940 are shown in this northeast-facing photograph of the intersection of North Polk Street and East Jeff Davis Avenue. In the background is the Rayne Jobbing Company on North Polk Street, where To-Go Mart is now located. (Courtesy of Sidney Stutes.)

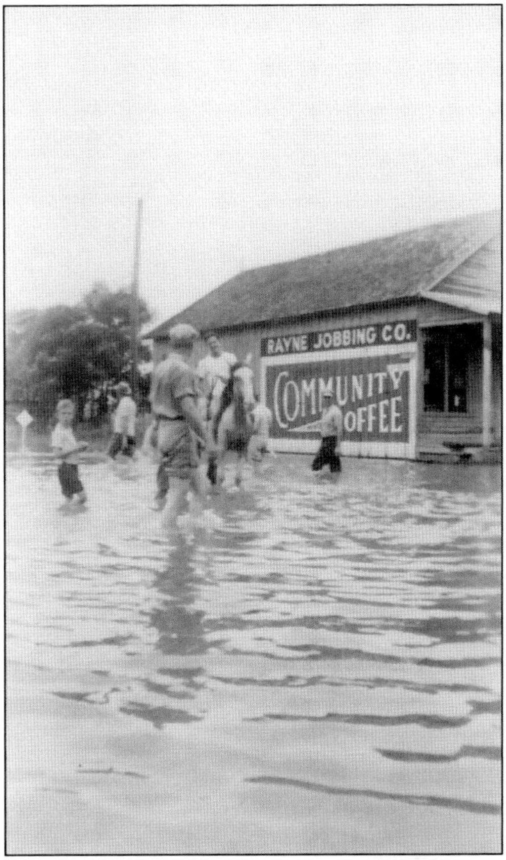

Olivier Broussard Sr. (right) stands inside his business, O. Broussard Pharmacy, located next to the Southern Pacific Railroad line on South Adams Avenue. The building still stands today as the W. Petitjean & Co. Building. Broussard and an unidentified employee are posing for a promotional photograph with a Parke-Davis Soap display. (Courtesy of Sidney Stutes.)

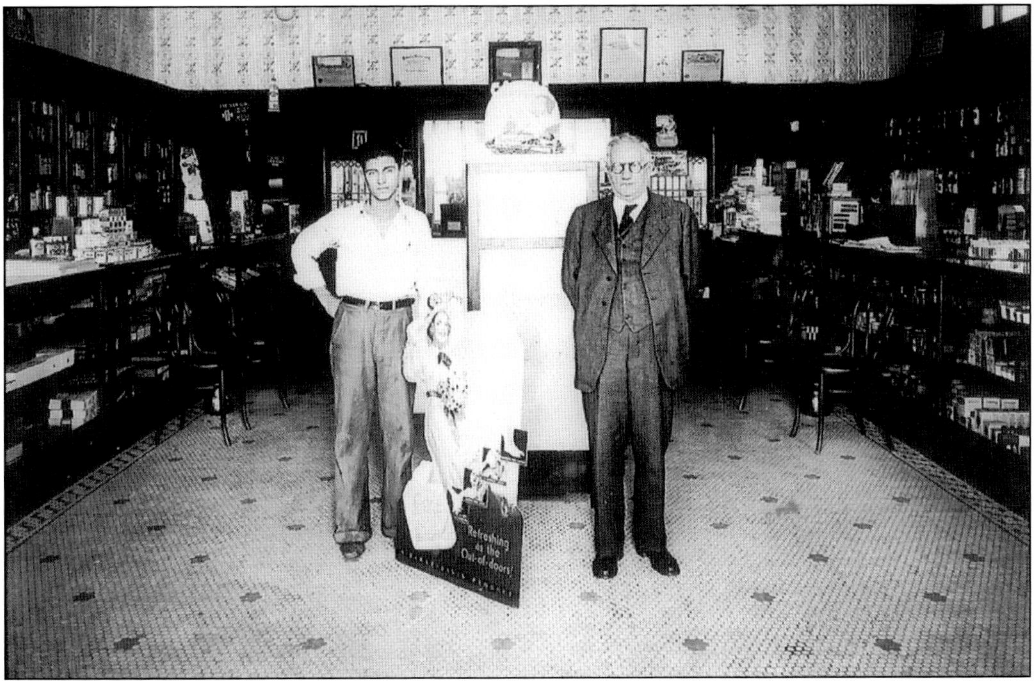

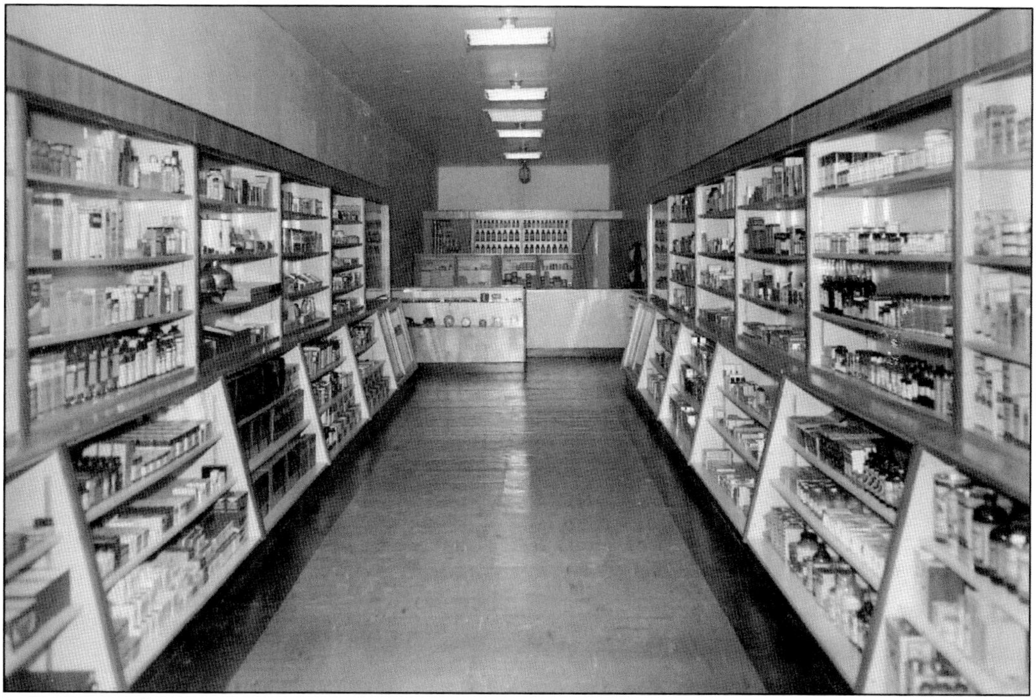

Lasseigne's Pharmacy is seen here when it opened for business in August 1946 in its original location, in the 200 block of North Adams Avenue. The rear of the pharmacy held the prescription and compounding department. Owned and operated by Mr. and Mrs. Paul Lasseigne, it moved to a second location, in the 100 block of North Adams Avenue, next to Koury's Jewelry. The Lasseignes then built their final location across from the new Rayne Branch Hospital on South Chevis Street. (Courtesy of Donald Petitjean.)

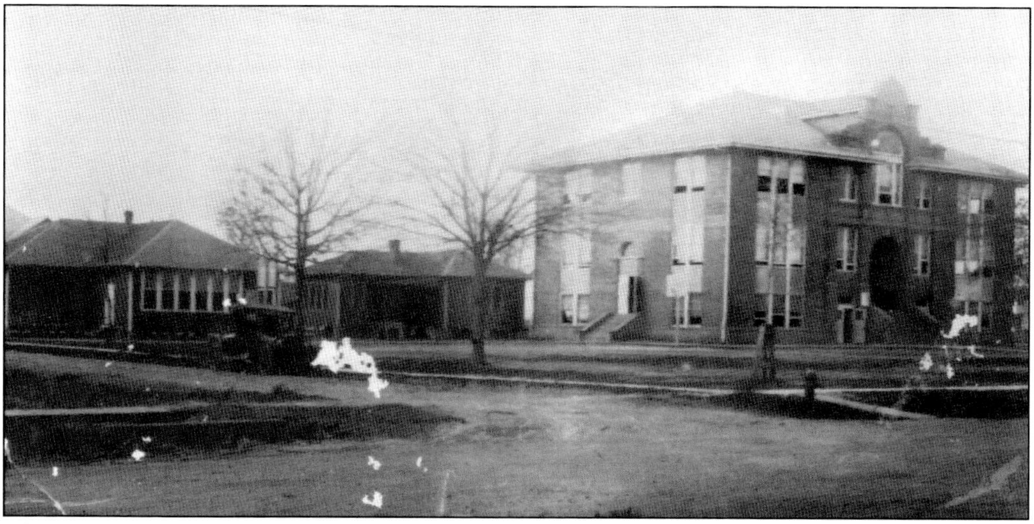

This is an early photograph of Rayne High School, which was built in 1912 at a cost of $20,000. It was located on North Polk Street, where Rayne Central Kindergarten is now located. This three-story school accommodated students from first through eleventh grade. The Home Economics Cottage can be seen directly behind the school. The trees were planted by the School Improvement League, headed by Mrs. R.C. Webb. (Courtesy of Sidney Stutes.)

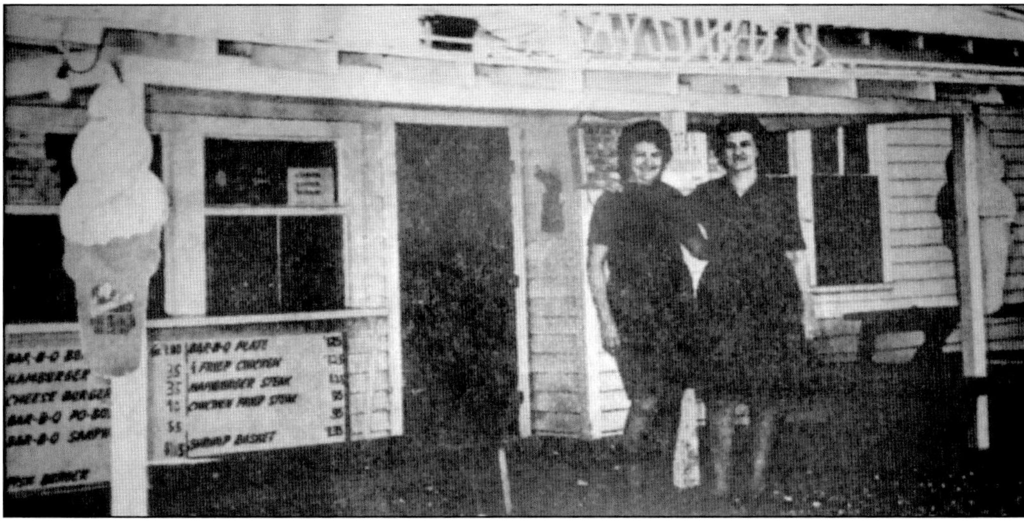

Terro Twins 7th Street Drive Inn offered barbecue pork chop plates with rice dressing and potato salad on weekends for $1.25. It was located at 210 Seventh Street and was owned by Ruby Terro Gautreaux and Ruth Terro Barton. The establishment opened in 1969. Originally, the building was owned by Boone and Sally Molbert, who ran a grocery store. (Courtesy of *Rayne Acadian-Tribune*.)

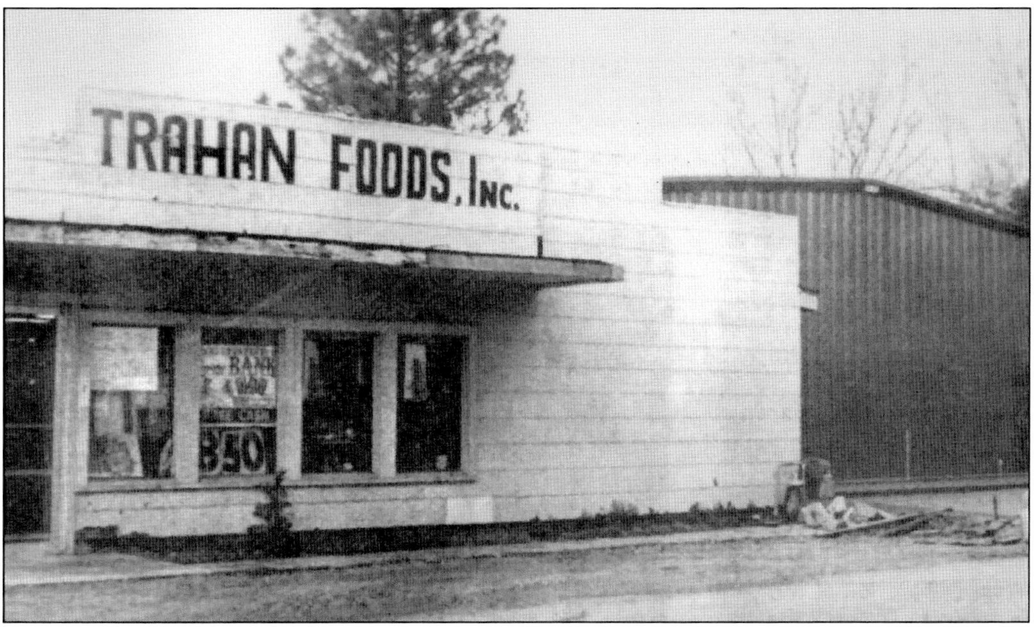

Out with the old, and in with the new. The original Trahan Foods Inc. (left) was founded by Mr. and Mrs. David Trahan in 1949. The new Trahan Foods building, erected by Ronnie and Mollie Trahan, is taking shape on the right in 1980. Trahan's is still in operation today, owned by Scotty and Marcia Menard. (Courtesy of *Rayne Acadian-Tribune*.)

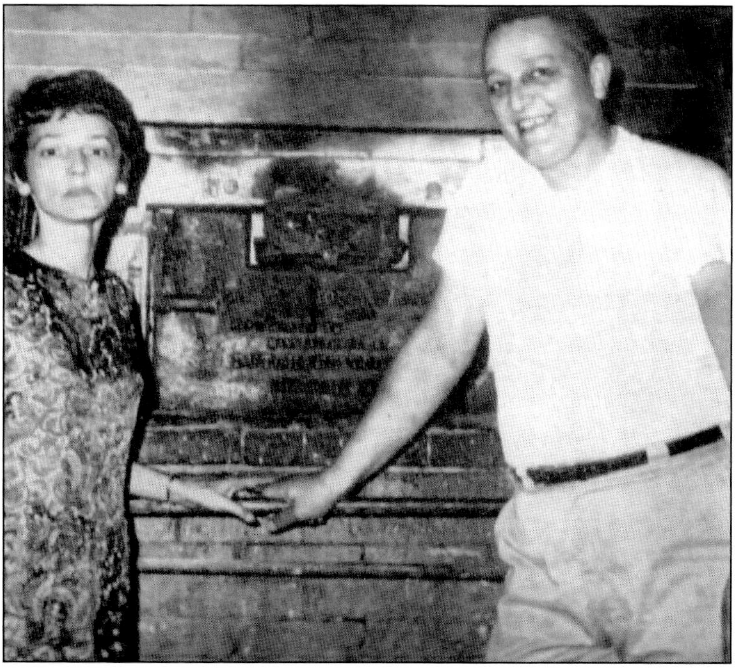

Julie Privat Ousse and her brother Tony Privat pose in front of the oven door at Privat's Bakery, which baked French bread since it was installed in 1924. Their father, Joe Privat, bought the business from his older brother Louis Privat, and the family ran it until it closed in June 1968. Jasper and Albert Johnson tore down the historic building for the lumber many years later. (Courtesy of *Rayne Acadian-Tribune*.)

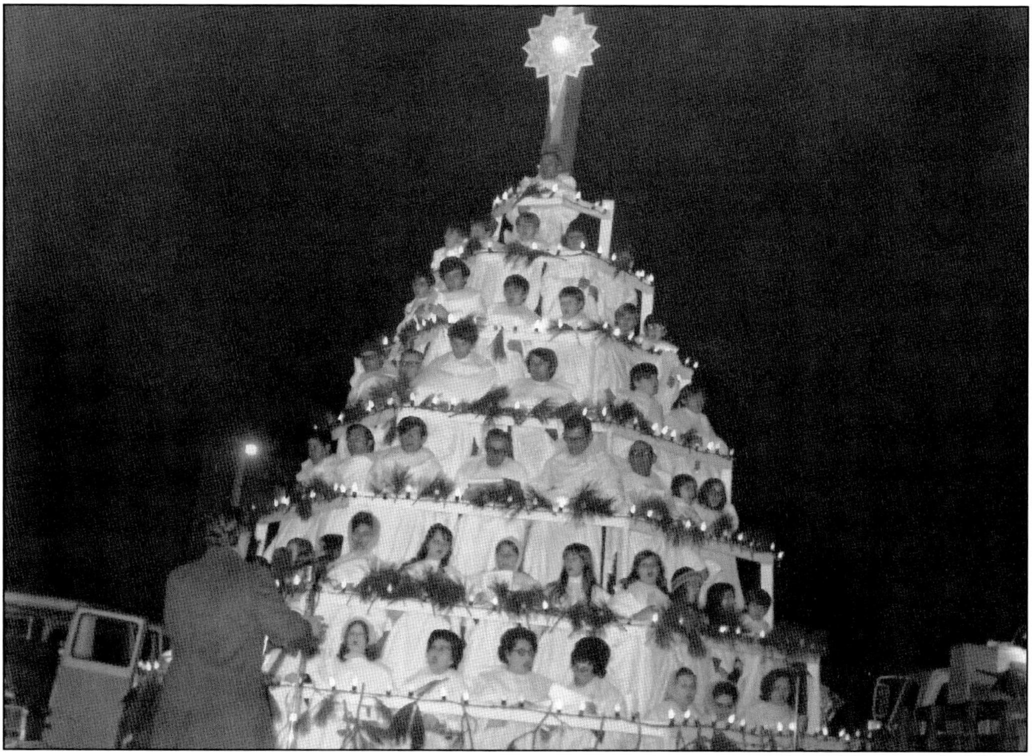

One of the most beautiful Rayne Christmas traditions was the singing Christmas tree, sponsored by the First Baptist Church of Rayne. When the original church was located on Clegg Street, this platform was catty-corner from the church, near The Boulevard's S-curve. The platform was up all year long. (Courtesy of *Rayne Acadian-Tribune*.)

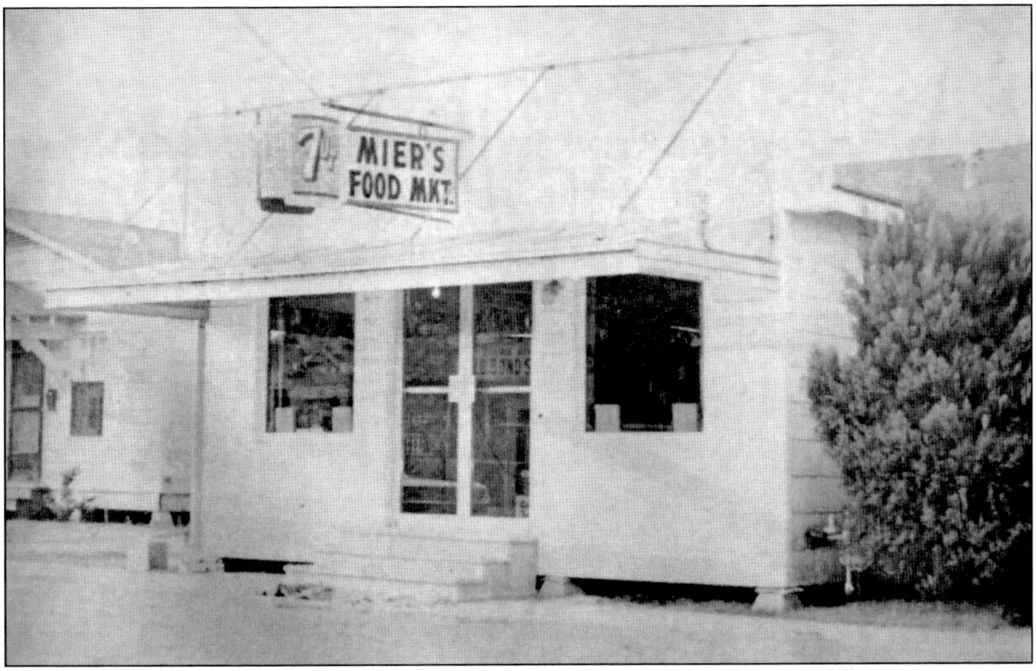

Mr. and Mrs. Alvin Mier operated Mier's Tip-Top Grocery and Market since January 1, 1958, at 702 Live Oak Street. Their business continued to expand until they erected a new building on South Adams Avenue and renamed it Mier's Grocery. It was located where Champagne's Grocery now stands. (Courtesy of *Rayne Acadian-Tribune*.)

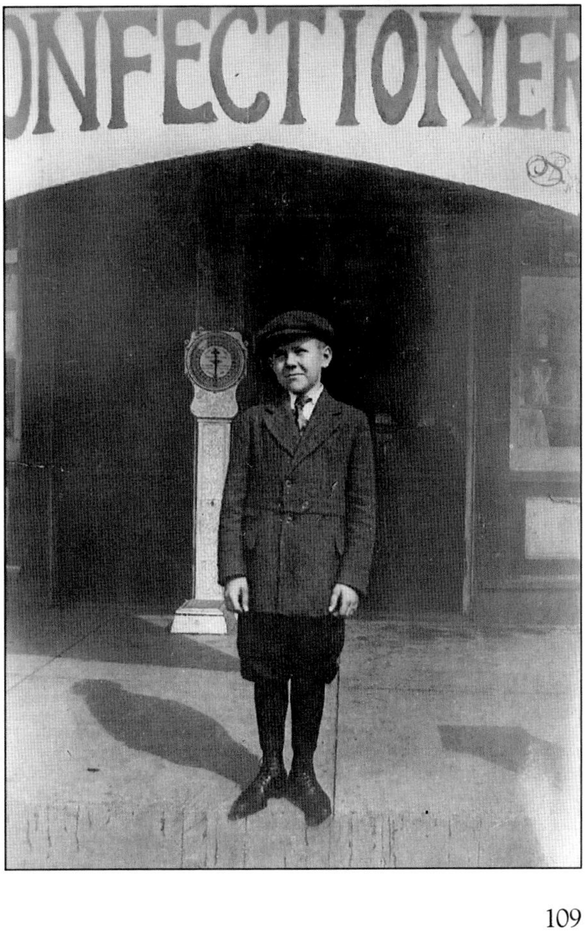

This Rayne lad poses in front of a confectionery on South Adams Avenue, next door to what is now the Hulin and Lormand Building. The business was later purchased by Oscar "Paco" Borne in 1933, who went into the restaurant business with the People's Café. Note some goods in the picture window, as well as the penny scale. (Courtesy of Ronnie Richard.)

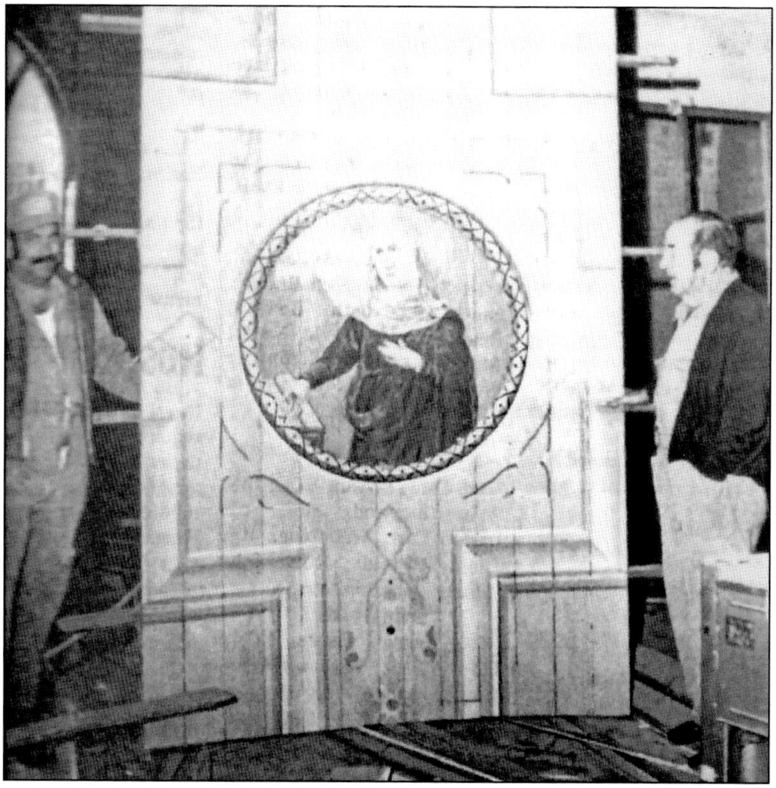

James Trahan (left) and Leroy "Happy Fats" LeBlanc pose with a piece of St. Joseph Catholic Church history. Trahan was tearing down the second St. Joseph Church and was able to cut out and save the painted murals on the high ceilings. The artist is unknown, as are the paintings' whereabouts today. The location of the old church on South Adams Avenue is a vacant lot today. (Courtesy of *Rayne Acadian-Tribune.*)

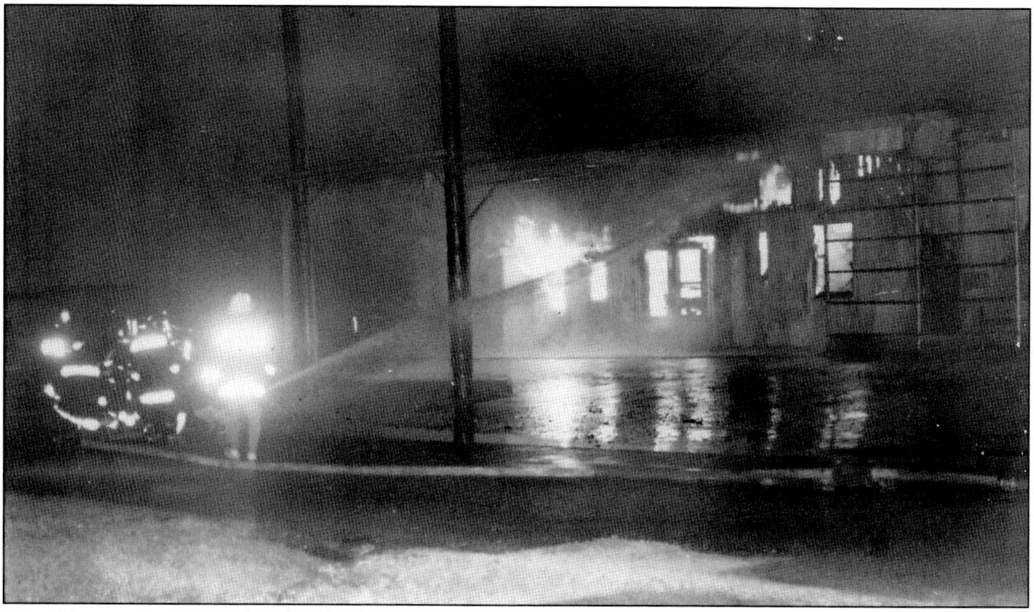

This blaze was reported to be the largest in the history of the Rayne Volunteer Fire Department. The Riviana Rice Mill, located on North Arenas Street, was being torn down at the time. The fire was fought by firefighters the majority of the day, and it smoldered for several days afterward. As the blaze started on Thanksgiving Day, not many of the firefighters were able to eat turkey that day. (Courtesy of *Rayne Independent.*)

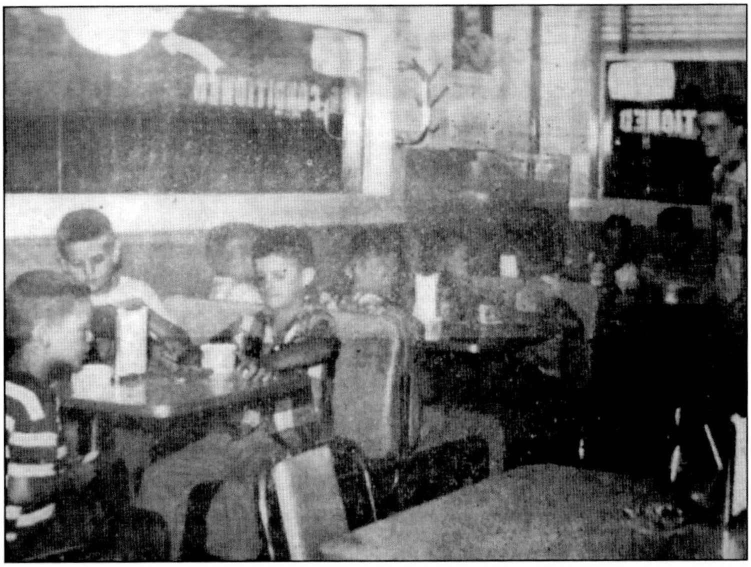

"A treat for Pee Wee Leaguers" was the headline for this June 1953 photograph. They played ball on Mondays, Wednesdays, and Fridays at St. Joseph's ball diamond and were treated to ice cream by Mr. and Mrs. Flemon Johnson at Johnson's Drive Inn on South Adams Avenue. None of the players was able to collect the top prize—a banana split—for hitting a home run. (Courtesy of *Rayne Acadian-Tribune*.)

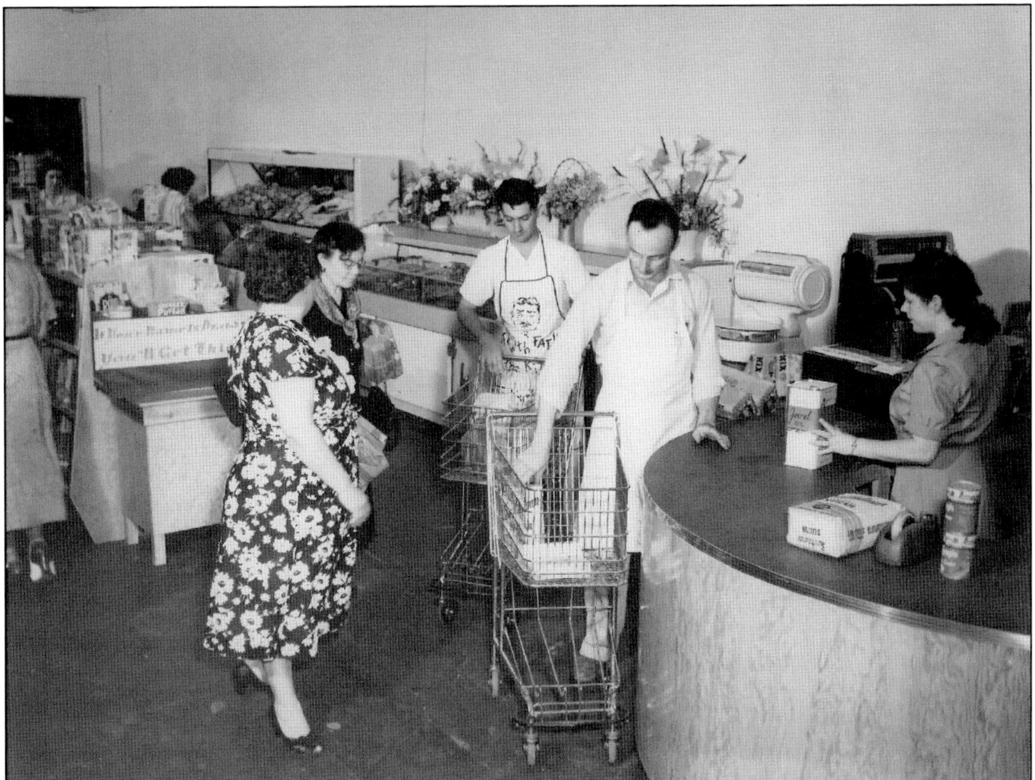

Mervine Kahn Company offered everything Rayne shoppers would need, including a grocery department. Here, a shopper checks out at the curved checkout counter. Edith Laperous is behind the counter, Purvis Richard unloads the cart at the counter, and Andrus Fontenot pushes the second cart. The other persons are unidentified. When the Cash and Carry and big grocery stores opened in Lafayette, Kahn's grocery department was forced to close. (Courtesy of Leonard J. Laperous, The Photo Shop.)

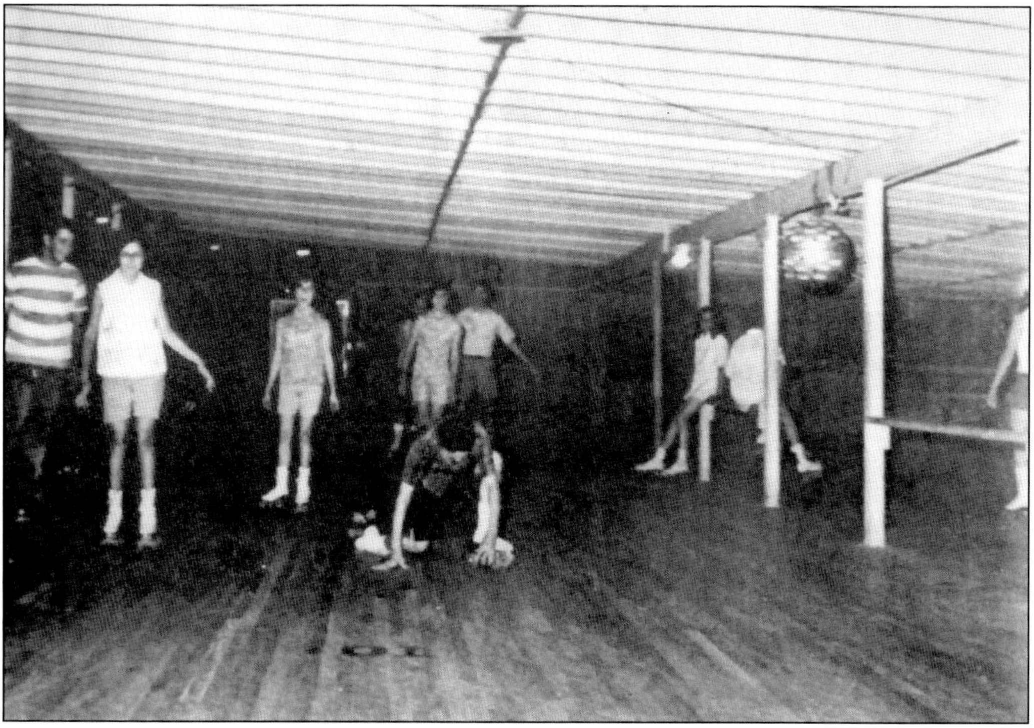

The St. Joseph Christian Youth Organization hosts a skating party at Ray's Skating Rink, owned by Raymond Credeur. Mrs. Overton Stelly, beloved counselor, is pictured after she fell. Originally opened by Ewell Latiolais, it was located in the 800 block of South Parkerson Street. Although the rink closed its doors in 2006, the building still stands today. During skates, the owners would turn out the lights and throw pennies on the floor, with red quarters in the mix. Skaters who found a red quarter received free skates on their next visit. (Courtesy of *Rayne Acadian-Tribune*.)

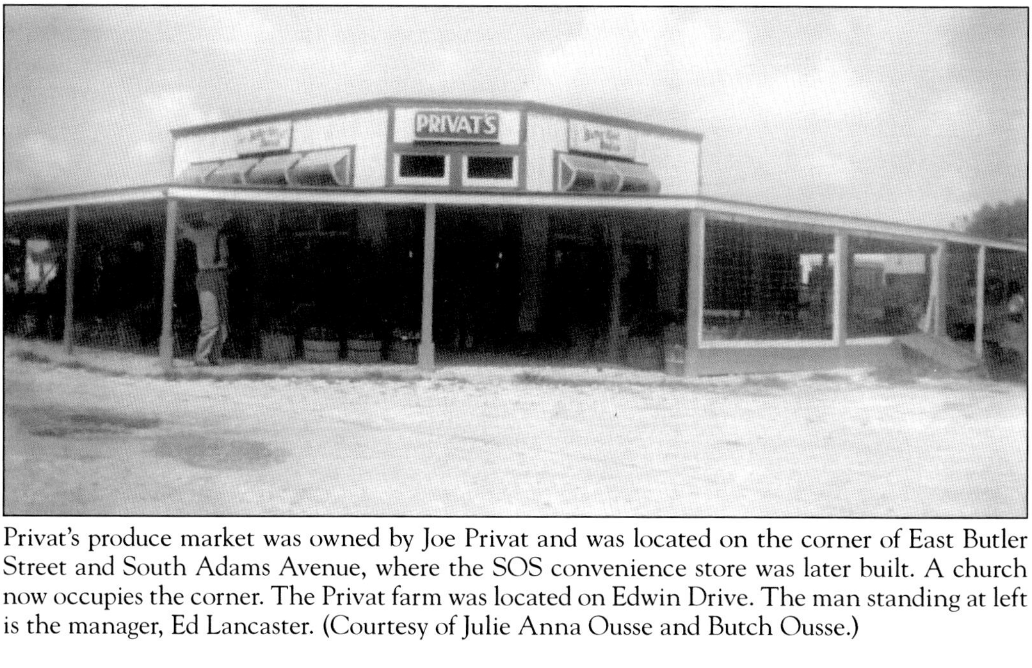

Privat's produce market was owned by Joe Privat and was located on the corner of East Butler Street and South Adams Avenue, where the SOS convenience store was later built. A church now occupies the corner. The Privat farm was located on Edwin Drive. The man standing at left is the manager, Ed Lancaster. (Courtesy of Julie Anna Ousse and Butch Ousse.)

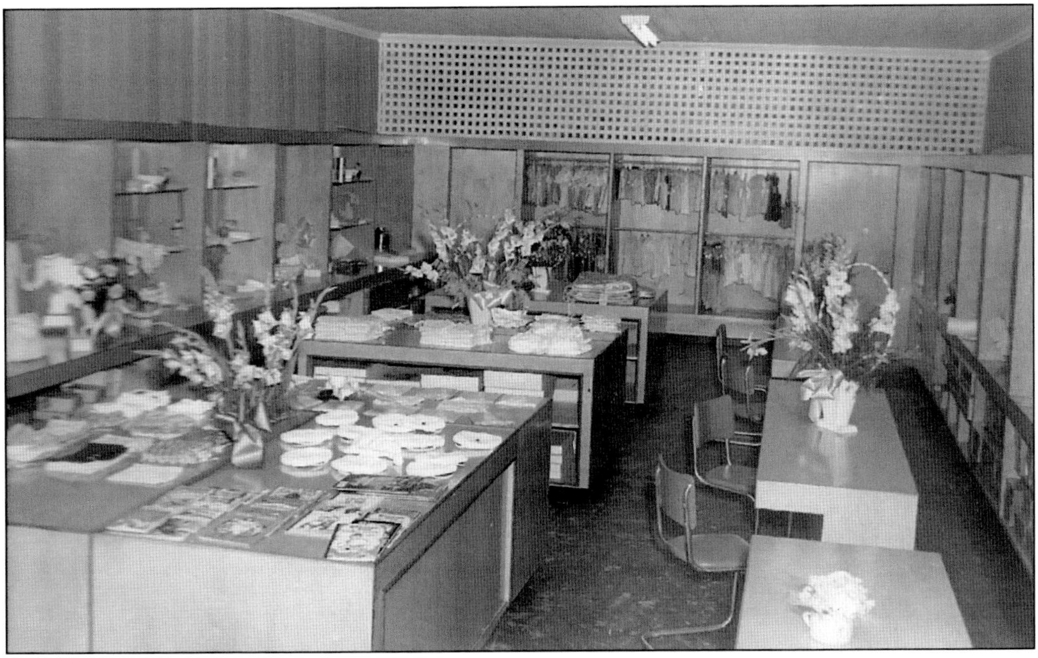

This is an inside view of Catherine's ABC shop, where baby clothes and accessories were sold. Owned by Catherine Kahn, it was opened in the mid-1940s and was in business for over 25 years on East Texas Avenue across from the Depot Square in the same building that housed the Rayne State Bank. Bercier Family Dentistry now occupies the building. (Courtesy of *Rayne Independent.*)

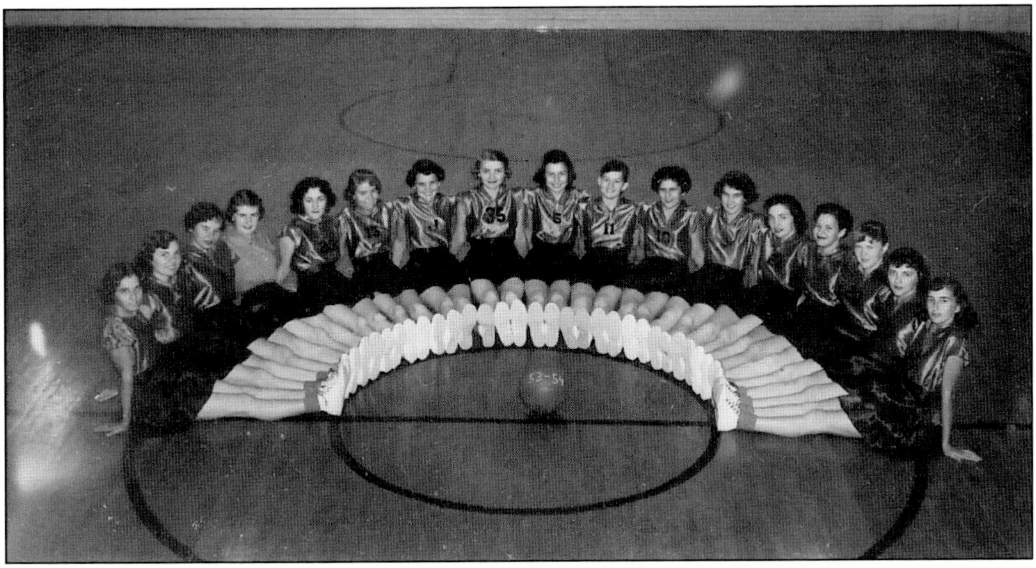

The 1953–1954 St. Joseph's High School ladies' basketball team poses at center court. Shown are, from left to right, Louise Habetz, Laura Trahan, Audrey Mier, Rose Marie Robichaux, Helen Dischler, Carol Jean Leger, Claudia Petitjean, Josie Heinen, Helen Gossen, Catherine Gossen, Martha Johnson, Barbara Arceneaux, Selma Faulk, Mary Alice Ruptier, Carol Myers, Lois Trahan, and Margie Nell Richard. They played three-on-three half-court basketball. Team A's offense played against team B's defense on one half of the court; on the other side, team A's defense played against team B's offense. (Courtesy of *Rayne Independent.*)

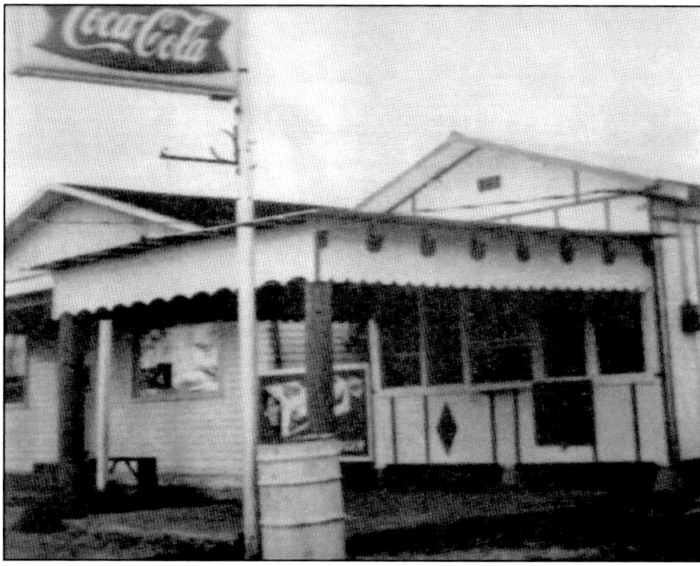

In July 1971, Thib's Burgers held its grand opening, selling burgers for a special price, four regular or three jumbo for 99¢. A free Coke was also given with each purchase. Located on Abbeville Highway, it also offered crab burgers, breaded oysters, and barbecue sandwiches. Next door to this building was the H&L store, owned by Harry Lee Bouillon. It was known for its meat department. (Courtesy of *Rayne Acadian-Tribune.*)

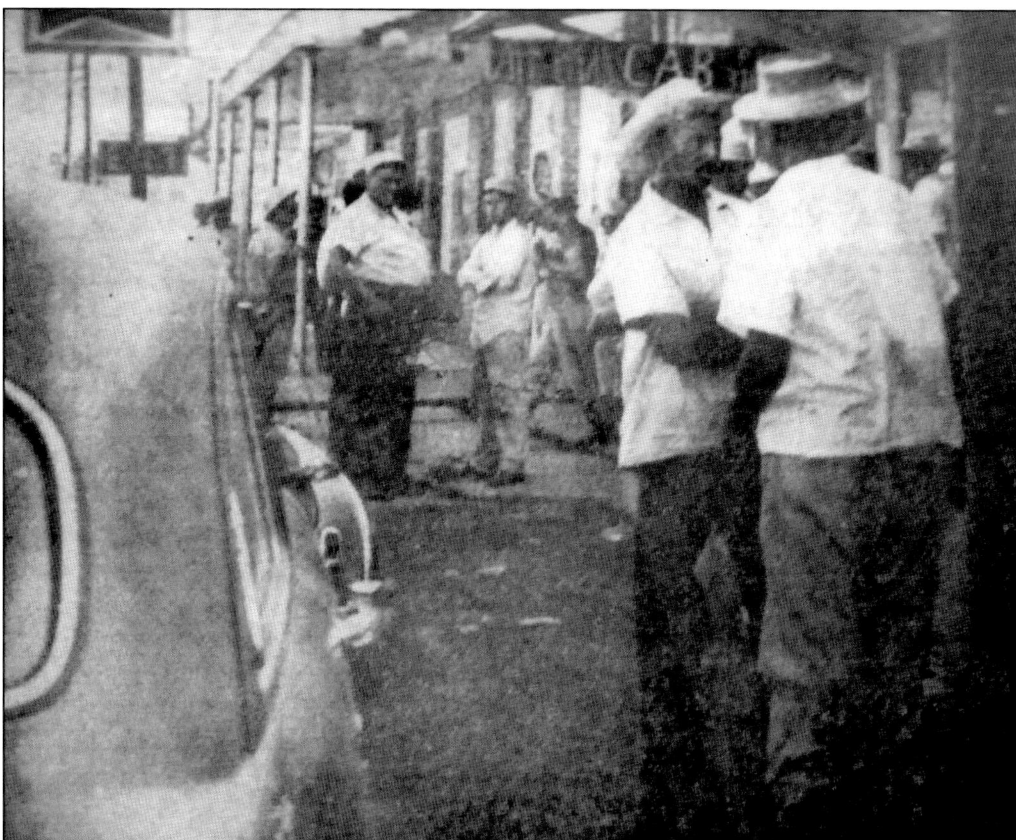

The sidewalk on East Texas Avenue near the Besse Café was buzzing with people hoping to get a job in July 1959. A construction company was looking to fill 50 union jobs at the new oil plant north of Rayne. Visible above the sidewalk is a sign for Alleman's Cab. At left is the familiar Besse Café "EAT" sign. (Courtesy of *Rayne Acadian-Tribune.*)

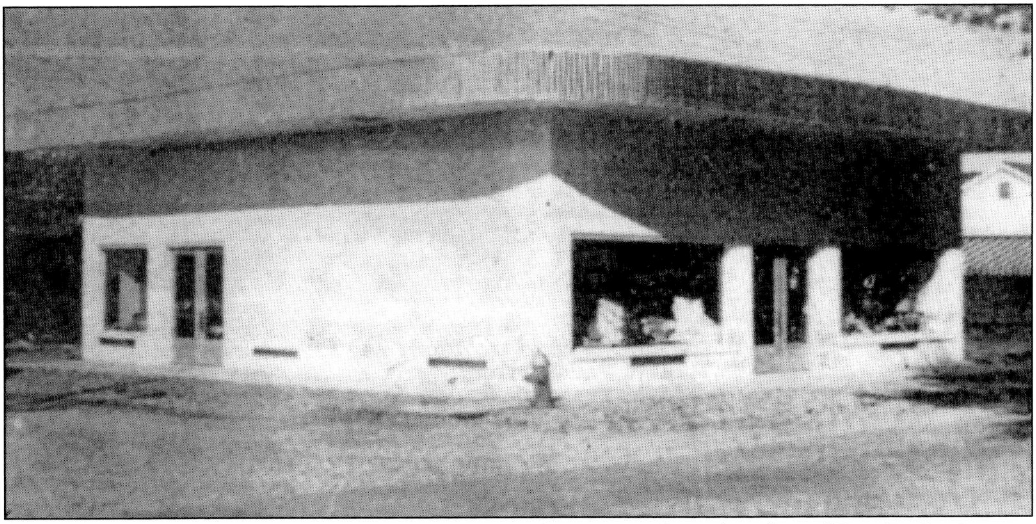

Jack's Cash Grocery opened in December 1947 on the corner of South Polk and East Butler Streets. It was owned by Jack Chaisson. His grand opening sale included the following deals: a carton of any brand cigarettes for $1.89, a bar of soap for 9¢, washing powder for 37¢, and five pounds of sugar for 47¢. It operated for many years until he turned the building into Jack's Washateria. The building was eventually torn down. Townhouses are now located on the corner. (Courtesy of *Rayne Acadian-Tribune*.)

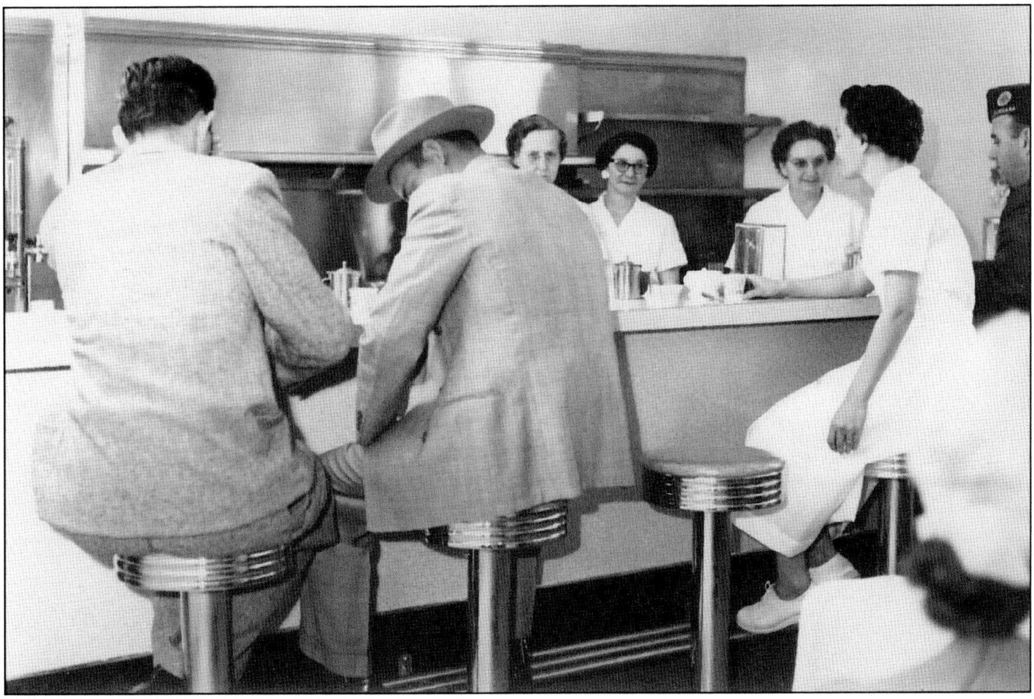

The Rayne Branch Hospital Cafeteria, located on South Chevis Street, is seen here shortly after its opening on February 19, 1958. From left to right are (seated) Dallas Domingue, Oscar Truell, Thelma Begnaud, and Herbert Hanks; (behind the counter) Zula Johnson, Ella Doucet, and Mrs. Ben Hoffpauir. With larger hospitals nearby, this establishment was forced to close its doors and is now abandoned. (Courtesy of Leonard J. Laperous, The Photo Shop.)

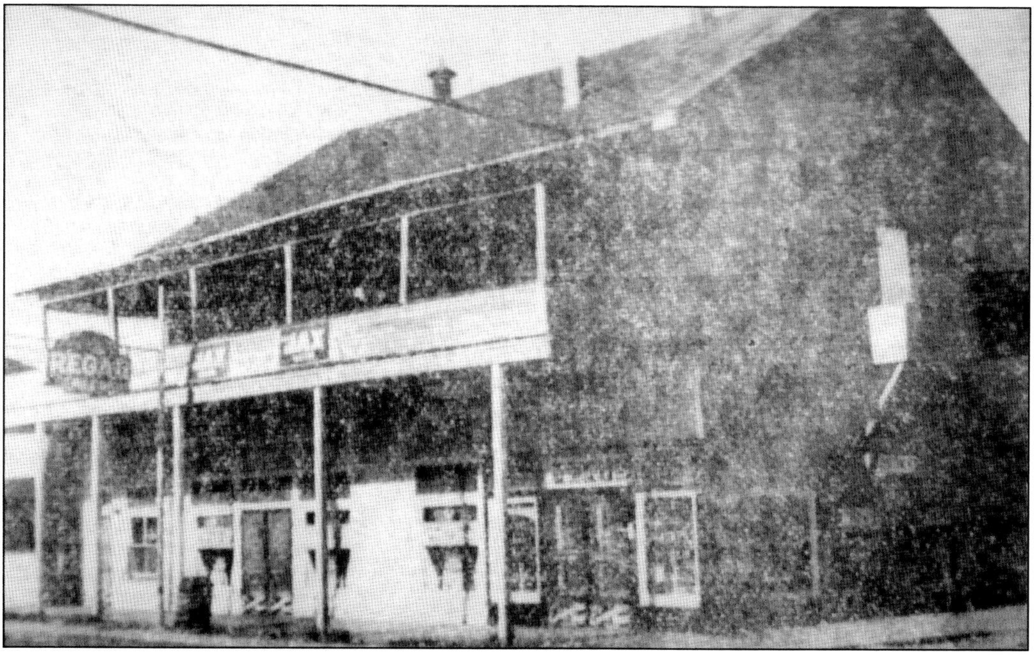

This was the home of many businesses, including Robicheaux's Meat Market, located on the right corner of the first floor. On the left side was Hanks's Bar, a barbershop, and the Greasy Spoon Café. The LaCroix family owned the building and lived on the second floor. This building was torn down by Wallace and Kootsie Simoneaux, and Kootsie used the wood to build the house he lives in today. Rayne State Bank was built on the corner of West Texas and South Adams Avenues. (Courtesy of *Rayne Acadian-Tribune*.)

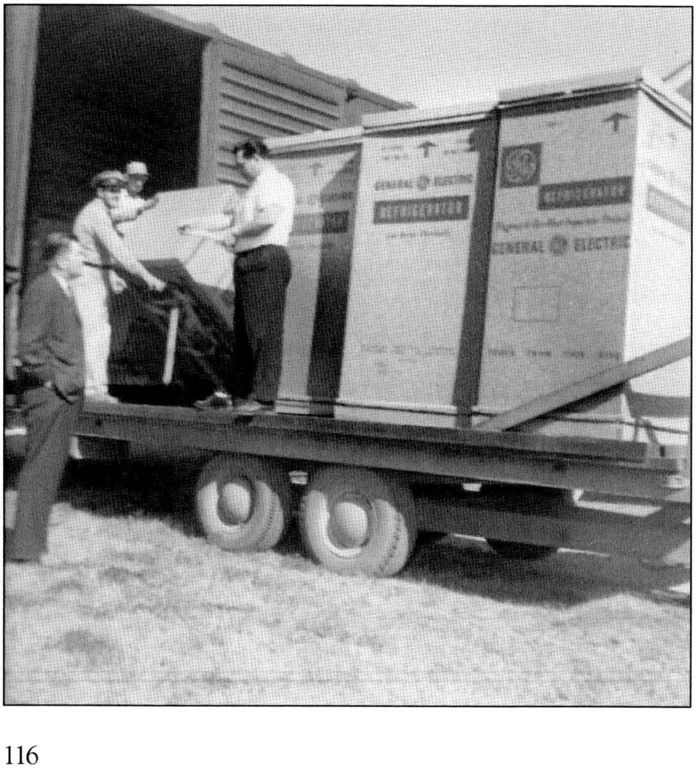

Before the majority of goods were shipped on Interstate 10 by 18-wheelers, the only way for Rayne businesses to receive goods was via Southern Pacific Railroad. Charlie Fremaux (left) of E.C. Fremaux's Hardware inspects a boxcar of GE refrigerators as they are offloaded. Standing at right, holding a clipboard, is Delton Soileaux. (Courtesy of *Rayne Independent*.)

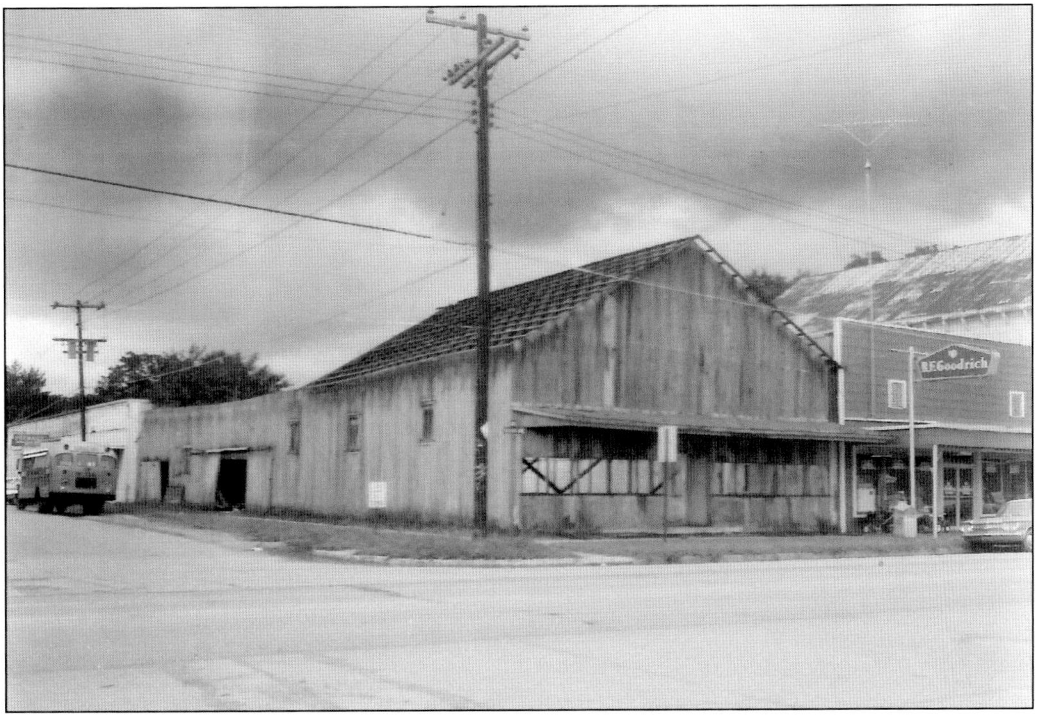

This livery stable, which was used by E.C. Fremaux's Implements Company as storage, was purchased by Raymond Mouton and torn down to make room for his Mouton Pharmacy. At left is the repair shop for Fremaux's, and at right is the storefront of Fremaux Hardware Store. (Courtesy of Donald Petitjean.)

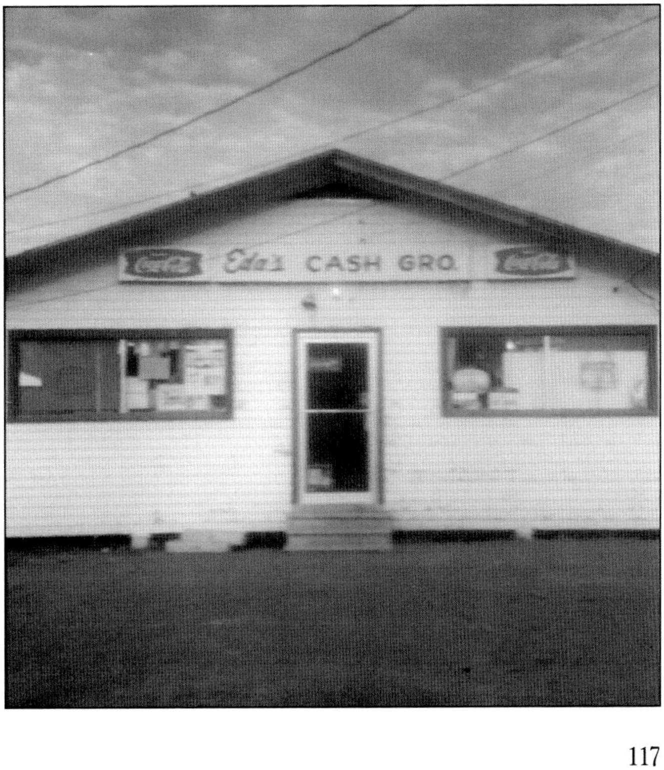

Eda's Cash Grocery was located at 614 Ann Drive. It was owned by Garland and Eda Daigle. They bought Labauve's Grocery from Eugene Labauve in 1970 and enlarged it in 1980. They were known for their meats and homemade boudin. The Daigles sold the business to Simon and Glenda Richard in 1985. The building later caught fire and was torn down. (Courtesy of Delores Daigle Lagneaux.)

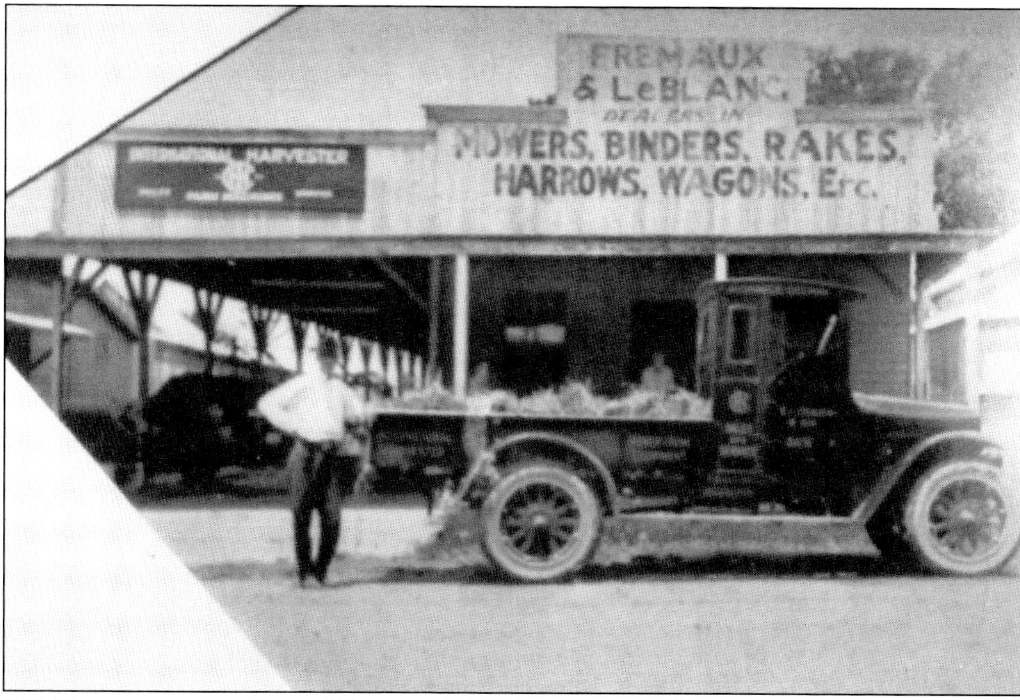

E.C. Fremaux poses in front of Fremaux & LeBlanc Farm Implement and Livery Stable, which he operated in partnership with Lynn LeBlanc. This business stood on South Adams Avenue, near the location of Paco's. Fremaux soon opened his own farm-implement and hardware store just down South Adams Avenue. (Courtesy of Sidney Stutes.)

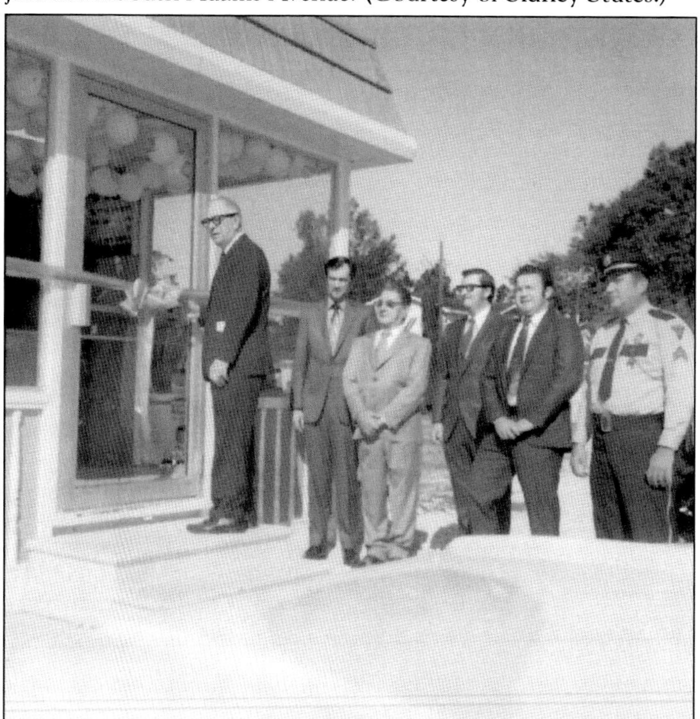

Mayor Bill Gossen (left) is about to cut the ribbon for the grand opening of Danny's Fried Chicken, located on the corner of North Polk Street and East Jeff Davis Avenue. The others are, from left to right, Ralph Stutes (mayor pro tem), Earl Colgin (owner), Gus Guidry (manager), George Melancon (chief of police), and Sgt. Wright Lavergne. (Courtesy of *Rayne Independent*.)

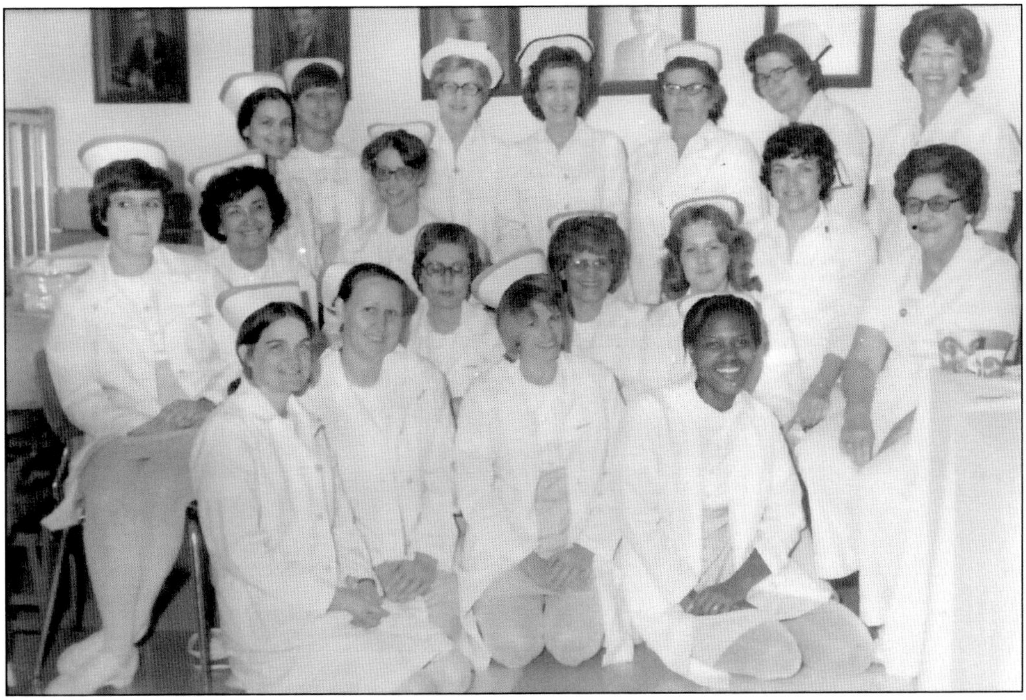

The nurses of Rayne Branch Hospital pose for a photograph in the lobby of the hospital in the 1970s. The only person identified is Gloria Hanks Domingue (top right), head of nursing for the hospital. (Courtesy of *Rayne Independent*.)

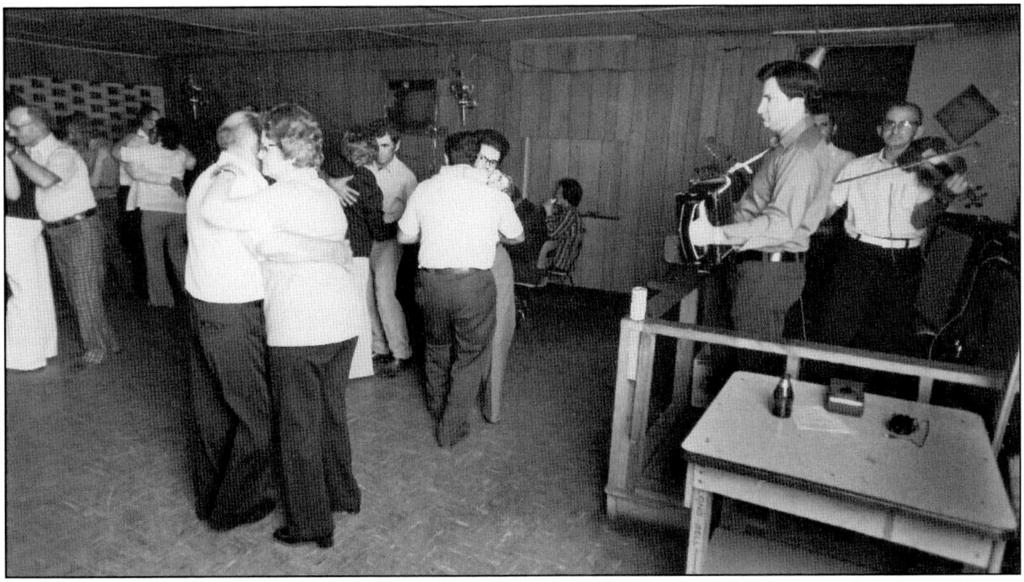

This is a typical dance at Kootsie's, located on South Polk Street, next door to the Town House Restaurant and across from the Depot Square. It had free dances on Wednesday, Friday, Saturday, and Sunday, and would charge an extra 25¢ to help pay for the band. A local band that drew large crowds was Aldus Mouton and the Scott Playboys (right). Anna Simoneaux said that the bar was so busy, the band could be paid before the first song was played. Behind the bandstand was the card room. (Courtesy of William "Kootsie" Simoneaux.)

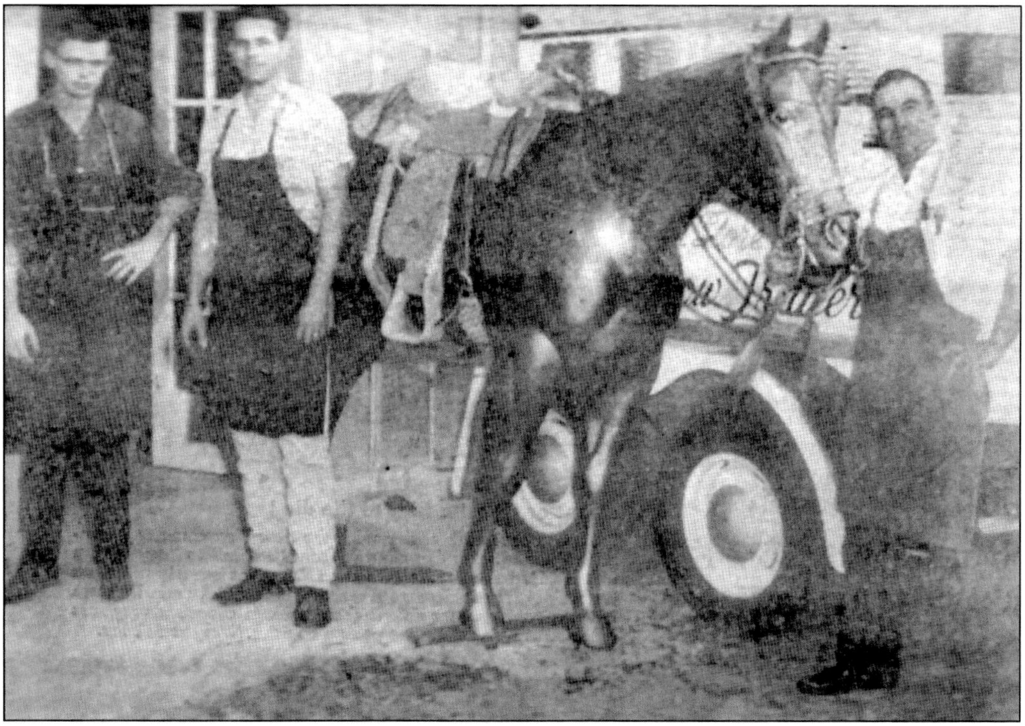

In 1962, employees of Boudreaux's Western Wear and Shoe Repair on South Adams Avenue pose with a full-size fiberglass quarter horse. It was made in California and picked up in Houston, Texas, in the horse trailer shown in the background. The men are, from left to right, Alpha Trahan, Cliff Huval, and Elmo Boudreaux. According to Boudreaux, there was a similar horse at Rayne Hardware Store about 10 years earlier, and he always wanted one. This horse was later brought to Huvals's in Crowley and then sold to a business in Opelousas. (Courtesy of *Rayne Acadian-Tribune*.)

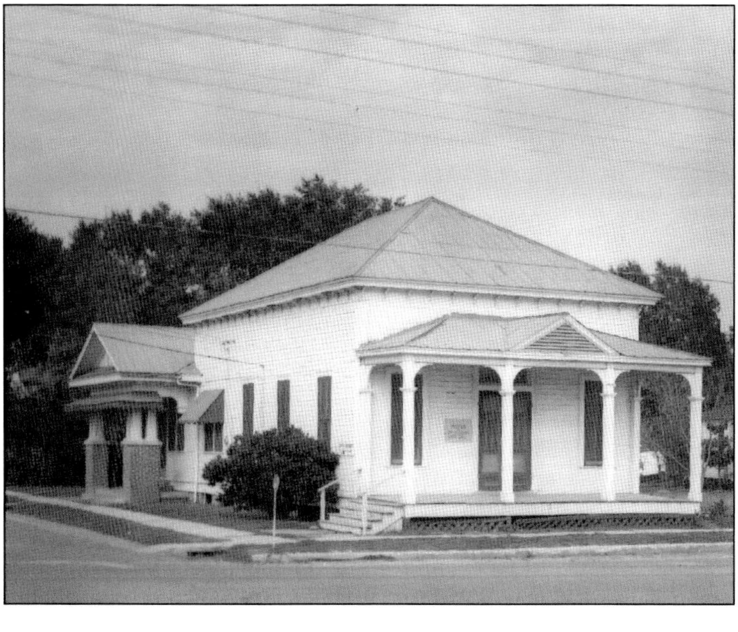

The original Rayne City Hall was located on the corner of East Louisiana Avenue and North Parkerson Street. The larger building in the front was torn down in 1952 to make room for a modern brick building. The rear section was moved and is now a rental property in the 1000 block of Louisa Avenue, near Rayne High School. (Courtesy of Leonard J. Laperous, The Photo Shop.)

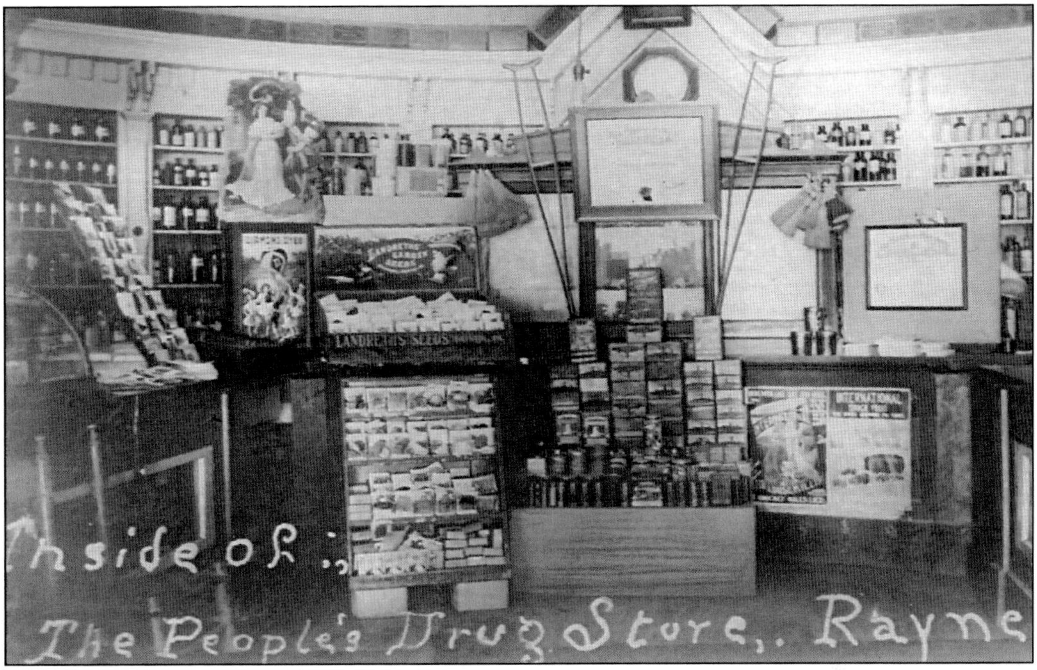

This early 1900s photograph shows the wares offered by the People's Drug Store, located at the corner of North Polk Street and East Louisiana Avenue. Established by Dr. Morris and later run for many years by the Kahn family, it was later purchased by Randal and Verelda Girouard. They later partnered with David Reed, and the establishment is still operating today as Rayne Pharmacy on Curtis Drive. (Courtesy of Marguerite Kahn Hoskin.)

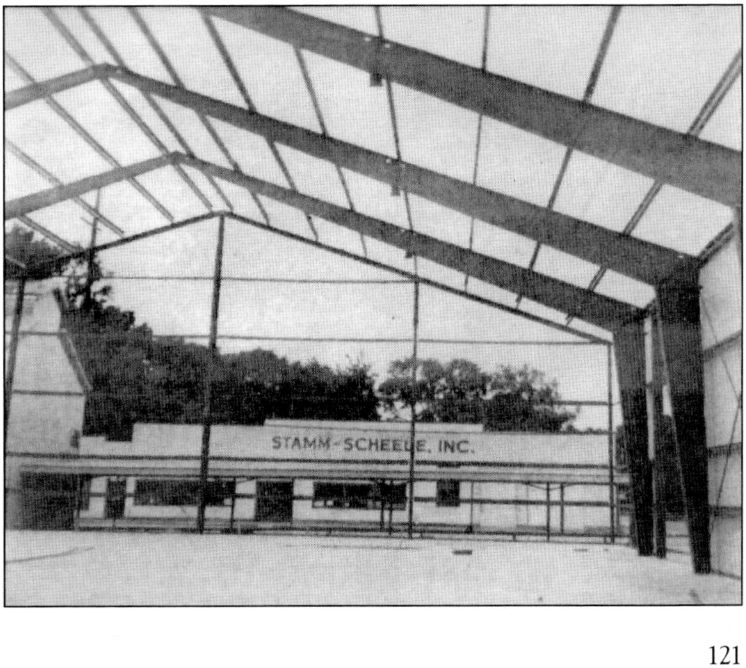

In 1976, an exciting change was documented when a *Rayne Acadian-Tribune* photographer captured this image of the old Stamm-Scheele offices on West Edwards Street while standing inside the new building on West Louisiana Avenue. Stamm-Scheele later sold out to Layne Christensen, which is still in business at that location today. (Courtesy of *Rayne Acadian-Tribune*.)

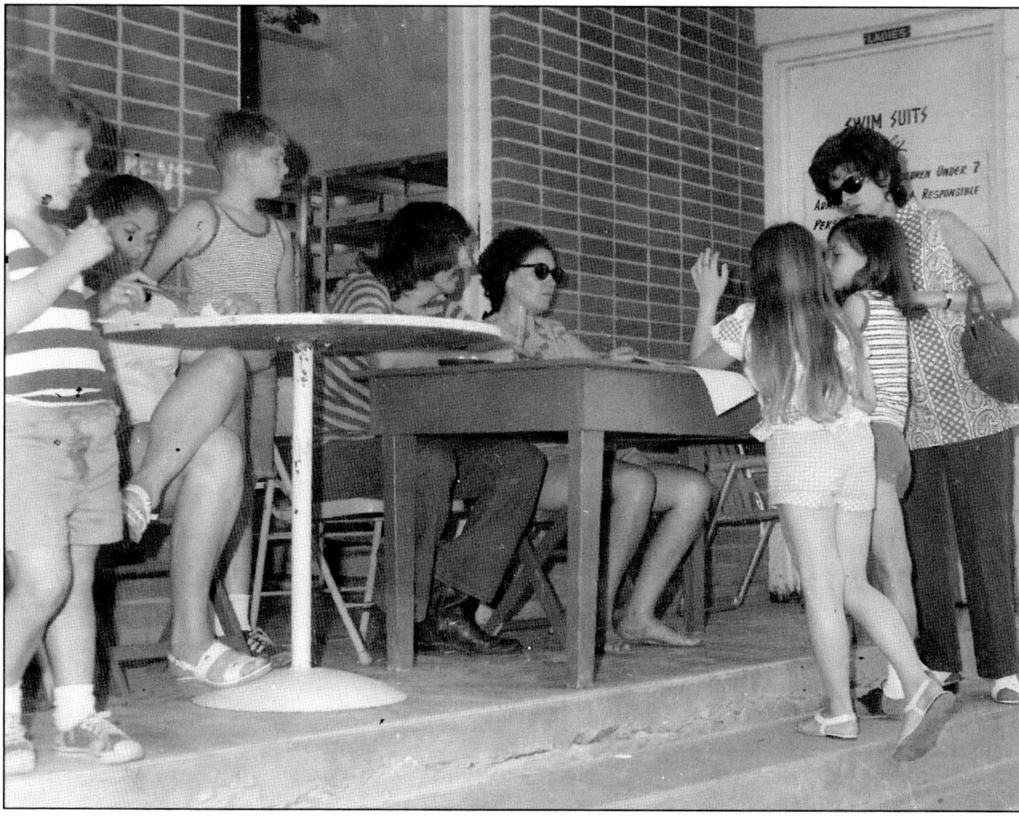

This is the front entrance of the Rayne Municipal Pool, then under the direction of Gene Henry. These children are registering for summer swimming lessons. The ladies' dressing room can be seen on the right; the men's was on the left, out of view. The fee to swim was 50¢. Patrons put their clothes in a basket and were given a large laundry pin with their basket number that they could attach to their swimming suits. Those wishing to dive off the diving board had to swim across the pool four times to prove to the lifeguards that they could swim. (Courtesy of Sidney Stutes.)

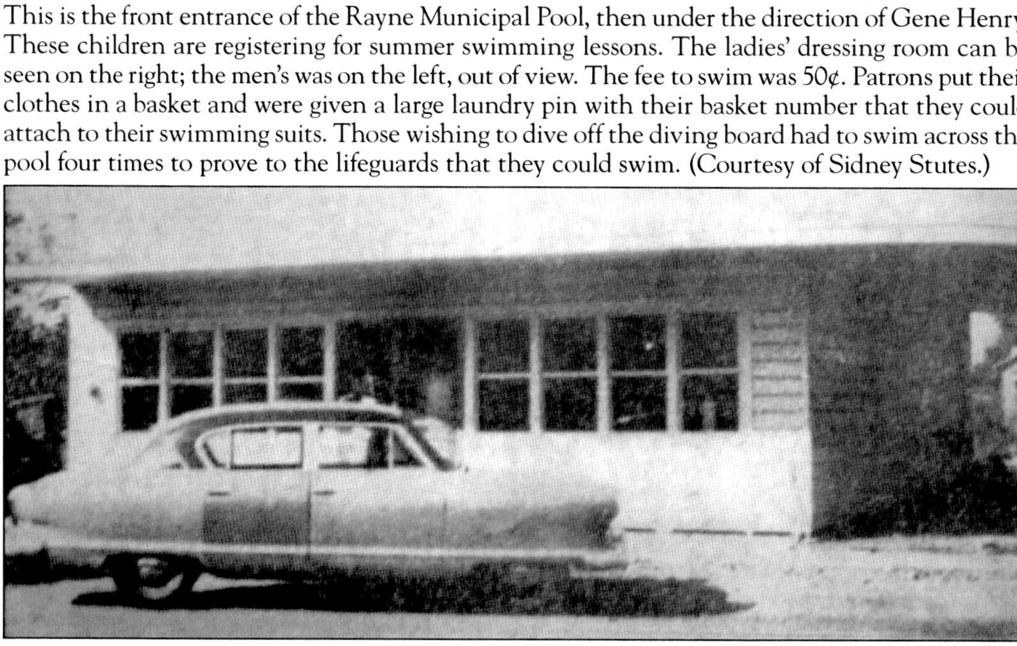

The Theobert Daigle Grocery Store is shown during its grand opening in 1954. The store was located at 306 Fourth Street. The building still stands today and is used as a church. (Courtesy of *Rayne Acadian-Tribune*.)

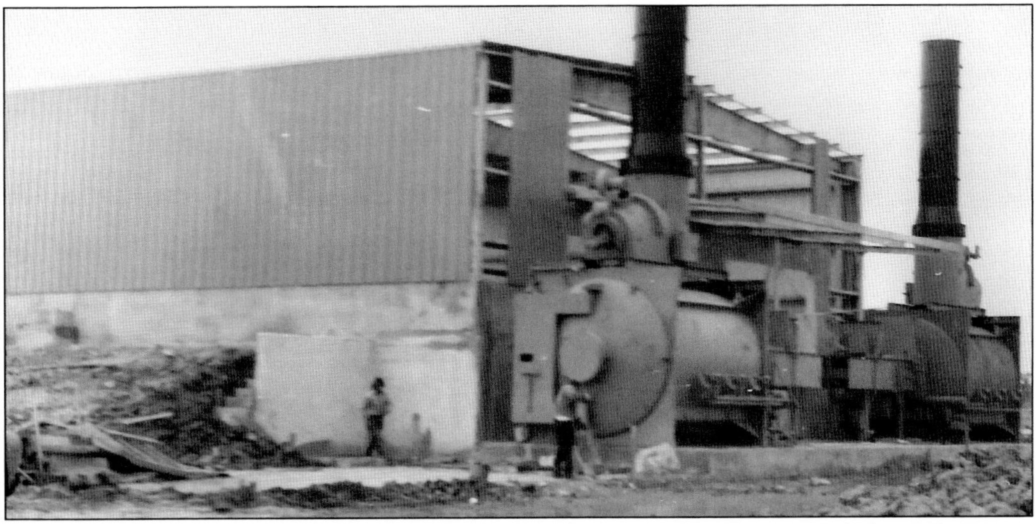

These two incinerators were installed by BFI in March 1974 on Section Street, behind the Rayne Plaza Shopping Center. With the ability to burn trash, the City of Rayne's trash pile on Roberts Cove Road was shut down. The incinerators gained attention when 30 tons of marijuana were later burned there by the Louisiana State Police. Many jokes went around town that the whole city was getting high. (Courtesy of *Rayne Acadian-Tribune.*)

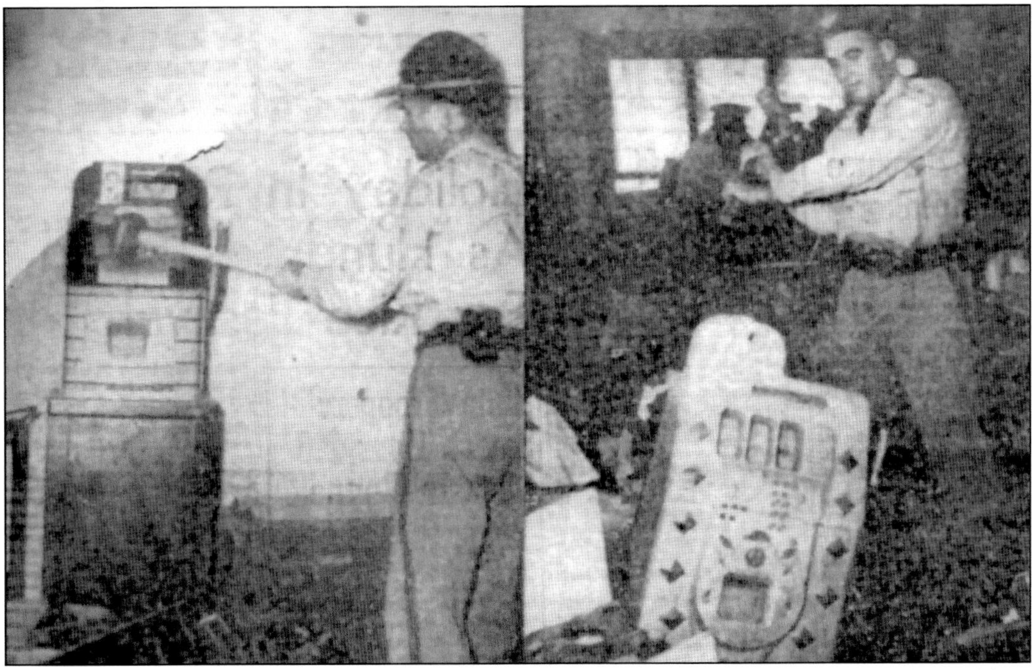

In 1953, Louisiana State Police superintendent Francis Grevemberg ordered that all gambling devices be destroyed. Before this order was handed down, gambling was illegal, but the law was rarely enforced. Troopers came to Rayne for two days with sledgehammers in hand and broke close to 200 slot machines. On the first day, machines were destroyed at the warehouse of United Novelty Co., said to belong to Eddie Floyd, Theo Mier Sr., and George Larriviere. The next day, another raid was conducted on machines said to be owned by Eddie Floyd and another man, identified as George Broussard. (Courtesy of *Rayne Acadian-Tribune.*)

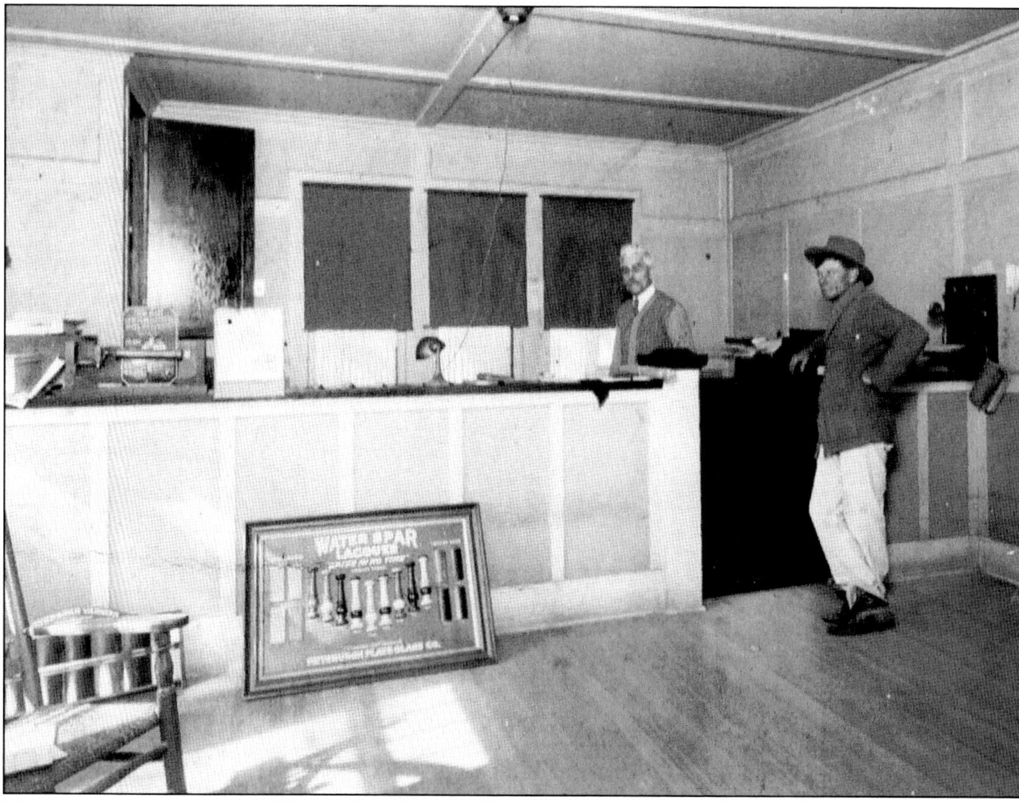

This is an interior view of Rayne Lumber Yard on West Texas Avenue across from the American Legion Home. The owner, Joseph Gossen, stands behind the counter. This building was later home to Gossen lumber yard and, for many years, housed Ernest Suiter's Quality Parts. (Courtesy of Sidney Stutes.)

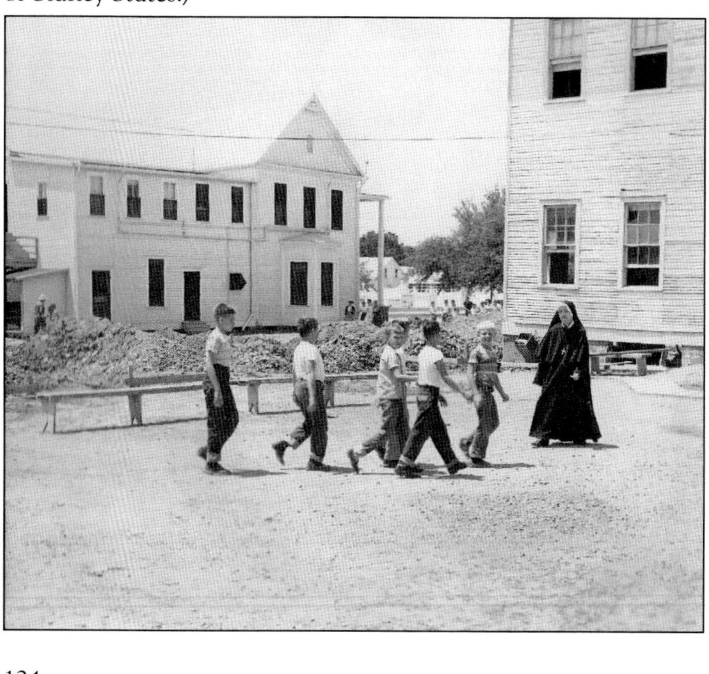

Construction is under way in 1954 for the new St. Joseph High School as these students head back to class under the watchful eye of a Mount Carmel nun. The convent can be seen on the left, and the back of the two-story wood school is at right. The school was replaced by a modern brick building, and a new brick convent was built by Martin Petitjean and dedicated to his wife, Thelice Petitjean. (Courtesy of Leonard J. Laperous, The Photo Shop.)

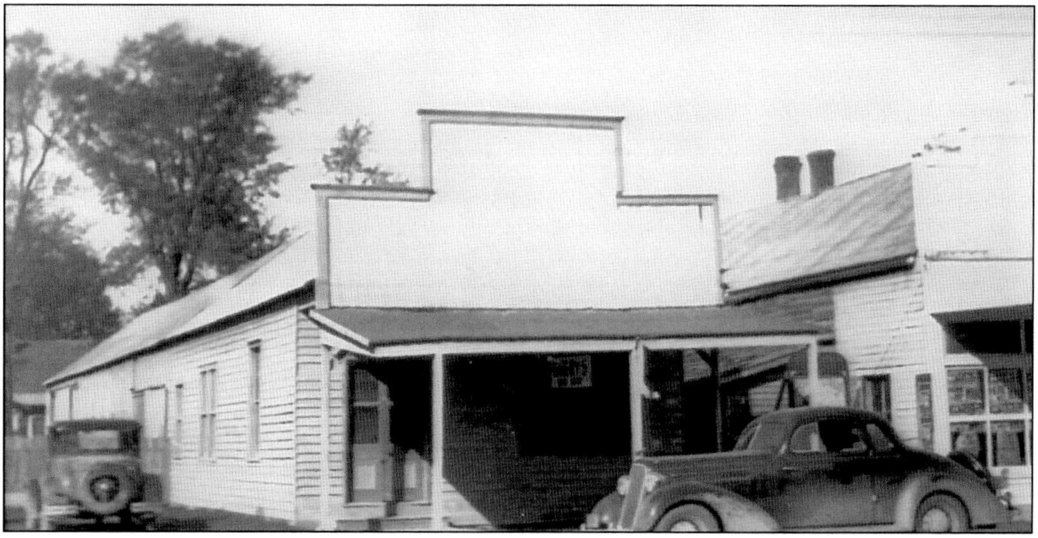

This 1940s photograph shows Guidry's Shoe Shop. It was in the 200 block of South Adams Avenue, to the north of Plattsmier-Hulin Grocery Store. McBride's Grocery Store, owned by Edward McBride Sr., is visible on the right. Guidry was from Church Point. When he retired, the business was bought by Elmo "T.T." Boudreaux, then by Cliff Huval. (Courtesy of Sidney Stutes.)

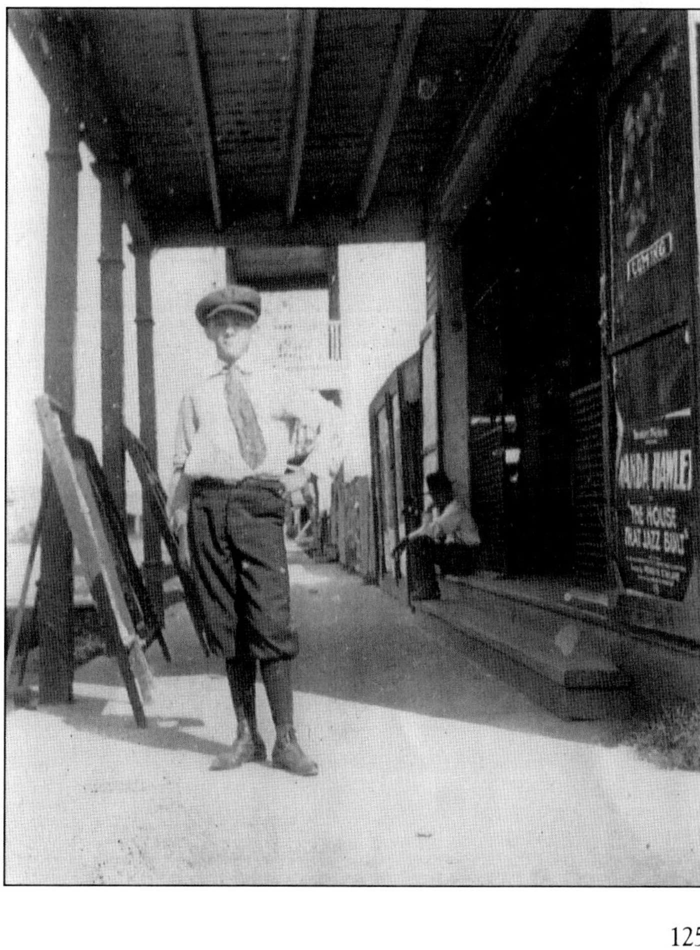

This Rayne youth poses in front of the Moulin Rouge Theater in 1921. Back then, a different movie played at the theater each day; the movie on this day was *The House that Jazz Built*. The Moulin Rouge, owned by Jacques Weil, was on the corner of East Texas Avenue and South Polk Street. This wooden building was torn down in 1946, and the new brick Joy Theater was built in its place. It is being used today by Knight Oil Tools. (Courtesy of Ronnie Richard.)

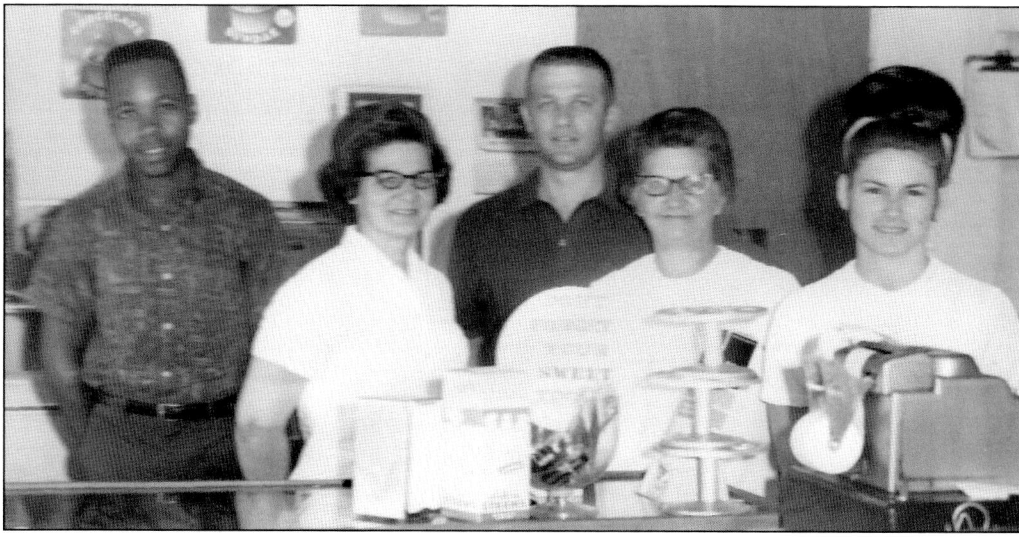

The staff at Johnson's Drive Inn are ready to serve customers. It was owned by Peter Comeaux, who purchased the business from the Johnsons. After a short time on South Adams Avenue, he moved the building in 1969 to The Boulevard, where the city was growing around Interstate 10. The building is in use today as Gabe's Cajun Foods. Shown here are, from left to right, Ronald White, Frances "Pat" Comeaux Myers, Charles "Peter "Comeaux (owner), Pearl Dore' Comeaux, and Eldine Broussard Arabie. (Courtesy of *Rayne Independent.*)

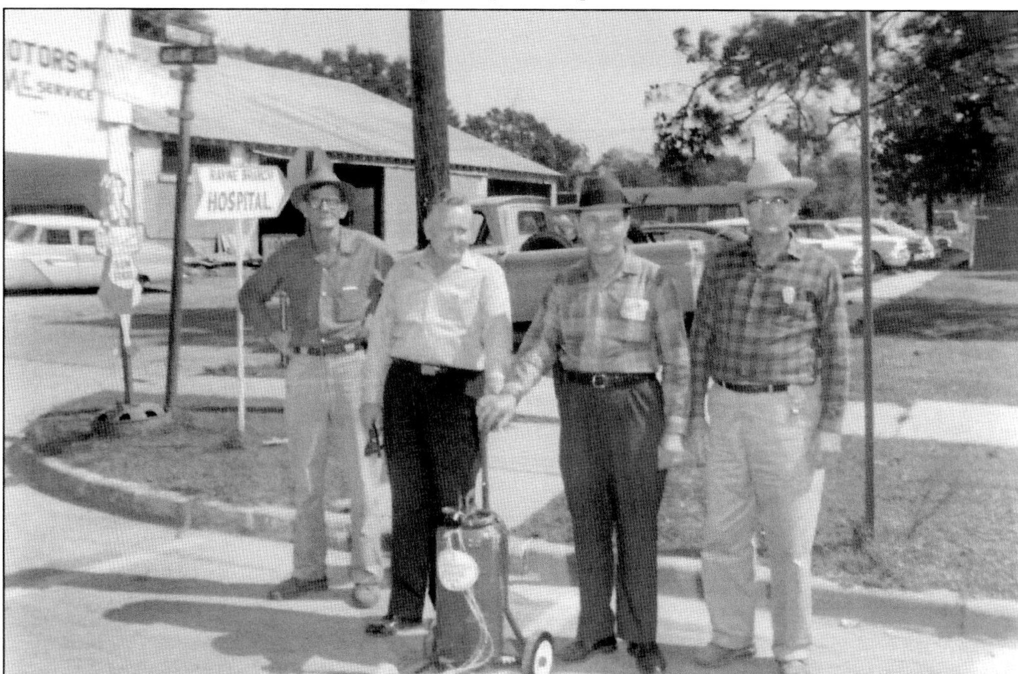

These City of Rayne employees display a new road line paint machine at the corner of East Perrodin Street and South Adams Avenue. At left is a sign directing vehicles to Rayne Branch Hospital, as well as a familiar sight, the Evangeline Maid "Slow School" safety sign. The Rayne Motors service garage can be seen in the background. (Courtesy of *Rayne Independent.*)

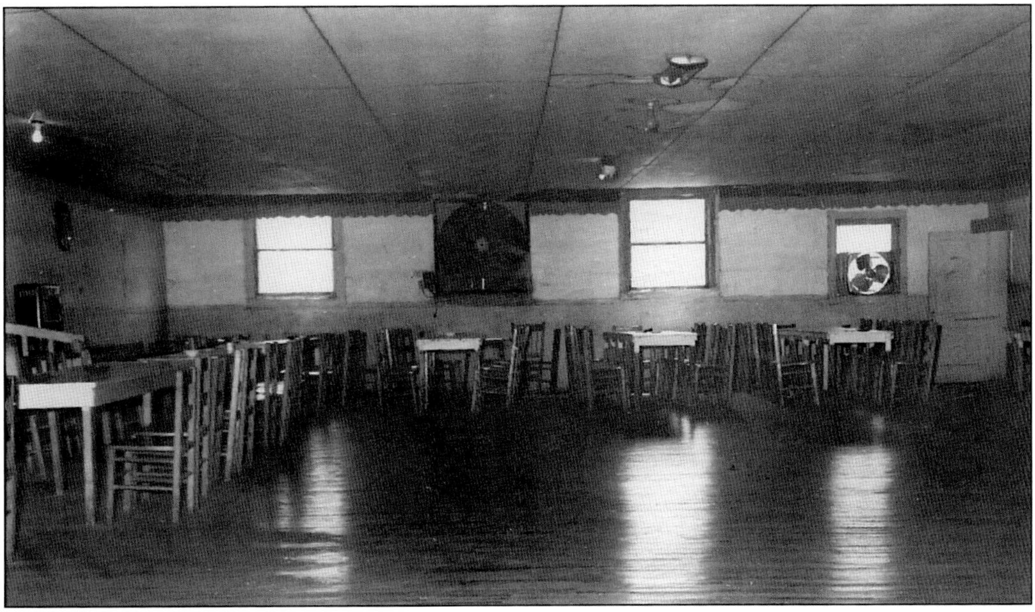

Thousands of people have "cut the rug" on the dance floor of the OST Dance Hall, built in 1924 by Mr. and Mrs. Joe Latour and Leo Clement on the Old Spanish Trail at its intersection with South Adams Avenue, on land leased from Edward Junot. The dance hall stood where Rayne Plastic Signs is now located. In 1927, Lozen Leger bought the land where the OST Dance Hall stood and wanted to build a new structure. The dance hall was then moved four blocks east, to the corner of East Branche and South Arenas Streets. It later served as a church before it caught fire and was torn down. (Courtesy of *Rayne Independent*.)

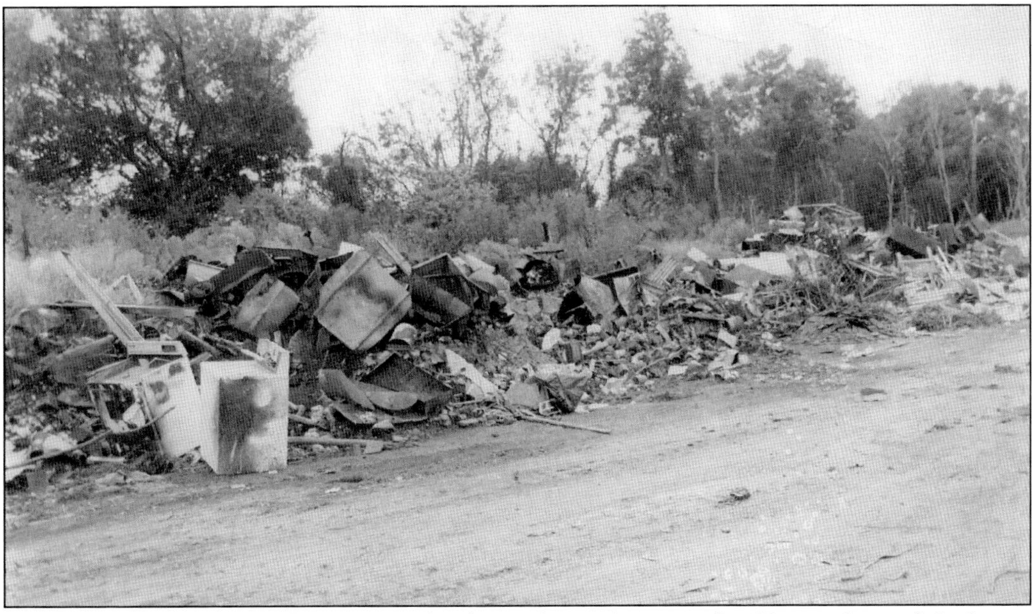

For many years, the City of Rayne's trash pile was located just north of Rayne, beyond the bayou bridge on Roberts Cove Road. It was cleaned up in 1974 when the new BFI incinerators were put into use. This is where much of "lost Rayne" ended up, but the memories will be forever etched in residents' minds. (Courtesy of *Rayne Independent*.)